The Unvarnished
GOSPELS

The Unvarnished
GOSPELS

Translated from the original Greek by
Andy Gaus

THRESHOLD BOOKS 1988

Threshold Books is committed to publishing books of spiritual significance and high literary quality. All Threshold books have sewn bindings and are printed on acid-free paper.

We will be happy to send you a catalog.
Threshold Books, RD 4, Box 600, Putney, Vermont 05346

ISBN 0-939660-25-3
Library of Congress Catalog Number: 87-51539
Cover: *Christ and His Apostles,* George Rouault
Design by Edmund Helminski
Typesetting: Letterforms, Brighton, MA
Printed in the United States

9 8 7 6 5 4 3

Library of Congress Cataloging-in-Publication Data
Bible.   N.T.   Gospels.   English.   Gaus.   1988.
The unvarnished Gospels.

I. Gaus, Andy, 1946·   II. Title.
BS2553.G38 1988   226.05209   87-51539
ISBN 0-939660-25-3

CONTENTS

ACKNOWLEDGMENTS

I'd like to thank the World and Time for wheeling around just long enough to bring this book to publication day. Thanks also to Judith Gibian of Allston, Massachusetts, the good friend and smart shopper who saw a Greek New Testament in a used bookstore and decided that was for me; to Camille Adams Helminski and Edmund Helminski of Putney, Vermont and George Witterschein of Jersey City, New Jersey, my principal supporters and critics at every stage; and to Victoria Reck at Threshold Books and Jeffrey Heehs at Letterforms for respectively moving the manuscript forward and freezing the type in place. And thanks above all to you, the fair-minded and inquisitive reader who is giving this work a hearing.

After all, the person who picks up this book is in for a surprise. My publisher's initial reaction to a first draft of Matthew was that it went beyond the bounds of proper translating to alter the text as much as I obviously had; why should the reader be any less suspicious? What have I "done" to the text?

Actually, no more than any translator, and rather less than some translators. In any event, this *is* a translation rather than an adaptation or popularization: it's intended not to simplify the Gospels but to reproduce the simplicity of style they already have. In short, the surprise is not in what has been done to the text, but in what the text is like in the first place.

It used to be accepted on faith that the evangelists were divinely inspired to produce Greek as pure and perfect as that of any classic author of the fifth century B.C.—and in just the same Attic dialect used by those authors back then.

As a matter of fact, New Testament *is* amazingly close to Attic Greek considering the half-millennium in between: you could just about overlook the differences by trying very hard. But differences are there: irregular verbs have become regular, religious and legal terms have been imported from Hebrew and Latin, and various words have gone in or out of fashion or have shifted in meaning. In all these matters the style of the Gospels doesn't correspond with that of the classic authors, whereas it does correspond with the style of various items of personal and business correspondence that have been preserved from the first century A.D.

Besides being current and not archaic, the Gospels show every sign of being conversational and not studied: the cavalier sequencing of person and number, as in "if each of you does not forgive your brother from your hearts" (Matthew 18:35); and the constant and very jarring mixture of present and past tenses, which sounds awfully ungrammatical but also conveys the vividness of memories at least 30 years old that seem like yesterday, as well as the urgency of a message brought by people who literally thought the sky was about to fall in.

If something current and conversational is required, then the King James Bible, beautiful though it is, doesn't convey an accurate impression of its original: in our ears, at least, it rings so distant and grandiose that it effectively refutes the incarnation by banishing all thought that Jesus could be human. Furthermore, it simply makes for very slow going, particularly if it's offered in an edition with double columns, small print, and verse numbers swarming all round like a cloud of pedantic mosquitoes. With such multiple obstacles, no wonder people think of the Gospels as hard reading. But perhaps the worst obstacle is the "daily lesson" approach to the Bible, which encourages interpretation out of context and discourages appreciation of the Gospels as a whole.

The amazing truth is that the Gospels are simple, lively, and short. And so this edition is dedicated to you, the general reader, in the hope that understandable English and legible type will embolden you to leave aside both your doubts and your daily lesson plan and do something radical: actually read the Gospels.

Boston
February 27, 1988

PREFACE

by George Witterschein

Some years ago, I developed the habit of reading the Gospel of St. John, in the Greek, at Easter time. My routine evolved into the following: on Good Friday, after hearing the sermon on the Seven Last Words in my nearby Catholic church, I would return home in the afternoon and start: *En archē ēn ho logos. . .*, "In the beginning was the word. . . ." I'd read about halfway through, then stop until Holy Saturday, when I'd all but finish. The ending, those last few pages that deal with the Resurrection and the final days Jesus spent on earth with his followers, I'd save for Easter Sunday itself.

What an exercise that is! How beautiful and simple, John's Greek sentences, and how affecting, in the way that only simple, heartfelt language can be! Each year, I find myself burning to share this Greek Gospel with my family and friends, indeed with everybody. I daydream that, all over the world, people will drop what they are doing, march off to the local traditional liberal arts college, and enroll in the Classics Department for *Introduction to the Greek of the New Testament*.

Which is not such a bad daydream. Anyone who did well at high school French can learn to read New Testament Greek in two semesters. But, of course, in our age of leisure, almost no one has that kind of free time. Those who are not flying off to Los Angeles for business meetings are flying off to Chicago for business meetings. Those who are not caring for children are caring for an elderly parent, or both. Andy Gaus, our translator, has gone a long way toward making my wish come true: without having to learn another language, the reader can now get a remarkable new perspective on the Gospels, a "feel" for them that is very like the experience I enjoy at Easter time. What Gaus has done is to translate the Greek of Matthew, Mark, Luke and John as if the nearly two thousand years of Christian history had not occurred. He has translated the Greek into modern American English, period. (Of course I speak relatively here. It is not possible to get those two thousand years – the "Christian era" – entirely out of one's mind. But the attempt is invaluable!) At first, this idea may not sound so astonishing. After all, hasn't every translator tried to do the same – to carry the ancient language over into a contemporary tongue? Well, yes and no. The versions of the New Testament we are familiar with all accept, to an overwhelming extent, a set of *interpretations* which arose some time after the Gospels were written. The important Church Councils, the work of great Christian translators (St. Jerome, Martin Luther, the King James scholars), the comments of theologians from St. Augustine to Karl Rahner, all turn on a "Christianized" view of the text.

But the text precedes that "Christianized" view, both in historical and religious-cultural time. The New Testament, written in clear, and for the most part straightforward, Greek, said what it said and meant what it meant *before* a Christianized interpretation of it came to be. In fact, the Greek texts of the Gospels apparently antedate "Christianity" itself.

Modern scholarship, as many readers are aware, has shown us that the followers of Jesus did not consider themselves to be members of a new religion called Christianity. They considered themselves to be Jews. To be sure, they felt something new and revolutionary had happened: the Anointed One, the Messiah, had come to fulfil the Jewish religion, establish the rule of the One God on earth, refute polytheistic paganism once and for all, and get rid of the Roman Empire. And to transform human life through love. . .

This Anointed One was called Jesus, and was a Jew, and nowhere in the Gospels did he say, "What I am doing is founding a new religion, called Christianity." That was to happen later, as more and more non-Jews joined the movement and eventually dominated it to the point where it broke conclusively with

Judaism. (The Jewish "Jesusites" lingered for a few centuries, then died out, leaving us with traditional Jews on the one hand and gentile Christians on the other. Was this something different from the original intent?)

The early sequence went something like this: first, there was the life of Jesus and the beginning of the community of his followers; then, after his departure, the community lived for a time with his memory, and with a fresh oral tradition, as their point of unity; then the community produced the Gospels, perhaps because the fresh tradition was fading and a written record could help compensate for the loss. These events occured before an organized church, calling itself "Christian," had emerged. Later on, beset with heresies, splinter groups, dissidents, Gnostics, pagan intellectual critics, Imperial Roman hostility, and the sheer weight of growing organizational momentum, Christianity took a look at itself and over time defined its tenets. Jesus is Christ; he is wholly God and wholly human; he is one of three members of the Trinity, that is, one of the three persons of God; he founded a church through his disciple Peter, and this church passes Peter's authority down through time to the bishops, especially the Bishop of Rome.

In short, Christianity took a while to come to be. Perhaps, now that I think of it, it is still coming to be.

But in any event the Gospels were there earlier. The words are on the pages; Andy Gaus has sought to revive them, in a modern language, for our sake; as I see it, he has tried to translate the Greek, period.

To say the least, the effect of this is refreshing. Anyone fortunate enough to read the Gospels in Greek is struck by the elementary power and simplicity of the vocabulary, and by the all-too-frequent loss of these qualities in the usual translations. "Sin," for example, connotes a deep separation between human will and God's will, a kind of flaw in our makeup that results in our acting wrongly. But the Greek word _hamartia_ is startlingly different: it is a term from archery, and means "missing the mark"!

The very word itself implies a much more optimistic view of human volition than "sin" does. With *hamartia* we are talking about something essentially correct in human nature, a part of us that wants to do what is good and right, but misses the bull's eye. Our goal is the right one; but somehow we miss it. (Gaus rightly prefers to render *hamartia* as "mistake" or "doing wrong.") Modern Greeks are fortunate in that their language has not changed so much that all this is lost. *Hamartia* is still the word. So is *pneuma*, "breath," for what we have seen translated as "spirit." Greeks (and the Gospel writers) talk about the Holy Breath, not the "Holy Spirit," and this is infinitely richer and more immediate. Breath is essential and intimate, one of the fundamental things of life, something we "do" constantly, an activity that contains elements of the voluntary and the involuntary, of the conscious and the unconscious, at one and the same time. "Spirit" is a remote and vaporous word in comparison. While derived from the Latin for "breath," "spirit" has lost its force and immediacy in English; the Holy Spirit sounds like something diaphanous wafting through lace curtains under moonlight. Breath, on the other hand, is moving in and out of me right now. At many points in the text, our translator has chosen to leave *pneuma* as "breath." And he points out in his glossary that while he uses "breath" and "spirit" interchangeably, they are one in the Greek.

Let's examine the difference this approach can make. *The New Jerusalem Bible* is certainly one of the great modern translations. It is a renowned work of academic scholarship, and it also succeeds to a large extent in capturing "the vitality and immediacy that the Bible had for the first Christians," as the Doubleday Reader's Edition claims.

In *The New Jerusalem Bible* John the Baptist speaks as follows (John 1:32-34) after seeing Jesus coming towards him:

> John also declared, "I saw the Spirit coming down on him from heaven like a dove and resting on him. I did not know him myself, but he

who sent me to baptize with water had said to me, 'The man on whom you see the Spirit come down and rest is the one who is going to baptize with the Holy Spirit.' Yes, I have seen and I am the witness that he is the Chosen One of God."

Compare this with Gaus:

And John has testified, saying, "I saw the breath descending like a dove from the sky, how it alighted upon him. And I didn't know him, but it was the one who sent me to bathe in water who said, 'Whoever you see the breath descending and alighting upon, that's the one who will bathe them in the sacred breath.' And I have seen and certified that this is the son of God."

Not only do we have "breath" and "sacred breath" instead of "Spirit" and "Holy Spirit." We also have:
– a much clearer image, at once palpable and mysterious: we watch breath, a movement of air, descend from the sky (not from "heaven"!) to mark the son of God.
– "to bathe in water" instead of "to baptize." *Baptizein* in Greek means "to bathe in water." A perfect example of Gaus letting the Greek, rather than Christian tradition, do the talking. To "bathe them in the sacred breath" is something we can feel on our very skins; that is not true of "to baptize with the Holy Spirit."
– "the son of God" instead of "the Chosen One of God." The Greek says *huios tou theou*, "son of God." Rather than interpret, Gaus leaves things as they are.
– a bit of superb English, ". . .like a dove from the sky, how it alighted upon him." That is every bit as noble, graceful, and evocative as the Greek.

Clearly, *The New Jerusalem Bible* rests on Christian interpretations of the vocabulary, which is exactly what Gaus's translation seeks to avoid. For all its accomplishments and excellence, the NJB suffers from being a derived, interpreted document.

To my eye the most startling difference between this version and all the others I know occurs in the famous Prologue to John's Gospel. Everyone has heard it: "In the beginning was the Word, and the Word was with God, and the Word was God." Now, one of the first things I noticed upon reading this passage in Greek was that it *doesn't say* "the Word was with God." It says: ". . .and the Word was towards God," or ". . .was going towards God."

Which is another matter altogether. If the Word was in motion towards God, instead of being literally and plainly identical with God, then St. John is introducing the notion of development (or process, or progression) within the divine nature, as the explanation for the origin of the created universe!

"Movement toward" implies a separation that is in process of being overcome. The movement of the Word towards God can then be seen as history: the history of the created universe, going back to its very beginning, is one of overcoming a separation from God, of a process of reunification.

Meditating on this "movement towards," we can even use the word *erotic* to describe a yearning for unity to overcome separation. In fact, to digress just slightly, that was how I first had it described to me, by Father Raymond York, the legendary Greek teacher at the Jesuit high school I attended. As Fr. York related it, the truth of the correct translation of the Prologue hit him like a thunderbolt one afternoon in the mid-1960s while he was in his room at the Jesuit Residence on Grand Street in Jersey City.

(A most curious aside: it is possible that both Edmund Helminski, the publisher of Threshold Books, and I were at different locations only a few hundred feet away from Fr. York at the time.)

Fr. York spent the brief remainder of his life meditating on this understanding of the Prologue. He felt that Christianity had made a grave error—had "missed the mark," perhaps—in failing to understand this "movement towards." The key to it all, he said, was the attraction between man and woman, which parallels (has the same source as) the attraction between the Word and God, and between the created universe and its origin in the separation between the Word and God.

This failure to understand John's Prologue, according to Ray York, accounts for the growing division between men and women, for our terrifying divorce and family break-up statistics, among many other things. (But not to worry: the good father believed it is America's function in world history to heal this rift, and that the hour of setting things right is at hand.)

I make this point in defense of Andy Gaus's translation. Certainly, I do not claim, in these paragraphs, to have explained the Prologue to the Gospel of St. John, one of the deepest, and in the best sense of the word, most mysterious passages in religious literature. But the fullness and depth, the richness, the possibilities, of the Prologue, are terribly reduced by saying "the Word was with God" instead of the much more suggestive (more mysterious) "the Word was towards God." And until now, you had to read Greek to get this distinction.

The example also illustrates the beauty of the basic premise of Gaus's translation. All the usual versions, relying as they do on developed Christian interpretation, have translated the Greek _pros ton theon_ as "with God" instead of "[going] towards God." This is despite the fact that _pros_ with the accusative case (_theon_) after the verb "to be" means "to go towards." (As Fr. York pointed out, this construction occurs scores of times in the New Testament, and typically means "to go towards.") Any high school Greek student could state as much.

Why then the "with" translation? My own suspicion is that doctrinal Christianity _had_ to mistranslate the Greek for two reasons, both of them a function of the long polemic the early church waged against Gnostics and other heretics. First, the notion of movement/separation/progress within God as the origin of the universe sounded too much like Gnostic creation myths. (There are many different ones but they seem to have in common the idea that the universe is the result of a cataclysm, division, or separation within the divine nature.) Second, if the Word was something other than God, or not quite identical with God, or was in some real sense separated from God, then several important points of doctrine were in apparent danger: the full, unmitigated divinity of Jesus Christ as the Second Person of the Trinity; and by extension the doctrine of the Trinity itself. As is so often the case, defensiveness leads to impoverishment.

It is Andy Gaus's good fortune – and the reader's – that he is not defending a body of doctrine. He is just translating as faithfully as he can, like the good German-American Midwesterner he was raised to be.

Andy Gaus succeeds at translating because he is hard-working, passionate, and scrupulous; and because he knows, somehow, the trick of making the English *sound* and *feel* like the original. The latter gift I cannot explain; but I accept its existence with gratitude.

And I believe the readers of these Gospels will also be grateful to the translator for his effort. And wonder, with me: Why didn't somebody do this sooner?

The Good Word According to
Matthew

1

THE BOOK of the birth of Jesus the Anointed, son of David, son of Abraham: Abraham had Isaac, Isaac had Jacob, Jacob had Juda and his brothers, Juda had Phares and Zara by Thamar, Phares had Esram, Esram had Aram, Aram had Aminadab, Aminadab had Naasson, Naasson had Salmon, Salmon had Boes by Rachab, Boes had Jobed by Ruth, Jobed had Jesse, and Jesse had David the king.

David had Solomon by Urius's wife, Solomon had Roboam, Roboam had Abia, Abia had Asaph, Asaph had Josaphat, Josaphat had Joram, Joram had Oziah, Oziah had Joatham, Joatham had Achaz, Achaz had Hezekiah, Hezekiah had Manasses, Manasses had Amos, Amos had Josiah, and Josiah had Jechoniah and his brothers at the time of the Babylonian migration.

After the Babylonian migration, Jechoniah had Salathiel, Salathiel had Zorobabel, Zorobabel had Abiud, Abiud had Eliachim, Eliachim had Azor, Azor had Sadoc, Sadoc had Achim, Achim had Eliud, Eliud had Eleazar, Eleazar had Matthan, Matthan had Jacob, and Jacob had Joseph, the husband of Mary, from whom was born Jesus, known as the Anointed One, or "Christ." So the generations from Abraham to David made fourteen generations, and from David to the Babylonian migration fourteen generations, and from the Babylonian migration to Christ fourteen generations.

The birth of Jesus the Anointed was like this: When Mary his mother was engaged to Joseph, before they got together, she was found to be carrying a child in her belly by means of holy spirit. Joseph, her husband, being decent and not wishing to make an example of her, decided to break off with her discreetly. He had that on his mind when one night a messenger of the Lord appeared in a dream and said to him: "Joseph son of David, don't be afraid to take Mary for your wife. What has been conceived in her is of holy spirit. She will have a son, and you will call his name Jesus [which means "The Lord is salvation"], because he is the one who will save the people from their own errors."

All this happened to fulfill what was said by the Lord, speaking through the prophet: "Look! the virgin shall carry a child and bear a son, and they will call his name Emmanuel" (which is translated "God-with-us"). Getting up from sleep, Joseph did as the messenger of the Lord commanded and took her for his wife, but he had no relations with her till she bore a son, and he called his name Jesus.

2

WHEN Jesus was born in Bethlehem, Judea, in the days of King Herod [the Great], one day wise men from the East showed up in Jerusalem, saying, "Where is the newborn king of the Jews? We saw his star in the East and came to adore him."

Hearing that, King Herod was disturbed and all of Jerusalem with him. And assembling all the high priests and canon-lawyers of the people he inquired of them, "Where has the Anointed One been born?"

They said to him, "In Bethlehem, Judea, because that's how it is written by the prophet:

And you, Bethlehem, land of Juda,
Are by no means the least of Juda's leaders,
Since from you shall come the leader
Who herds my people Israel."

Then Herod, secretly calling the wise men, ascertained from them the time of the appearing star, and sent them to Bethlehem, saying, "When you get there find out in detail about the child, and when you find him, report to me, so that I can go and adore him too." They, having heard the king, went on their way, and look! the star they'd seen in the East was guiding them, till it came and stood over where the child was. Seeing the star, they were delighted with a great delight indeed. And going into the house they saw the child with Mary his mother; and they fell down and adored him, and they opened up their treasure-chests and offered gifts to him: gold and incense and Arabian ointment. And being warned in a dream not to return to Herod, they went back to their country by another road.

When they had gone back, one night a messenger of the Lord appears* in a dream to Joseph and says, "Get up, take the child and his mother with you and flee to Egypt, and stay there until I tell you, because Herod is going to look for the child to kill him."

So he got up and took the child and his mother by night and went on into Egypt and was there until Herod's end, fulfilling what was said by the Lord speaking through His prophet: "Out of Egypt I called my son."

Then Herod, seeing he had been tricked by the wise men, was utterly enraged, and he sent out and disposed of all the children in Bethlehem and its environs two years old or younger, according to the time he had ascertained from the wise men. Then was fulfilled what had been said by Jeremiah the prophet:

A voice was heard in Rama,
Weeping and wailing aplenty:
Rachel crying for her children,
And she would not be consoled,
Because she has none.

When Herod died, a messenger of the Lord appears in a dream to Joseph in Egypt saying, "Get up and take the child and his mother with you and proceed to Israel, for those who wanted

*Yes, "appears" and "says" in the middle of an otherwise past-tense narrative. This mixing of present and past tenses is not illegal, as an occasional device, in either Classical Greek or the Greek of the New Testament period; but the constant use that Matthew, Mark, and John make of it, sometimes changing tenses in mid-sentence, would have to be rough in any language – and the best proof is that Luke is much more careful, keeping his past tenses past with few exceptions.

the life of the child are dead." So he got up and took the child and his mother and went on into Israel.

But when he heard that [Herod] Archelaus was king of Judea instead of his father Herod [the Great] he was afraid to go there; and being advised by a dream he proceeded to the regions of Galilee. And he went and settled in a town called Nazareth, to fulfill what was said by the prophets: "He shall be called a Nazarene."

3

IN THOSE DAYS John the Baptist appeared, preaching in the desert of Judea and saying, "Repent, for the kingdom of the skies is approaching."

He is the one described by Isaiah the prophet:

The voice of a crier in the desert:
"Prepare the road of the Lord,
Straighten his paths."

This same John had a robe of camel hair and a leather belt around his waist, and his food was locusts and wild honey. At that time all Jerusalem and all Judea and all the surrounding country of the Jordan was going out to see him, and they were being bathed by him in the Jordan River and admitting their mistakes.

Seeing many of the Pharisees and Sadducees coming for his bathing he said to them: "Children of the snake, who tipped you off to run from the coming fury? Bear the fruit proper to a change of heart and do not think you can say amongst yourselves, 'We have Abraham for our father!' I tell you, God can raise up children for Abraham out of these stones here. Already the ax is poised at the root of the trees. And so any tree not bearing good fruit gets cut down and thrown into the fire.

"Now I bathe you in water to change hearts, but the one coming after me is stronger than me: I'm not big enough to carry his shoes. He will bathe you in holy breath and fire. Winnowing-fan in hand, he will clean up his threshing floor, and collect the grain to be put in the silo and the husks to be burned in unquenchable fire."

Then Jesus showed up from Galilee on the banks of the Jordan where John was, to be bathed by him. But John stopped him: "I have need of being bathed by you, and you come to me?"

Jesus answered and said to him, "Go ahead: it's right that we should fulfill all the law." So John let him do it.

After being bathed, Jesus came straight out of the water. And all of a sudden the skies opened and he saw the breath of God descending like a dove and coming toward him. And just then there was a voice from the skies saying, "This is my son, my beloved son in whom I am delighted."

4

THEN Jesus was led into the desert by the spirit, to be tested by the devil. And after fasting forty days and forty nights, he was utterly starving. And drawing near, the Examiner said, "If you're the son of God, tell these rocks to turn into bread."

He answered: "It is written: 'Humanity shall not just live on bread, but on every word that comes from the mouth of God.'"

Then the devil takes him along into the holy city and sets him atop one wing of the temple and says to him, "If you're the son of God, throw yourself down, for it is written: 'His messengers have been instructed about you, and they will take you in their hands, so you don't stub your foot against a stone.'"

Jesus said to him, "It also says, 'You are not to experiment with the Lord your God.'"

Next the devil takes him along to a mountain way up high and shows him all the kingdoms of the world and their glory, and says to him, "I'll give these all to you if you fall down and adore me."

Then Jesus said to him, "Get out of here, Satan! It says, 'The Lord your God is whom you shall adore, and you shall serve only Him'!"

Then the devil left him alone, and just then holy messengers came and waited on him.

But when he heard that John had been handed over to the authorities, he moved on into Galilee. And leaving Nazareth, he went and settled in Capharnaum by the sea, in the regions of Zabulon and Nephthali, to fulfill what was said by the prophet Isaiah:

Earth of Zabulon and earth of Nephthali,
On the way to the sea, beyond the Jordan,
Galilee of the nationalities,
The people lying in darkness saw a great light,
And to those in that land lying in death's shadow,
A light rose in the sky.

After that Jesus began to proclaim and say, "Repent, for the kingdom of the skies is approaching!"

Walking by the sea of Galilee, he saw two brothers, Simon, known as Simon Rock ["Peter"], and Andrew his brother, casting their net into the sea, since they were fishermen. And he said to them, "Come along after me and I'll make you fishers of humanity." And they put their nets right down and followed him. And going on a ways he saw two more brothers, James, Zebedee's son, and John his brother, in the boat with their father Zebedee fixing their nets; and he called to them. And right away they left the boat and their father behind and followed him.

And he started traveling round all of Galilee teaching in their synagogues and proclaiming the good word of the kingdom and curing every disease and every infirmity among the people.

And word of him spread throughout all Syria. And they brought him everyone in bad health with all kinds of diseases, and people living with torments, and the possessed, and the insane, and the paralyzed; and he cured them. And giant crowds followed him from Galilee, the Decapolis, Jerusalem, Judea, and across the Jordan.

5

SEEING the crowds, he went up the mountain, and as he sat there his students came to him, and he opened his mouth and taught them, saying:

"The poor in spirit are in luck: the kingdom of the skies is theirs.

"The mourners are in luck: they will be consoled.

"The gentle are in luck: they will inherit the earth.

"Those hungering and thirsting for justice are in luck: they will get their fill.

"The merciful are in luck: they will be treated mercifully.

"The clean-hearted are in luck: they will see God.

"The peacemakers are in luck: they will be called God's sons and daughters.

"Those persecuted for the sake of justice are in luck: the kingdom of the skies is theirs.

"You are in luck – when they blame you and persecute you and tell all kinds of filthy lies about you, because of me. Be happy and delighted, because you will be well paid in the skies. After all, they persecuted the prophets before us the same way.

"You are the salt of the earth, but if the salt goes tasteless, what do you salt it with? It's good for nothing any more but to be thrown out and stepped on by everybody.

"You are the light of the world. A city can't be hidden lying on a mountaintop. Nor do people light a candle and cover it with a big basket; they put it up on a tall candlestick where it can shine for everyone in the house. That's how your light must shine in front of the world, so that people see your good deeds and give credit to your Father in the skies.

"Don't think I came to dissolve the law or the prophets: I didn't come to dissolve them, I came to fulfill them. I assure you, till the sky and the earth go away, not one letter or punctuation mark of the law will ever go away until everything has come to pass. So anyone who dissolves even one of the smallest commands and teaches others the same way, will be known as the lowest in the kingdom of the skies; whereas anyone who keeps the commands and teaches them too, will be known as someone great in the kingdom of the skies.

"I'm telling you, if you don't brim over with justice more than the canon-lawyers and Pharisees, you will not get into the kingdom of the skies.

"You've heard how your ancestors were told: 'You are not to murder. Whoever murders is liable to be brought to justice.' But I say everyone who gets angry at his brother will be subject to justice, and if he calls his brother 'swine,' it will go before the high court, and if he calls him 'idiot,' he's liable to be thrown into the fire of Gehenna.

"So if you're just about to put your offering upon the temple altar and then you remember that your brother has something against you, leave your gift on the floor and get out of there: first make up with your brother, and then go make your offering. Get friendly with your adversary fast, while you're still on the road with him, so your adversary doesn't hand you over to the judge, and the judge to the jailer, and you get thrown in jail; I assure you, you won't get out of there till you've paid off every last penny.

"You've heard how it was said, 'You are not to commit adultery.' But I say any man who looks at a woman and really wants her has already slept with her in his heart. If it's your right eye that gets in your way, pull it out and throw it off: you're better off losing one of your members than having your whole body thrown into the Gehenna fire. And if it's your right hand that gets in your way, cut it off and throw it aside: you're better off losing one of your members than if your whole body goes into the Gehenna fire.

"It was said, 'Whoever separates from his wife must present her with a divorce decree.' But I say anyone who divorces his wife for any reason but whoring is setting her up for adultery, and anyone who marries a divorced woman is living in adultery.

10

"You've also heard how your ancestors were told, 'You are not to break oaths, you give your oaths to the Lord.' But I say don't swear at all: don't swear by heaven, it's the throne of God. Don't swear by the earth, it's the footrest under His feet. Don't swear by Jerusalem, it's the city of the great king. Don't swear by your own head, you can't make a single hair white or black. Let your way of talking be 'yes' and 'no'; anything more than that comes from the Evil One.

"You've heard it said, 'An eye for an eye and a tooth for a tooth.' But I say don't stand up to the villain: if somebody raps you on the right side of your jaw, give him the other side, and if somebody sues you for your shirt, give him your coat too. And if somebody drags you a mile out of your way, go two miles with him. Give to those who ask you, and don't turn the person away who wants to borrow from you.

"You've heard it said, 'You are to love those close to you and hate your enemies.' But I say love your enemies and pray for your persecutors if you want to be children of your Father in the skies, because He shines his sun on villains and saints and rains on the innocent and the guilty.

"If you love those who love you, what pay do you get? Don't the tax collectors do that much? And if you only say hello to your brothers, what are you doing special? Don't pagans do that much? So be perfect the way your heavenly Father is perfect.

6

"BE CAREFUL not to put your virtue in front of people to be noted by them. If you do, you will get no pay from your Father in the skies. So when you contribute to charity, don't have a trumpet-player go before you, like the fakes do in temples and down alleyways, so people will glorify them; believe me, they have already been paid their wages. But when _you_ give to charity, your left hand shouldn't know what your right hand is doing, so that your charity is on the sly; and your Father, watching on the sly, will pay you back.

"And when you pray, don't be like the fakes who love to pray standing in the temples and on streetcorners so as to show off for everybody. Believe me, they have already been paid their wages. When *you* pray, duck into the store-room and lock the door and pray to your Father on the sly. And your Father, watching on the sly, will pay you back.

"When you pray, don't babble on like pagans who think they can make themselves heard with a great glut of words. Don't act like them, because your Father knows what you need before you ask Him.

"So pray like this:

Our Father in the skies,
Let Your name be sanctified.
Let Your kingdom come,
May Your will be seen
On the earth, just as in the sky.
Give us day by day the next day's bread,
And forgive our debts
The same as we forgave the debts that others owed us.
And do not put us to the test,
But snatch us from the Evil One's clutches, let it be so.

"If you forgive people for stepping out of line, your heavenly Father will forgive you too. But if you don't forgive other people, your Father also won't forgive you for stepping out of line.

"When you fast, don't be like the grim-looking fakes who disguise their faces so they'll look to people like they're fasting. Believe me, they have already been paid their wages. When *you* fast, put on a fragrance and wash your face, so you *don't* look to people like you're fasting, except to your Father on the sly. And your Father, watching on the sly, will pay you back.

"Don't save up your treasures on the earth, where moths and rust eat away at them and thieves tunnel in and steal them. Save up your treasures in the sky, where no moth and no rust eats away and thieves don't tunnel in and steal. Because where your treasure is, your heart will be too.

12

"The lamp of the body is the eye. So if your eye is in one piece, your whole body is lighted; whereas if your eye is bad, your whole body is in darkness. So if the light inside you is dark. . . what a lot of darkness!

"No one can serve two masters: either he'll hate one and love the other, or he'll put up with the one and despise the other. You can't serve God *and* the Almighty Dollar.*

"That's why I tell you, don't trouble your heart about what you will eat and drink or clothe your body with. Isn't the soul more important than food, and the body more important than clothing? Look at the birds in the sky: they don't plant, don't harvest, and don't fill silos, and your heavenly Father still feeds them. Don't you make more difference to Him than they do? Can any of you, by being vastly concerned, add a foot to your height? And why do you worry about clothing? Study how the lilies of the field grow: they don't work, and they don't spin cloth. But I am telling you that not even Solomon in all his glory was ever dressed like one of them. If that's how God clothes the wild grass of the field, there today and thrown into the furnace tomorrow, won't He do much more for you, unbelievers?

"So don't worry, saying, 'What will we drink? What will we wear?' The pagans ask for all these things, but your heavenly Father knows that you need all these things. Ask first for the kingdom of God and His justice, and these other things will be delivered to you. So don't worry about tomorrow, because tomorrow can worry about itself. Each day's evil is enough for the day.

7

"DON'T judge, so that you won't be judged; you will be sentenced to the same sentence that you sentence others, and by

---

*"Mammon"—the Syrian god of riches, a word the Jews used in describing the paganistic worship of money. The use Jesus makes of the word here crystallizes a recurrent theme of his teaching: not money, but the deification of money, turns a person away from God.

whatever standard you measure you will be measured. Why do you look at the splinter in your brother's eye but don't notice the log in your own eye? And how can you say to your brother, 'Let me get that splinter out of your eye,' with that log there in your own eye? You fake, first get the log out of your own eye, and then you can see about getting the splinter out of your brother's eye!

"Don't give the holy of holies to dogs, and don't throw your pearls at the feet of pigs, or else they'll trample them with their hooves and then swing round and knock you down.

"Ask and you will receive, look and you will find, knock and you will be admitted. For the asker always gets, the seeker finds, and whoever knocks is admitted. Is there any person among you who, being asked by his son for bread, would give him a stone, or being asked for a fish, would give him a snake? If you, villains that you are, know enough to give good things to your children, how much more will your Father in the skies give good things to those asking Him!

"So everything you want people to do for you, you do the same for them, because that's the law and the prophets.

"Go in the narrow door; because the door is wide and the road is broad leading off to destruction, and many people are going that way. Whereas how narrow the door and how constricted the road leading off to life, and how few people find it!

"Be careful of pseudoprophets who come to you in the clothing of lambs and are rapacious wolves inside. You'll know them by the fruit they bear: you don't get grapes from a thorn-tree or figs from a thistle-bush, do you? Likewise, every good tree bears good fruit, while the rotten tree bears bad fruit. A good tree can't bear bad fruit, and a rotten tree can't bear good fruit either. Any tree not bearing good fruit gets cut down and thrown into the fire. So definitely you'll know them by the fruit they bear.

"Not everyone saying 'Lord, Lord' to me will get into the kingdom of the skies, but only those who do the will of my Father in the skies. Many will say to me on that day, 'Lord, Lord, didn't we prophesy in your name and exorcise demons in your name and work many wonders in your name?'

"And I will say to them, 'I must confess I never met you; go away from me, workers of lawlessness.'

"So anyone who hears these words from me and does them, will become like a sensible man who built his house on bedrock, and the rain came down and the floods came and the winds hurled themselves at the house, and it didn't fall because it was grounded on the rock. And anyone who hears these words from me and doesn't do them, will become like a stupid man who built his house on sand, and the rain came down and the floods came and the winds beat at the house, and it fell, and its downfall was tremendous."

And it happened that when Jesus finished these words, the crowds were dumbfounded at his teaching, because he was teaching them as if on his own authority, not like their canon-lawyers.

8

COMING DOWN from the mountain he was followed by giant crowds. And suddenly a leper came forward and bowed before him, saying, "Lord, if you want to, you can heal me."

And he reached out and touched him saying, "I do want to; be healed." And immediately his leprosy was washed away. And Jesus said to him, "Careful, don't talk to anyone, just go show yourself to the priest and bring the offering specified by Moses, as a testimony for them."

As he was going into Capharnaum, a captain, the leader of a hundred soldiers, came up to him, pleading with him and saying, "Lord, my child back home has been left paralyzed, suffering horribly."

And he said to him, "I'll come cure him."

And the captain answered, "Lord, I'm not important enough for you to come under my roof; just say it in words, and my child will be cured. After all, I'm a man under authority too, with soldiers under me, and if I tell one of them Go, he goes, and if I tell another Come, he comes, and if I tell my slave Do this, he does it."

Jesus was amazed to hear that and said to the onlookers, "Believe me, I never found that kind of trust in anyone in Israel. I tell you, many will come in from east and west and sit down to eat with Abraham, Isaac and Jacob in the kingdom of the skies, while the heirs of the kingdom will be thrown out into the darkness beyond, where the wailing and gnashing of teeth will be." And Jesus said to the captain, "Go home, and let it be for you as you have trusted." And the child was cured at that hour.

And going into Peter's home Jesus saw Peter's mother-in-law struck down with a fever; and he touched her hand, and the fever left her, and she got up and was at his service.

As it got late, they brought him many people with demons; and he threw the spirits out with his words and cured everyone in bad health, fulfilling what was said by Isaiah the prophet:

He himself took on our weaknesses
And bore our diseases.

Seeing the crowd around him Jesus gave orders to shove off for the other shore. And a clerk came up and said to him: "Master, I'll follow you wherever you go."

And Jesus said to him, "Foxes have holes, and the birds of the sky have places to camp, but the son of humanity doesn't have anywhere to lay his head."

Another of his students said to him, "Lord, let me go bury my father first."

Jesus said to him, "Follow me and let the dead bury their own dead."

And as he got on board the boat, his students followed him. Next thing you know there was such a great shaking in the sea that the boat was hidden under the waves – but he was sleeping. And they went over and roused him, saying "Lord! Help! We'll be killed!"

And he says to them, "What cowards you are, unbelievers." Then he got up and yelled at the winds and the sea, and there was a great calm.

The people were amazed and said, "Where did this guy come from who can make the winds and the sea listen to him?"

And when he got across to the country of the Gadarenes, he was met by two possessed men coming from the graveyard, extremely dangerous men, so much so that no one could go by that way. And just then they started shouting, "What have we done to you, son of God? Did you come to start torturing us ahead of time?"

Now off a ways from them there was a big herd of pigs grazing. So the demons started pleading with him, saying, "If you throw us out, send us into the herd of pigs."

And he told them, "Go ahead." And they came out and went into the pigs. And all of a sudden the whole herd of them rushed off the cliff into the sea and were killed in the waves. As for the herders, they ran away, and when they got into town they reported all about the possessed men. And look, the whole town came out to meet Jesus, and when they saw him they begged him to go away from their neighborhood.

9

AND HE got on the boat and went back across and returned to his own town. And next thing they were bringing him a paralyzed man lying on a stretcher, and Jesus, seeing their faith, said to the paralytic, "Take heart, son, you are forgiven your errors."

And at that, some of the canon-lawyers said to each other, "That's blasphemy!"

And Jesus, seeing their mood, said, "Why are you brooding evil in your hearts? Which is easier to say: 'You're forgiven your errors,' or 'Get up and walk away'? Well then, so you'll know that the son of humanity has authority to forgive errors on earth –" at that point he said to the paralytic, "Get up and take your stretcher and go home." And he got up and went back to his house. Seeing that, the crowds were terrified and praised God for giving that kind of power to mortal beings.

And passing through there, Jesus saw a person sitting at the toll-station, name of Matthew, and says to him, "Follow me." And he stood up and followed him.

And it happened that as he was seated at table in his house this crowd of tax-collectors and godless people came in and sat down with Jesus and his students. And the Pharisees, seeing that, said to his students, "Why does your teacher eat with tax-collectors and godless people?"

He heard that and said, "It's not the healthy who need a doctor, but the sick. Go find out what 'I want mercy and not sacrifice' means. I came here, not to call the saints, but to call the godless people."

Then John's students came up to him and said, "Why is it that we and the Pharisees fast a lot, while your students don't fast?"

And Jesus said to them, "The wedding party can't be in mourning while the groom is with them, can they? There will come days when the groom will be taken away from them, and then they can fast. No one patches an old cloak with a scrap of brand-new cloth. It takes away the cloak's completeness, and a worse split results. Nor do they put new wine in old wineskins, because if they do, the skins break and the wine pours out and the skins are ruined; instead, they put new wine in new skins, and both are preserved."

As he was saying these things to them, next a high official came and bowed before him, saying, "My daughter has just died, but go and put your hand on her, and she'll live." And Jesus got up and followed him, and so did his students.

And then this woman who had been bleeding excessively for twelve years came up from behind and touched the bottom of his cloak, saying to herself, "If I just touch his cloak, I'll be saved."

Jesus, turning and seeing her, said, "Courage, daughter, your trust has saved you." And the woman was all right from that time on.

And Jesus, going into the official's house and seeing the flute-players and the noisy crowd, said, "Be on your way: the girl didn't die, she's sleeping." And they were laughing at him. But when the crowd was thrown out he went in and took her hand, and the girl woke up. And that story went out across the country.

And as he passed through there Jesus was followed by two blind men shouting, "Have mercy on us, son of David."

When he got back to his house the blind men came up to him and Jesus says to them, "You believe I can do this?"

"Yes, Lord," they say to him.

Then he touched their eyes, saying, "Let it be for you according to your trust." And their eyes were opened. And Jesus thundered at them, saying, "Make sure no one finds out!" But they went and publicized him throughout the country.

Then as they were going out, now look, they brought him a mute person with a demon. And with the demon thrown out, the mute man talked, and the crowds were amazed saying, "Nothing like this was ever seen in Israel!"

But the Pharisees said, "He throws out demons by the power of the demon king."

And Jesus made the rounds of all the towns and villages, teaching in their synagogues and proclaiming the good word of the kingdom and curing every disease and every infirmity.

Seeing the crowds, he felt sorry for them, because they were lying scattered and torn like sheep without a shepherd. Then he says to his students, "An ample harvest, and few workers. So ask the harvestmaster to send workers out into his fields."

10

THEN, calling his twelve students together, he gave them authority over unclean spirits, to throw them out and cure every disease and every infirmity.

The twelve apostles' names are as follows: first Simon, the one known as Simon Peter, and his brother Andrew; James son of Zebedee and his brother John; Philip; Bartholomew; Thomas;

Matthew the tax-collector; James son of Alpheus; Thaddeus; Simon of Canaan; and Judas Iscariot, his betrayer.

Jesus sent out these twelve after first giving them orders saying, "Don't go off on the road to the pagans and don't go to the Samaritan city. Instead go after the lost sheep of the Israel family. Go and announce that the kingdom of the skies is approaching. Cure the sick, raise the dead, wash lepers, throw out demons. Accept free gifts, and give for free. Don't have gold, silver, or brass in your belts. Don't take a knapsack on the road, or a second tunic, or shoes, or a cane. For the worker is worth his feed. When you get to a city or town, find out who there is appropriate, and stay there until you move on. Salute the house as you go into it, and if it's worthy, your peace will come over it; if it's not worthy, your peace will come back to you. And whoever doesn't receive you and doesn't listen to your words, when you get out of that house or that city shake its dust off your feet. I assure you, Sodom and Gomorrah will be in better shape on Judgment Day than that town.

"Here I am sending you out like sheep amid wolves, so be smart as snakes and innocent as doves.

"Be careful of the world, because they'll hand you over to the judges and flog you in their synagogues. You'll be haled before governors and kings because of me, as a testimony to them and the pagans. But when they hand you over, don't worry how you'll talk or what you'll say: you will be given something to say at that time, because it isn't you talking, it's the breath of the Father talking through you.

"Brothers will hand each other over to be executed, and fathers their children; children will rise up against their parents and kill them. And you will be hated by everybody because of my name. Whoever endures to the end, that's who will be saved.

"If they hound you in one city, escape to the next: believe me, you won't exhaust the cities in Israel before the son of humanity comes.

"No student is better than his teacher and no slave better than his master. It's enough for the student to become like his teacher and the slave like his master. If they called the head of the house Beelzebub, what will they call the servants there?

"So don't be afraid of them; because there's nothing covered that won't be opened up and nothing hidden that won't be found out. What I tell you in the darkness, say in the light; what I whisper in your ear, announce on the rooftops.

"And don't be afraid of those who kill the body but can't kill the soul. Instead, fear Him who can annihilate both soul and body in Gehenna-fire. Aren't sparrows sold two for a quarter? Not one of them falls on the ground without your Father, and every hair on your head is accounted for. So don't be afraid: you matter more than a heap of sparrows.

"So everybody who speaks up for me in front of the world, I'll speak up for them in front of my Father in the skies; and everybody who says they don't know me in front of the world, I'll say I don't know them in front of my Father in the skies.

"Don't think I came to cast peace across the land. I didn't come to cast peace, I came to wield a sword, because I came to divide a man against his father and a daughter against her mother and a bride against her mother in law, and to make a man's servants his enemies.

"Whoever prefers father or mother over me is not worthy of me; and whoever prefers son or daughter over me is not worthy of me; and whoever does not take his cross and follow after me is not worthy of me. Whoever found his life will lose it, and the one who lost his life because of me will find it.

"Whoever receives you receives me, and whoever receives me, receives my Sender. Whoever receives a prophet by the name of a prophet will receive a prophet's wages; whoever receives a just man by the name of a just man will receive a just man's wages. And whoever gives one of these lowly people even just a glass of cold water by their name as one of my students, I promise you, he will not forfeit his pay."

11

AND as it happened, when Jesus finished giving orders to his twelve students, he moved on from there to teach and spread the word in their towns.

Now John, hearing in jail of the works of the Anointed, sent word to him through his students, saying to him, "Are you the one who's coming, or shall we expect another one?"

And Jesus said in answer to them: "Go back and report to John what you hear and see: blind people see and lame people walk, lepers are washed clean and deaf people hear; and corpses rise; and the poor are given the good news. And the person is in luck who doesn't let me down."

As they were leaving, Jesus started telling the crowds about John: "What did you go out in the desert to see? A reed shaken by the wind? Come on, what did you go out to see? A person dressed in nice soft clothes? Look, the people wearing the soft clothes are in the houses of kings. Come on, what did you go out to see? A prophet? Yes, I tell you, a prophet and more: He's the one about whom it is written:

Look, I'm sending my messenger before your face,
To prepare your road ahead of you.

"I assure you, among all those born of women no one has arisen greater than John the Baptist – but the lowest person in the kingdom of the skies is greater than him. Ever since the days of John the Baptist, right up to now, the kingdom of the skies has been suffering violence and violent people are laying hands on it. For the prophets and the law prophesied as far as John, and if you wish to receive him, he is the Elijah to come. Those with ears to hear, hear!

"What can I compare this generation to? They're like children sitting around the marketplace hollering at the others:
We-played-the-flute-and-you-wouldn't-dance,
We-beat-our-breasts-and-you-wouldn't-mourn!

"After all, John came along not eating or drinking, and they say, 'He's possessed.' The son of humanity came along eating and drinking, and they say, 'Look at this wine-drinking gourmand who's friendly with tax-collectors and godless people.' But wisdom always was vindicated by its works."

Then he began to complain that in the towns where his greatest wonders were worked, they didn't come round. "The worse for you, Chorazin! The worse for you, Bethesda! Because if the wonders had occurred in Tyre and Sidon that have occurred in you, they would long since have come round in sackcloth and ashes. Except I'm telling you, Tyre and Sidon will be better off on Judgment Day than you! And you, Capharnaum, won't _you_ be exalted to the heavens? You'll sink into hell! Because if the wonders had occurred in Sodom that have occurred in you, it would still be there today. But I'm telling you, the Land of Sodom will be better off on Judgment Day than you."

At that point Jesus reacted by saying: "I praise you, Father, lord of the sky and the earth, that you hid these things from scholars and wits and opened them up to babies—yes, Father, because that's how your divine pleasure could be manifested before you.

"Everything was handed to me by my Father, and no one knows the son but the Father, and no one knows the Father but the son and those he decides to reveal himself to.

"Come here to me, all you drudges and overburdened ones, and I will give you a rest. Put my yoke on and learn from me: I am gentle and humble of heart, and you will find rest for your souls, because my yoke is kindly and my load is light."

12

DURING that time Jesus once traveled through the grain fields on the Sabbath. And his students got hungry and started picking ears of grain and eating them. The Pharisees, seeing that, said to him, "Look, your students are doing what isn't allowed on the Sabbath."

And he said to them, "Haven't you ever read what David did when he and those with him began to starve, how he went into the house of God and they ate the sacramental loaves which he himself wasn't allowed to eat, nor those with him, but only the priests? Or didn't you ever read in the law how on the Sabbath the priests in the temple break the rules of the Sabbath but aren't guilty? And I'm telling you, there's something greater than the temple here. If you'd found out what 'I want mercy and not sacrifice' means, you wouldn't have charged those who aren't guilty. After all, the son of humanity is superior to the Sabbath."

And moving on from there he went into their synagogue, and there was this fellow with a withered hand. And they questioned him, saying, "Is it all right to cure people on the Sabbath?" so that they would be able to charge him.

And he said to them, "Which of you, if you had one sheep and it fell into a ditch, would not take hold and haul it out again because it was the Sabbath? So how much more important is a person than a sheep? Enough that it's all right to do good on the Sabbath." Then he says to the fellow, "Reach out your hand." And he reached it out, and it was restored to health like the other one.

But the Pharisees went out and had a meeting about him and how to get rid of him.

Jesus, learning of that, withdrew from those parts, and giant crowds followed him, and he cured all of them and strictly warned them not to make him famous, fulfilling what was spoken by Isaiah the prophet:

Here is the child of mine, whom I chose,
My beloved child, in whom my soul has delighted.
I will put my breath upon him,
And he will announce a verdict to the nations.
He will not squabble, he will not shout,
Nor will they hear his voice in the streets.
He will not snap a reed that's bruised

Nor douse a wick that's smoking,
Till he pronounces the decision for victory
And nations set their hopes on his name.

Then a man with a demon was brought to him, blind and mute, and he cured him, so the mute man could talk and see. And the crowds were all thunderstruck and said "Is this the son of David?"

But the Pharisees heard, and said, "This guy only throws out demons through the power of Beelzebub, the demon king."

Sensing their feelings, he said to them: "Any country split in opposition to itself gets wiped out and any city or house split in opposition to itself won't stand up. And if Satan throws out Satan, that splits him in opposition to himself, so how will his country stand up? And if I'm throwing out demons by Beelzebub's power, whose power are *your* sons throwing them out by, and won't they condemn you on that account? But if I'm throwing out demons by the breath of God, then the kingdom of God has caught up with you. How can a person go into a strong man's house and steal his stuff without first tying up the strong man? *Then* he can rob his house. Who isn't with me is against me, and who doesn't unite with me scatters from me.

"For that reason I tell you, every wrong and every curse will be forgiven people, but cursing the spirit won't be forgiven people. If someone says something against the son of humanity, he will be forgiven; but if he speaks against the breath of the holy, he will not be forgiven in this century or the coming one.

"Either you have a good tree with its good fruit, or you have a rotten tree with its rotten fruit; because the tree is known by its fruit. Children of the snake, how can you say good things if you are bad? since the mouth speaks out what the heart is brimming over with. The good person dispenses good from his good treasury, and the bad person dispenses bad from his bad treasury. I tell you, every idle word that people say, they will have to account for on Judgment Day, because by your words you will be acquitted, and by your words you will be condemned."

Then some of the canon-lawyers and Pharisees answered him saying, "Master, we want to see a sign from you."

But he answered them: "This low and adulterous breed demands a sign, and they will be given no sign but the sign of Jonah the prophet. Because just as Jonah was in the hollow of the whale for three days and three nights, so the son of humanity will be in the heart of the earth for three days and three nights. Men of Niniveh will stand up on Judgment Day alongside this breed and condemn them, saying *their* minds were changed by the preaching of Jonah, and there's more than Jonah right here. The Queen from the South will rise in the middle of the judgment alongside this breed and condemn them, because *she* came from the ends of the earth to hear the wisdom of Solomon, and there's more than Solomon right here.

"When the unclean spirit goes out of a person it passes through arid regions, looking for a place to rest and not finding it. Then it says, 'I'll go back home where I came from,' and when it gets there it finds the place vacant, all swept and tidied up. Then it goes and brings along with it seven other spirits nastier than itself and goes in and settles down there, and the person ends up worse off than before. And that's what will happen to this vile race."

While he was still speaking to the crowds, there was his mother and his brothers and sisters standing on the outskirts, wanting to talk with him. And someone told him, "Your mother and your brothers and sisters are standing out there and they want to talk with you."

And he said to the person speaking, "Who is my mother, and who are my brothers and sisters?" And gesturing toward his students, he said, "Here's my mother and my brothers and sisters: whoever does the will of my Father in the skies, that's who my brother and my sister and my mother is."

13

THAT same day Jesus went out of his house and sat by the sea. And such great crowds were drawn to him that he got in a boat and sat down, while the crowd all stood along the shore.

And he talked to them a lot in metaphors, saying: "Once there was a man who went out sowing his seed. And in the course of his sowing some fell by the roadside, and the birds came and ate it up. Some fell on the rocky ground where there wasn't much soil, and it sprang right up, there being no depth to the soil; but when the sun came up it got scorched and dried out for lack of roots. Some fell on thorns, and the thorns came up and choked it off. And some fell on good soil and bore fruit, a hundred here, sixty there, thirty there. Those with ears, hear!"

And his students came up to him and said, "Why do you speak to them in metaphors?"

He answered, "To you it is given to know the mysteries of the kingdom of the skies; to them it isn't given. Because whoever has shall be given more and more, while whoever has nothing, even what he has will be taken away from him. That's why I talk to them in metaphors, so that when they see they don't see, and when they hear they don't hear or understand." (So the prophesy of Isaiah was fulfilled for them, the one saying:

With your ear you hear and never understand,
And when you look, you look but never see.
Because the heart of this people was weighted down,
And with their ears they heard sluggishly,
And their eyes were kept closed,
Lest they see with their eyes,
And hear with their ears,
And understand with their heart,
And come back and I heal them.)

"How lucky your eyes are to see and your ears are to hear! Because believe me, many prophets and upright people longed to see what you are seeing and never saw it, and longed to hear what you are hearing and never heard it.

"So you heard the metaphor of the sower. If anyone hears the word of the kingdom and doesn't understand, the Evil One comes and robs what was sown in their heart: that's the seed sown by the roadside. The seed sown on rocky ground, that's the person who hears the word and joyfully seizes it at once. But it has no root in them, it's only temporary; and if there's pressure or persecution because of the word, that immediately trips them up. The seed sown among thorns, that's the person who hears the word, and then the worries of the times and the strategy of moneymaking strangle the word and it becomes unable to bear fruit. The seed sown on good soil, that's the person who hears the word and understands it, and who really does bear fruit, a hundred here, sixty there, and thirty there."

He put another metaphor before them, saying: "The kingdom of the skies was once compared to a man who sowed good seed in his field. But while everybody was sleeping his enemy came and sowed weeds in the middle of the wheat and went away. But as the grain sprouted and bore fruit, then the weeds appeared too.

"So the landlord's servants came and said to him: 'Sir, didn't you sow good seed in your field? So where does it get these weeds from?'

"And he said to them, 'Some enemy did this.'

"And the servants said to him, 'Do you want us to go pull them out?'

"He said, 'No, because in pulling out the weeds you might uproot the wheat along with them. Let both grow together till the harvest, and at harvest-time I'll tell the harvesters, *First pull up the weeds and tie them in bundles to be burned, then collect the wheat and put it in my silo.*'"

He put another metaphor before them, saying: "The kingdom of the skies is like a seed of the mustard-plant that a man took and planted in his garden. Though it's the smallest of all seeds, when it grows it's bigger than the vegetables and turns into a tree, till the birds of the sky come and camp in its branches."

Another metaphor he spoke to them: "The kingdom of the skies is like yeast which a woman took and mixed in with three sacks of flour till it all rose." Jesus said all these things to the crowds in metaphors, and said nothing to them without metaphors, so as to fulfill what was spoken through the prophet saying,

> _I will open my mouth in metaphors,_
> _I will spew out things hidden since the founding of the world._

Then he dismissed the crowds and went home, and his students came up to him saying, "Clarify the metaphor of the weeds in the field for us."

He replied, "The sower of good seed is the son of humanity. The field is the world, the good seed is the sons of the kingdom, the weeds are the sons of the Evil One. The enemy who sowed them is the devil. The harvest is the culmination of time, and the harvesters are messengers. So just as the weeds are collected and burned in the fire, that's how it will be in the culmination of time. The son of humanity will send his messengers and round up all the obstacles in his kingdom and all the workers of lawlessness and throw them into the furnace of fire, where the wailing and gnashing of teeth will be. Then the innocent will shine like the sun in the kingdom of their Father. Those with ears to hear, hear!

"The kingdom of the skies is like a treasure hidden in the field, which a person finds and re-hides, and in his joy goes off and sells all he has and buys that field.

"Again, the kingdom of the skies is like a businessman looking for high-quality pearls. Finding one costly pearl he went off and sold all he had and bought it.

"Once again, the kingdom of the skies is like a large net thrown in the sea, collecting some of every species, which, when it was full, they dragged onto dry ground, and sat down and sorted the good fish into their creels and threw the bad ones out. That's how it will be in the culmination of time. The messengers will ride out and separate the evil from the just and throw them into the furnace of fire, where the wailing and gnashing of teeth will be.

"Do you understand all that?"

They told him, "Yes."

And he said to them, "Because of this, any scholar versed in the kingdom of the skies is like the head of a household who brings out of his treasury new things and old."

And as it happened, when Jesus finished these metaphors, he moved on from there. And he went back to his home town and taught them in their synagogue, till they were stunned and said, "Where does he get this wisdom and these powers? Isn't this the carpenter's son? Isn't his mother named Mary and aren't his brothers named James, Joseph, Simon, and Jude? And aren't his sisters all with us? So where does he get all this?" And they were offended by him.

But Jesus said to them: "A prophet is never dishonored if not in his home town and in his own house." And he didn't work many wonders there because of their lack of faith.

14

AT THAT TIME Herod [Archelaus] the governor heard of Jesus's reputation and said to his children, "It's John the Baptist! He came back from the dead, and that's why these powers work in him!"

(You see, Herod had seized John, tied him up, and put him in jail on account of Herodiada, his brother Philip's wife; because John had said to him, "You aren't allowed to have her." And though he wanted to kill him he was afraid of the masses, because they considered him a prophet.

But when it was Herod's birthday, Herodiada's daughter danced in front of everybody; and Herod liked her so much he swore under oath to give her whatever she asked. She – urged on by her mother – said, "Give me the head of John the Baptist on a tray." And the unhappy king, because of his oath and the other guests there, ordered it to be given to her, and sent out and had John beheaded in jail. And the head was brought to her on a tray and given to the girl, and she brought it to her mother. And his students came and took the body away and buried it and went and reported that to Jesus.)

Jesus, hearing that, headed out of there in a boat for a deserted place by himself. And the crowds, when they heard, followed him on foot out of the cities. And he came out and saw a great crowd and felt sorry for them and cured those of them that were sick.

When it got late, his students came up to him and said, "This place is in the middle of nowhere and it's already late. Send the crowds off so they can go into the villages and buy food for themselves."

But Jesus said to them, "They don't have to go away; give them something to eat yourselves."

They said to him, "We don't have anything here but five loaves of bread and two fish."

He said, "Bring them here to me." And after telling the crowds to sit down on the grass, he took the five loaves and two fish, looked up to the sky and blessed them, then broke the loaves and gave them to his students, and his students gave them to the crowds. And they all ate and had their fill. And they cleared away twelve basketfuls of leftover scraps. And those eating were about five thousand men, exclusive of women and children.

And right after that he made his students get in the boat and bring him to the other side until he could disband the crowds. And after disbanding the crowds he went up the mountain by himself to pray. When it got late he was there alone. But the boat was already several hundred yards offshore and being buffeted by the waves, since the wind was against them. Then during the fourth watch of the night he came toward them walking on the sea. His students, seeing him walking on the sea were disturbed and said "It's a ghost!" and cried out in fear.

But Jesus spoke right up and said to them, "Courage, it's me, don't be afraid."

And Peter answered him, saying, "Lord, if it's you, command me to come toward you on the waters."

And he said, "Come on." And getting down out of the boat Peter walked on the waters and went toward Jesus. But seeing the strong wind he got scared, and cried out as he started to sink, saying, "Lord, save me!"

And Jesus stretched his hand right out and took hold of him and says to him, "Unbeliever, what did you hesitate for?" And when they climbed back into the boat the wind cut down.

And those in the boat bowed before him, saying, "You really are God's son."

And after crossing over they went on land to Gennesareth. And when they recognized him, the men of that place sent word into all the surrounding countryside, and they brought him everyone in bad health. And they asked him if they could just touch the edge of his cloak, and those who touched it were healed.

15

THEN Pharisees and canon-lawyers from Jerusalem come up to Jesus saying, "Why do your students overstep the tradition of the elders? Why, they don't wash their hands when they eat bread."

He answered, "Why do you overstep the command of God on account of your tradition? After all, God said, 'Do right by your father and your mother,' and 'Whoever denounces father or mother, let them end in death.'

"But you say, 'Whoever says to his father or mother, *I'm giving to religion whatever you might have gotten from me,* doesn't have to worry about his father or his mother.' And you invalidate the word of God on the basis of your tradition. You fakes, Isaiah prophesied very well about you when he said,

These people honor me with their lips
But their heart is far away from me.
Pointlessly they worship me,
Teaching as their doctrine the commandments of the world."

And calling the crowd closer he said to them, "Hear and understand: it isn't what goes into your mouth that pollutes a person, it's what comes out of your mouth – that's what pollutes a person."

Then his students come up and say to him: "You know the Pharisees were offended to hear those words?"

But he answered, "Every plant not planted by my heavenly father will be uprooted. Let them go. They are blind guides for the blind. But if one blind person guides the other around, both fall into the ditch."

Peter answered him saying: "Tell us about this metaphor."

He said: "Even *you* still don't understand? Don't you see that everything that goes into the mouth passes into the belly and is thrown out into the toilet? But what comes out of the mouth comes from the heart, and those things pollute the person. For out of the heart come evil designs, murders, adulteries, whoring, thefts, perjuries, blasphemies. . . those things pollute a person, but eating with unwashed hands doesn't pollute a person."

And going out of there Jesus proceeded into the parts of Tyre and Sidon. And this Canaanite woman from those regions came out and cried, "Pity me, Lord, son of David! My daughter is terribly possessed."

But he didn't answer her. And his students came up to him and asked him, "Set her free, she's screaming after us."

He answered, "I was only sent to the lost sheep of the Israel family."

And she came and bowed before him, saying, "Lord, help me."

He answered, "It isn't right to take the children's bread and throw it to the dogs."

But she said, "Yes it is, Lord! Even the dogs get to eat the scraps falling from their master's table."

Then Jesus answered her, "Madam, your faith is tremendous. Let it be for you as you wish." And her daughter was cured from that hour on.

And moving on from there Jesus went down by the sea of Galilee, and he went up the mountain and sat down there. And giant crowds came to him, bringing with them people who were lame, blind, deformed, mute, and all kinds of things, and threw them at his feet, and he cured them, so that the crowd was astonished to see mute people talking, deformed people sound, lame people walking, and blind people seeing. And they glorified the God of Israel.

But Jesus, calling his students to him, said, "I feel sorry for the crowd, because they've been following me around for three days and they don't have anything to eat. And I don't want to send them off still hungry because they might drop on the way."

And his students said to him, "Where in the middle of nowhere do we get enough bread to satisfy a crowd this size?"

And Jesus says to them, "How much bread do you have?"

They said, "Seven loaves, plus a few small fish." And after telling the crowd to sit down on the ground he took the seven loaves and the fish, gave thanks, broke them, and gave them to his students, who gave them to the crowds. And they all ate their fill, and they cleared away seven basketfuls of leftover scraps. (Those eating were four thousand men, exclusive of women and children.)

And after sending the crowds away he got in the boat and went to the regions of Magadan.

16

AND the Pharisees and Sadducees came up to him and, testing him out, asked him to show them a sign from the sky. He answered them, "When it gets late you say, 'Nice day tomorrow, the sky's red,' and in the morning, 'A storm today, the sky's red and gloomy.' You know how to make out the face of the sky, but you can't make out the signs of the times? This low and adulterous breed demands a sign, and they won't be given any sign except the sign of Jonah." And he left them behind and went away.

And in crossing to the other bank his students forgot to bring bread. And Jesus said to them: "Watch and guard against the yeast of the Pharisees and Sadducees."

And they discussed that with each other saying, "We didn't *bring* any bread!"

Jesus, knowing that, said: "Why are you talking amongst yourselves, unbelievers, about how you didn't bring any bread? You don't know any more, you don't remember any more about the five loaves that fed five thousand and how many basketfuls you cleared away, or the seven loaves that fed four thousand and how many basketfuls you cleared away? How can you not see that I'm not talking to you about bread? But be careful of the yeast of the Pharisees and Sadducees." Then they understood that he hadn't said to guard against the yeast of their bread, but to guard against the teaching of the Pharisees and Sadducees.

After Jesus went into the regions of Philip Caesarea he asked his students, "Who do people say the son of humanity is?"

They said, "Some say John the Baptist, others say Elijah, the rest say Jeremiah or one of the prophets."

He said, "And you, who do you say I am?"

Simon Rock [that is, Peter] answered, "You are the Anointed, the son of the living God."

Jesus answered him, "You are in luck, Simon Johnson: flesh and blood didn't reveal this to you, but my Father in the skies. And I say to you that you *are* a Rock, and on this rock I will build my assembly, and the gates of the underworld will not overpower it. I will give you the keys to the kingdom of the skies, and what you bind on earth will be bound in the skies, and what you release on earth will be released in the skies." Then he ordered his students to tell nobody that he himself was the Anointed.

After that Jesus began to show his students how he had to go off to Jerusalem, and have many things done to him by the elders and chief priests and canon-lawyers, and be killed, and rise up on the third day. And Peter, taking him aside, began to remonstrate with him, saying, "Mercy on you, Lord! This won't happen to *you!*"

But he turned and said to Peter, "Out of my sight, you devil! You are an obstacle to me, because you're thinking about human concerns, not God's concerns." Then Jesus said to his students, "If anyone wishes to walk in my footsteps, let them repudiate themselves and pick up their cross and follow me, because whoever tries to save their life will lose it, whereas whoever loses their life because of me will find it. After all, what will a person gain if he wins the whole world and loses his life? Or what shall a person give in exchange for his life? Remember, the son of humanity is going to come with his messengers in the glory of his Father, and then he will pay back each person according to their deeds. I assure you, there are some among those standing here who will never taste death before they see the son of humanity coming in his monarchy."

17

AND six days later Jesus takes Peter, James, and James's brother John with him and takes them up a high mountain off by themselves. And he was transformed before their eyes, and his face shone like the sun, and his clothes became as white as light. And suddenly there appeared to them Moses and Elijah talking with him. Peter reacted by saying to Jesus, "Lord, it's good for us to be here. If you want, I will put up three tabernacles here, one for you, one for Moses, and one for Elijah."

Even as he spoke, a cloud of light enveloped them, and suddenly there was a voice from the cloud saying, "This is my son, my beloved son, in whom I am delighted: listen to him!"

And hearing that, his students fell on their faces and panicked completely. And Jesus came over to them and touched them, saying, "Get up and don't be afraid." Lifting their eyes they saw no one but Jesus alone.

And as they went down the mountain Jesus commanded them, "Don't tell this vision to anyone till the son of humanity has come back from the dead."

And his students asked him, "So why do the scribes say, 'First Elijah must come'?"

He answered, "Elijah is coming and will restore everything. Yet I'm telling you that Elijah came already, and they didn't recognize him; instead, they did with him as they pleased. And the son of humanity will be treated the same way by them." Then his students understood that he was talking to them about John the Baptist.

And as they went toward the crowd a fellow came their way who fell on his knees and said, "Lord, have mercy on my son; he is insane and suffering horribly. He falls into the fire repeatedly and into the water repeatedly. And I brought him to your students, but they couldn't cure him."

And Jesus answered, "You unbelieving and perverse-minded crew! How long will I be with you? How long will I put *up* with you? Bring him here to me." And Jesus yelled at him and the demon came out of him, and the child was cured from that time on.

Then his students came up to Jesus privately and said, "Why couldn't *we* throw it out?"

He said to them, "Because of your lack of faith. I assure you, if you have a mustard-seed's worth of faith, you'll tell this mountain to move from here to there and it will move; nothing will be impossible for you."

As they were making the rounds of Galilee Jesus told them, "The son of humanity will be betrayed into the hands of the world, and they will kill him, and on the third day he will rise up." And they were deeply saddened.

As they were going into Capharnaum those who collected the fifty-cent toll came to Peter and said, "Your teacher doesn't pay his fifty cents?"

And he said, "That's right!"

And when he got home Jesus was there ahead of him, saying, "What do you think, Simon? On whom do the kings of the earth impose their taxes and their tolls? On their own children or on other people's?" And when he said "Other people's," Jesus said to him, "Then their own children go free. But so as not to get in these people's way, go down to the sea and throw in a hook and take the first fish that comes up, and you'll find a silver dollar in its mouth. Take it and give it to them for you and me."

18

AT THAT HOUR Jesus's students came to him saying, "Tell us, who is the greatest in the kingdom of the skies?"

And he called to a child and put the child in front of them and said, "I assure you, if you don't turn round and become like children, you'll never get into the kingdom of the skies. So whoever brings himself down to the level of this child, that's who the greatest in the kingdom of the skies is. And whoever receives any child like this one in my name, receives me.

"Whereas whoever trips up one of these little ones who believe in me, would be better off to have a giant millstone hung around his neck and sink in the vastness of the sea.

"Woe to the world for stumbling-blocks! Because stumbling-blocks must come along, but woe to the person through whom they come! If your hand or your foot gets in your way, cut it off and throw it away. You're lucky if you enter deformed and crippled into Life, and aren't thrown with both hands and both feet into the everlasting fire. And if your eye gets in your way, pluck it out and throw it off. You're lucky if you enter with one eye into Life, and aren't thrown with both eyes into the fire of Gehenna.

"Watch out and don't be contemptuous of these little ones, because I tell you that their messengers at all times see the face of my Father in the skies.

"What do you think? If a fellow has a hundred sheep and one of them wanders off, isn't he going to leave the ninety-nine on the hillside and go look for the lost one? And if he manages to find it, I can tell you for sure that he will be happier about that one than about the ninety-nine that never wandered. In the same way, there is no desire on the part of your Father in the skies that the least important of these people should be lost.

"If your brother wrongs you, go have it out with him, just you and him. If he listens to you, you've gained your brother back. If he doesn't listen, bring one or two along with you, so that everything said stands on the word of two or three witnesses. If he won't listen to them, speak up at meeting. If he won't listen to the assembly, let him be the same to you as the foreigner and the tax-collector.

"I assure you, whatever you bind on the earth will be bound in the sky, and whatever you release on the earth will be released in the sky.

"Again, I tell you truly that if two of you on the earth agree about anything they ask for, it will come to them from my Father in the skies, because where two or three are assembled in my name, there I am in their midst."

Then Peter came up to him and said, "Lord, how many times shall my brother wrong me and I forgive him? Up to seven times?"

Jesus says to him, "I'm not telling you up to seven times, I'm telling you up to seventy-seven times.

"In this connection, the kingdom of the skies could be compared to a certain king who wanted to settle accounts with his slaves. As he started the settlement, they brought before him one who was indebted for ten million dollars. Since he didn't have it to pay back, the master ordered him and his wife and his children and everything he had to be sold in repayment. So the slave fell down and bowed before him, saying, 'Have patience with me, and I will pay it all back to you.' And the master, feeling sorry for that slave, let him go and forgave him the loan.

"Then that slave went out and found one of his fellow slaves who owed him a hundred dollars, and seized him and started choking him, saying, 'If you owe it to me, pay up!'

"So his fellow slave fell down and pleaded with him, saying, 'Have patience with me, and I will pay you back.' But he wouldn't hear it, and instead went off and threw him in jail till he should pay the debt.

"So his fellow slaves, seeing these events, were most unhappy, and went and informed their master about everything that had happened. Then the master, calling him before him, said to him, 'Wretched slave, I let you off from your entire debt, because you pleaded with me. Shouldn't you also have pitied your fellow-slave, as I pitied you?' And in a rage the master handed him over to the torturers till he should pay back everything he owed. And that's what my heavenly father will do to you, if each of you does not forgive your brother from your hearts."

19

AND as it happened, when Jesus finished these words, he headed out of Galilee and went into the regions of Judea across the Jordan. And giant crowds followed him, and he cured them there.

And the Pharisees came up to him testing him out and saying, "Is a man allowed to divorce his wife for whatever cause?"

He answered, "Didn't you ever read that the Creator made them male and female from the beginning, and that he said, 'Because of this a man is to leave his father and his mother behind and stick with his wife, and the two are to become one living thing, so that they aren't two anymore, they're one living thing?' So what God joined together, let no man divide."

They said to him, "Why did Moses say to present her with a divorce decree and divorce her?"

He said to them, "Moses, in view of the hardness of your hearts, allowed you to divorce your wives, but it wasn't like that from the beginning. I tell you that whoever divorces his wife for anything but whoring and marries another is living in adultery."

His students said to him: "If the guilt of a man with a woman is so great, it doesn't pay to get married."

And he said to them, "Not all have room for this idea, it has to be given to you: but some eunuchs were born that way from their mother's bellies, and some eunuchs were made that way by others, and some make themselves that way for the kingdom of the skies. Whoever can encompass it, let them do so."

Then some children were brought to him so he could put his hands on them and pray for them, but his students yelled at them. But Jesus said, "Leave the children alone and don't keep them back from coming toward me; the kingdom of the skies belongs to such as them." And after laying his hands on them he traveled on from there.

And someone came up to him and said: "Teacher, what good shall I do in order to have everlasting life?"

He said to him, "Why do you ask me about good? You only have one good Person. But if you wish to enter into that life, keep the commandments."

He says to him, "Which?"

Jesus said, " 'You are not to murder,' 'You are not to commit adultery,' 'You are not to steal,' 'You are not to perjure,' 'Do right by your father and your mother,' and 'You are to love those close to you as you love yourself.' "

The young man says to him, "I have kept all those. What do I still need?"

Jesus said to him, "If you want to be perfect, go sell what you have and give it to the poor, and you will have a treasure in the skies, and come here and follow me." Hearing those words the young man went away in mourning, because he was the owner of many possessions.

Jesus said to his students, "Believe me, a rich person won't find it easy to get into the kingdom of the skies. On the contrary, I tell you, it's easier for a camel to squeeze through the eye of a needle than for a rich person to get into the kingdom of God."

Hearing that, his students were completely stunned and said, "Then who *can* be saved?"

Looking straight at them, Jesus said, "For human beings it's impossible, but for God everything is possible."

Then Peter answered him, "Look at us: we left everything and followed you; so what will be ours?"

Jesus said to them, "I assure you that you who have followed me, in the time of rebirth when the son of humanity sits upon the throne of his glory, you too will sit on twelve thrones judging the twelve tribes of Israel. And everyone who left behind houses or brothers or sisters or father or mother or children or lands because of my name will get it back a hundred times over and inherit everlasting life. And many of the first will be last and many of the last will be first.

20

"YOU SEE, the kingdom of the skies is like a certain landowner who went out with the dawn to hire workers for his vineyard. After agreeing with the workers on a drachma a day he sent them off to his vineyard. And going out around nine o'clock he saw others standing around the marketplace idle and said to them: 'You go off to my vineyard too, and I will pay you what is reasonable,' and they went. Going out around noon and three he did the same.

"Around five o'clock he went out and found others standing and says to them, 'Why are you standing here all day with nothing to do?'

"They say to him: 'Nobody hired us.'

"He says to them, 'You go off to my vineyard too.'

"So when it got late the owner of the vineyard says to his foreman: 'Call the workers and pay them their wages going from last to first.' And the ones from five o'clock came forward and received a drachma apiece. And when the first ones came forward, they thought they'd get more, but they got a drachma apiece too.

"On receiving it they started grumbling at the landowner saying, 'These last ones worked one hour, and you make them equal to us who bore the burden and the heat of the day!'

"But he answered one of them, saying, 'I'm not cheating you, pal. Didn't you agree with me on a drachma? Take what's yours and go your way. I wish to give this latecomer the same as you; can't I do what I want with my own possessions? Must you cast an evil eye upon my being kind?' That's how the last will be first and the first will be last."

And going up to Jerusalem Jesus took his twelve students aside and said to them on the way: "Here we go up to Jerusalem, and the son of humanity will be handed over to the high priests and canon-lawyers, and they will condemn him to death and hand him over to the pagans to be made fun of, and whipped, and crucified; and on the third day he will rise again."

Then the mother of the sons of Zebedee came up to him with her sons, bowing before him as if asking him for something. He said to her, "What do you want?"

She says to him, "Say that these two sons of mine may sit one on your right and one on your left in your kingdom."

Jesus answered, "You don't know what you're asking. Can you drink the cup that I'm going to drink?"

They say to him, "We can."

He says to them, "Then you will drink my cup, but sitting at my right and left is not mine to give, it's for whoever my Father has prepared it for."

And the other ten were outraged at the two brothers. So Jesus called them together and said, "You know how the rulers of nations lord it over them and big men use their power. Among us it's not going to be like that: on the contrary, if you want to be big, be everybody's servant, and if you want to be number one, be everybody's slave – just as the son of humanity didn't come to be served, but to serve and to give his life as a ransom for many."

And as they traveled out from Jericho a large crowd followed him. And these two blind men sitting by the road, hearing that Jesus was going by, shouted, "Have mercy on us, son of David!" The crowd yelled at them to be quiet, but they shouted all the louder, "Have mercy on us, Lord, son of David!"

And Jesus stopped and called out to them, "What do you want me to do for you?"

They say to him, "Make our eyes open, Lord." And Jesus was moved, and touched their eyes, and immediately they could see, and they followed him.

21

AND WHEN they got close to Jerusalem and came to Bethphage on Mount Olive, at that point Jesus sent off two of his students, saying to them, "Go on into the village ahead of you, and right away you'll come upon a donkey tied up and her foal with her. Untie them and bring them to me. And if anyone says anything to you, you'll say, 'The master needs these,' and they'll

send them right back with you."* This happened so as to fulfill
what was spoken by the prophet:

Tell your daughter Zion,
Here comes your king,
Gently, mounted on donkey-back,
And on its foal, the beast of burden's son.

The students, going on their way and doing as Jesus ordered,
brought back the donkey and the foal and spread their cloaks
on them, and he sat down on top of them. And a very large
crowd spread their cloaks in the roadway, while others cut
branches from trees and strewed them in the road. And the
crowds going ahead of him and the crowds following shouted,
"Hooray for the son of David! Bless him who comes in the name
of the Lord! Hooray to the highest heavens!"

And as he came into Jerusalem the whole city was shaken up,
saying, "Who is this?"

And the crowds said, "This is the prophet Jesus, from Nazareth, Galilee."

And Jesus went into the temple, and threw out all those buying and selling in the temple, and overturned the tables of the
moneychangers and the chairs of the pigeon-sellers. And he says
to them, "It is written, 'My house will be known as a house
of prayer,' whereas you make it a den of thieves."

And blind and lame people came up to him in the temple
and he cured them. But the high priests and the canon-lawyers,
seeing the wonders he had worked and the children shouting
"Hooray for the son of David!" in the temple, were outraged
and said to him, "Do you hear what these ones are saying?"

*These instructions and similar ones given in advance of the Last Supper in
Matthew, Mark, and Luke, have been interpreted at least three ways: 1) Jesus
can say "go into town and you'll see this and that" by prophetic power;
2) Jesus can rely on the customs of Middle Eastern hospitality; 3) Jesus has
arranged something like a spy rendezvous with a well-to-do secret sympathizer.
The third explanation explains the most, including "go into town and see
So-and-so" and "you'll see a fellow with a water jug" (usually women and
not men carried water).

And Jesus says to them, "Yes. Didn't you ever read where it says, 'I will round out my praise in the mouths of babies and toddlers?'" And he left them behind and went out of town to Bethany and camped there.

The next morning, going back into town, he got hungry. And seeing a fig tree on the way he went toward it and found nothing but leaves on it, and said to it, "Let no fruit come from you ever again," and it dried up in a flash.

And his students were amazed to see that and said, "How could the fig tree dry up in a flash?"

Jesus answered, "Believe me, if you have faith and don't hesitate, not only will you do this business with the fig tree, but if you tell this mountain here, 'Get up and throw yourself into the sea,' it will happen; and everything you ask for in your prayers, if you believe, you will get it."

And after he'd gone into the temple, the high priests and the elders of the people come up to him as he was teaching and said, "What authority do you have to do this? Who gave you any such authority?"

Jesus answered, "I also want to ask you something, and if you tell me that I'll also tell you what authority I have to do this: Where did the washing of John come from? From heaven or from the world?"

They discussed that among themselves saying, "If we say from heaven, he'll say to us, 'Then why didn't you believe in him?' But if we say from the world, we have the crowd to be afraid of, since they all consider John a prophet." And they answered Jesus, "We don't know."

And he in his turn said to them, "I won't tell you what authority I have to do this either.

"What do you say? A fellow had two children: and he went to the first one and said, 'Son, go work in my vineyard today,' and he answered, 'I don't want to,' but later he thought better of it and went. And he went to the other one the same way, and he answered, 'Yessir,' and didn't go. Which of the two did the will of his father?"

They said, "The first."

And Jesus says to them, "Believe me, the whores and the tax-collectors will get into the kingdom of God before you, because John came toward you on the path of justice, and you didn't believe, while the whores and the tax-collectors *did* believe him. And you, even after seeing him, didn't convert to believing in him afterwards.

"Listen to another comparison. Once there was a certain land-owner who planted a vineyard and put a fence around it and dug out a wine cellar in it and built a tower and contracted it out to some farmers and left the country. So when the harvest time got close, he sent his slaves to the farmers to get his produce. And the farmers, seizing the slaves, flogged one, killed another, and threw stones at a third.

"Again he sent some more slaves, more numerous than the first, and they did the same thing to them. Finally he sent his son to them, saying, 'They will respect my son.'

"But when the farmers saw his son they said to each other, 'This guy is the heir. Here, let's kill him and get his inheritance,' and they seized him and took him outside the vineyard and killed him. So when the owner of the vineyard comes, what will he do to those farmers?"

They say to him, "He'll get rid of those evil people by evil means and give the vineyard out to other farmers who will deliver the produce to him in good season."

Jesus says to them, "Haven't you ever read in the Scriptures:

A stone that the builders rejected,
That one ended up the corner-stone:
That was made by the Lord
And is the admiration of our eyes?

"Because of that, I tell you that the kingdom of God will be taken away from you and given to a nation that bears its fruits. And whoever falls on that stone will be crushed, and whoever it falls upon, it will scatter in pieces."

And when the high priests and Pharisees heard his comparisons they realized he was talking about them. And though they wanted to seize him they were afraid of the masses, since they regarded him as a prophet.

22

AND Jesus again continued speaking to them in metaphors, saying, "The kingdom of the skies was once compared to a certain king who arranged a wedding for his son. And he sent his servants to call the guests to the wedding, and they wouldn't come. Again he sent some more servants, saying, "Tell the guests, 'Look, I've prepared the dinner, the steers and fat calves have been slaughtered, and everything's ready: come to the wedding.' But they ignored him and went away, one to his fields, another about his business; and others seized the servants, did violence to them, and killed them. So the king flew in a rage and sent out his army and got rid of those murderers and burned their city down. Then he says to his servants, 'The wedding is ready, but the guests didn't deserve it. So travel around the exits of the highways and invite whoever you find to the wedding.' And those servants went out into the streets and brought back whoever they found, bad and good alike, and the wedding was filled with guests. But when the king came in to look the guests over he saw a fellow there not dressed for a wedding, and said to him, 'Pal, how did you come here without wedding clothes?' But the man kept his mouth shut. Then the king said to his servants, 'Tie him hand and foot and throw him out into the darkness beyond, where the wailing and gnashing of teeth will be, because many are called, but few are chosen.'"

Then the Pharisees went out and had a meeting about how to trap him in his words. And they sent out their students to him with Herod's men, saying, "Teacher, we know that you're truthful and that you teach the word of God truthfully without being concerned about anybody, because you don't look to the face of the world. So tell us what you think: Is it all right to pay taxes to Caesar or not?"

Jesus, sensing the evil in them, said, "What are you testing me for, you fakes? Show me the coin paid in taxes." And they brought him a drachma. And he says to them, "Whose picture and inscription is this?"

They say to him, "Caesar's."

Then he says to them, "So give Caesar's things to Caesar, and God's things to God." And they were amazed to hear that, and left him alone and went away.

That same day Sadducees, who said there was no resurrection, came up to him and asked, "Teacher, Moses said, 'If someone dies without children, let his brother take his widow to wife and continue his brother's seed.' So in our town there were seven brothers: the first one married and died, and having no children, he left his wife to his brother. The second brother did the same, and the third, and so on for all seven, and the woman died last of all. So in the resurrection, which of the seven's wife will she be? After all, they all had her."

Jesus answered, "You're wandering in circles, knowing nothing of the scriptures or the power of God, because in the resurrection there are no brides and no grooms; instead, they're like the messengers in the sky. As for the resurrection of the dead, didn't you ever read what was spoken by God: 'I am the God of Abraham and the God of Isaac and the God of Jacob'? There is no god of the dead, only of the living." And the crowds were stunned to hear his teaching.

So then the Pharisees, hearing that he'd shut the Sadducees up, all got together in the same place. And one of them versed in law asked him as a test, "Teacher, which commandment in the law is important?"

He said to them, "You are to love your lord God with all your heart and all your spirit and all your mind. That is the important and first commandment. The second one is similar: You are to love those close to you as you love yourself. All the law and all the prophets hang from these two commands."

With the Pharisees assembled, Jesus asked them this question: "What do you think about the Anointed One? Whose son is he?"

They told him, "David's."

He says to them, "Then how does David in the spirit call him Lord, saying,

A lord said to my lord,
Sit at my right,
While I pin your enemies underneath your feet?

So if David calls him Lord, how is he his son?"

And no one could give him an answer for that, nor did anybody dare to ask him any more questions after that day.

23

THEN Jesus talked to the crowds and his students, saying, "Where Moses sat, the Pharisees and the canon-lawyers now sit. So do and keep what they say to you, but don't go by what they do, because they say things and then don't do them. They shackle us with unbearably heavy taxes and lay that on people's shoulders, but they let no taxes come within arm's length of *them*. Everything they do is done to be observed by the world: their phylacteries with big broad strips, their cloaks with nice wide hems. They love their seats at the head tables of banquets and in the front pews of churches, and everyone saying hello to them downtown, and having people call them 'Master.'

"Don't you be called 'Master': you only have one teacher, all of you are brothers. And don't call your father on the earth your father, you only have one heavenly Father. And don't be called leaders, because you only have one leader, the Anointed. The highest person among you is to be the servant of you all, so those who exalt themselves will be humbled and those who humble themselves will be exalted.

"Woe to you canon-lawyers and Pharisees, you fakes, for shutting the door to the kingdom of the skies in humanity's face:

you don't go in yourselves and you don't let anybody else go in either.

"Woe to you canon-lawyers and Pharisees, you fakes, for traversing land and sea to make a convert, and then when one is made, turning him into a son of Gehenna twice as bad as yourselves!

"Woe to you, blind pathfinders, when you say, 'If you swear _by the temple,_ that's nothing, but if you swear _by all the gold in the temple,_ that's swearing.'* Blockheads and blind men, which is more important, the gold, or the temple that sanctifies the gold?

"And you say, 'If you swear _by the temple altar,_ that's nothing, but if you swear _by the offerings on the temple altar,_ that's swearing.' Blind men, which is more important, the offering or the altar that sanctifies the offering?

"In other words, if you swear 'by the altar,' you're swearing by it _and_ by everything on top of it, and if you swear 'by the temple,' you're swearing by it _and_ by its inhabitant, and if you swear 'by heaven!', you're swearing by the throne of God and by its occupant.

"Woe to you canon-lawyers and Pharisees, you fakes, for singling out the mint, the dillweed, and the curry-powder of the law and leaving aside the hard parts, like judgment and mercy and faith! _Those_ were the parts you should have done – and then the others shouldn't be omitted. Blind pathfinders, if there's a gnat in your soup, you strain it out; if there's a camel in your soup, you drink it down!

"Woe to you canon-lawyers and Pharisees, you fakes, for cleaning off the rim of your cup and saucer while on the inside you're bursting with greed and wild appetites. Blind Pharisee, wash out the inside of the cup and saucer first, if you want the outside to end up clean!

---

*_By the temple_ doesn't count as a curse to the Pharisees because it's so short it can be said without thinking and has become so common that it has no force anymore; while _by all the gold in the temple_ is considered more deliberate because it's longer, and more of a conscious choice because it's rarer.

"Woe to you canon-lawyers and Pharisees, you fakes, for being like dusty monuments that look pretty on the outside but on the inside are full of the bones of corpses and all kinds of rot. You likewise from the outside appear to the world to be decent, but inside you're full of hypocrisy and ways around the law.

"Woe to you canon-lawyers and Pharisees, you fakes, for building monuments to the prophets and decorating the graves of the just, and saying, 'If we'd been around in our fathers' time, we'd have had no part in shedding the prophets' blood.' So you testify yourselves that you're the children of those who *did* murder the prophets. And you fully come up to the standard of your forefathers. Vipers, offspring of snakes, how will you run from the sentence of Gehenna?

"For this reason I hereby send you prophets, wise men and scholars. Some of them you'll kill, some of them you'll crucify, some of them you'll have flogged in the synagogue and hounded from town to town. So that there will come back upon you all the innocent blood poured out upon the earth from the blood of Abel the innocent to the blood of Zachariah the son of Barachiah, whom you murdered between the temple and the altar. I assure you, that will all come back upon this generation.

"Jerusalem, Jerusalem, killer of prophets, stoner of ambassadors to the city, how often I wanted to gather your children together the way a bird gathers her little birds under her wing – and you didn't want to. And now look, your house is left in ruins. I tell you, you won't see me again from now until you say

Bless him who comes in the name of the Lord!"

24

AND Jesus went out of the temple and on his way, and his students came to him to show him the temple buildings. But he said to them, "You see all that? I assure you, not one stone will be left on top of another stone without being demolished."

As he sat on Mount Olive, his students came to him privately saying, "Tell us, when will that happen, and what will be the sign of your presence and of the culmination of time?"

And Jesus answered them, "Watch out, don't let anyone fool you, because there will be many people coming in my name and saying, 'I am the Anointed,' and they will fool a lot of people. You're going to hear wars, and reports of wars. Be careful, don't be afraid, because it has to happen, that's how it is at the end: race will rise up against race and country will rise up against country, and there will be famines, and places hit by earthquakes. All that is the beginning of the death-throes.

"Then they'll hand you over into torment and kill you off, and you'll be hated by people of every kind because of my name. And then many will be tripped up, and will betray each other and hate each other. And many pseudoprophets will come along and fool a lot of people. And on account of the full-scale lawlessness, the love in the hearts of the masses will be chilled. But whoever endures to the end, that's who will be saved. And this good word of the kingdom will be announced to all the inhabited earth as a testimony to all nations, and then comes the end.

"So when you see the monster of destruction, as spoken of by Daniel the prophet, standing in the holy place, when you recognize it, remember: those in Judea, evacuate into the mountains; those standing on housetops, don't go down to get anything from your house; those in the fields, don't go back to get your cloak. Woe to those with a child in their belly or nursing in those days!

"Pray that your flight doesn't happen in winter or on the Sabbath. For there will be trouble then like there has never been from the beginning of the world till now, and never will be again. And if those days were not cut short, no living thing would be left at all, but because of the chosen ones, those days will be cut short.

"If someone says to you then: Look here, it's the Anointed! or, Over here! don't believe them, because many pseudo-Christs and pseudoprophets will come along and give such great signs and portents as to fool, if possible, even the chosen ones: I hereby warn you in advance. So if they say to you, 'There he is, out in the desert,' don't go out there; or if they say, 'There, in the secret chambers,' don't believe them. Like the lightning that comes shining from east to west, that's what the presence of the son of humanity will be like. Wherever the body is, the vultures gather.

"Then right after the troubles of those days, the sun will go dark, and the moon won't give her beams, and the stars will fall from the sky, and the powers of the skies will be shaken.

"And then the sign of the son of humanity will appear in the sky, and then all the tribes of the earth will weep, and they will see the son of humanity coming upon the clouds of the sky with power and great glory. And he will send out his messengers with a big trumpet, and they will collect the chosen ones out of the four corners of the earth, from peak to peak of heaven.

"Take a lesson from the fig tree: when the shoots are tender, and the leaves are out, you know the harvest is near. The same with you: when you see all these things happening, you'll know it's right at your doorstep. I assure you that this generation will not go by before all this happens. The sky and the earth will go by, but my words will not go by.

"As for the date and time, no one knows, not even the messengers of the sky, not even the son, only the Father alone.

"Just like the days of Noah, that's what the presence of the son of humanity will be like. Just as in those days before the cataclysm they were eating and drinking and taking husbands and wives, and didn't notice anything till the cataclysm came and took them all, that's what the presence of the son of humanity will be like. Then there will be two men working in the fields; one will be taken along and one will be left behind.

Two women grinding at the mill: one will be taken along and one will be left behind.

"So keep awake, because you don't know what day your master is coming. This much you do know: if the owner of the house knew at what hour of the night the thief was coming, he'd stay awake and not let his house be tunneled into.

"Tell me, who is the faithful and prudent slave whom the master put in charge of his household to give them their food on time? Lucky for that slave if the master comes and finds him doing just that. I assure you, he will put him in charge of all his possessions. But if that lousy slave says to himself, 'My master is taking a while to get here,' and starts to beat up his fellow slaves and eat and drink with drunkards, that slave's master will show up on a day he wasn't expecting and at a time he didn't know, and will have him drawn and quartered and throw his portion to the hypocrites, where the wailing and gnashing of teeth will be.

25

"THEN the kingdom of the skies will be like ten maidens who took their lanterns and went out to meet the bridegroom, but five of them were stupid and five were sensible. You see, the stupid ones took their lanterns without taking any oil with them, whereas the sensible ones took cans of oil with their lanterns. The bridegroom being delayed, they all got drowsy and lay down. Then at midnight the cry went up: 'Here comes the bridegroom, everybody out to meet him.' Then all those maidens got up and fixed their lanterns. But the stupid ones said to the sensible ones: 'Give us some of your oil, our lanterns are going out.'

"And the sensible ones answered, 'There may not be enough for us and you; you'd better go to those who sell it and buy yourselves some.' After they went off to buy oil, the bridegroom came, and those who were ready went in with him to the wedding, and the door was shut.

"Then later the other maidens came along saying, 'Master, master, open up for us.'

"But he answered, I swear I don't know you.' So stay awake, because you don't know the date or the time.

"You see, it's like a fellow who was going away and called his slaves and entrusted his goods to them: and he gave five bars of silver to one, two to another, and one to a third – to each according to his ability – and went away. The one who got the five bars went right out and did business with them and earned another five bars; likewise, the one who got the two bars earned another two. But the one who got the one bar went off and dug a hole and hid his master's silver.

"After a long time the master of those slaves comes back and settles accounts with them. And the one who got the five bars came forward and presented the other five bars, saying, 'Master, you entrusted me with five bars of silver; see, I earned another five bars.

"And his master said to him, 'Well done, good and faithful slave! You were trustworthy in small things, I'll put you in charge of many things. Welcome to your master's joy.'

"And the one who got two bars also came forward and said, 'Master, you entrusted me with two bars of silver; see, I earned another two bars.'

"His master said to him, 'Well done, good and faithful slave! You were trustworthy in small things, I'll put you in charge of many things. Welcome to your master's joy.'

"Then the one who got the one bar also came forward and said, 'Master, knowing you to be a tough fellow, who reaps what he didn't sow and collects what he didn't scatter, I was afraid and went off and hid your bar of silver in the ground; here it is.'

"His master answered, 'Bad and cowardly slave, if you knew that I reap what I didn't sow and collect what I didn't scatter, then you should have put my silver in the bank, so I could have gone and gotten my money back with interest. Take the bar of silver away from him and give it to the one with ten bars: he who has everything shall be given more and more; whereas he who has nothing, even what he has shall be taken away from him. And throw the useless slave out into the darkness beyond, where the wailing and gnashing of teeth will be.'

"When the son of humanity comes in his glory and all his messengers with him, then he will sit upon a throne of his glory, and all the nations will be assembled before him, and he will separate them from each other, just as the herdsman separates the sheep from the goats, and he will put the sheep on his right and the goats on his left. Then the king will say to those on his right, 'Come here, you blessed of my father, inherit the kingdom prepared for you from the beginning of the world. After all, I was hungry and you gave me something to eat, I was thirsty and you gave me something to drink, I was wandering and you took me in, I was naked and you clothed me, I was sick and you looked after me, I was in jail and you came to see me.'

"Then the innocent will answer, 'Lord, when was it that we saw you starving and we fed you, or saw you thirsty and gave you something to drink? When did we see you wandering and take you in, or see you naked and clothe you? When were you sick or in jail and we came to see you?'

"And the king will answer, 'Let me assure you, however much you did it for any of the least important of these brothers and sisters of mine, you did it for me.' Then he will say to those on his left, 'Away from me, damned souls, into the everlasting fire prepared for the Devil and his messengers! Why, I was hungry and you wouldn't give me anything to eat, I was thirsty and you wouldn't give me anything to drink, I was wandering and you didn't take me in, I was naked and you didn't clothe me, I was sick and in jail and you didn't look after me.'

"Then they will also answer, 'Lord, when did we see you hungry or thirsty or wandering or naked or sick or in jail and we didn't take care of you?'

"Then he will answer, 'Let me assure you, however much you wouldn't do it for any of the least important of these people, you wouldn't do it for me either.' Then those ones will ride off to everlasting punishment, while the innocent ride off to everlasting life.'"

26

AND it happened when Jesus finished all these words, he said to his students, "You know, in two days it will be Passover, and the son of humanity will be handed over to be crucified."

Then the high priests and elders of the people got together in the meeting-hall of the high priest named Caiaphas and exchanged ideas about some trick to lay hold of Jesus and kill him. But they said, "Not during the feast days, the people will make too much noise."

Jesus being in Bethany at the house of Simon Leper, a woman came to him with a bottle of expensive perfume and poured it over his head as he sat at dinner. His students were outraged to see that and said, "Why this waste? After all, this could have been sold for a lot and given to the poor."

Jesus, noticing this, said to them, "Why are you giving this woman grief? She did a fine thing for me. Remember, you always have the poor around, but you don't always have me around. Why, this woman who poured this perfume on my body made me ready for burial. I promise you, wherever this good word is proclaimed in all the world, what she did shall also be told in her memory."

Then off went one of the twelve, the one called Judas Iscariot, to the high priests and said, "What will you give me if I hand him over to you?" And they set thirty silverpieces on him. So from that time on he was looking for the right time to hand him over.

On the third day of the unleavened bread Jesus's students came to him and said, "Where do you want us to get things ready for you to eat the seder?"

He said, "Go into town and see So-and-So and tell him, 'The master says, *My time is near, I'm celebrating Passover with you, along with my students.'"* And his students did as Jesus ordered them and got the seder ready.

When it got late he sat down with the twelve. And while they were eating he said, "I tell you for sure, one of you is going to hand me over."

And they, deeply pained, started saying to him one by one, *"I* couldn't be the one, could I, Lord?"

He answered, "The one who dips his hand in the bowl with mine, that's the one who will hand me over. Yes, the son of humanity must go now, just as it was written about him, but woe to that person by whom the son of humanity is handed over. Better for him if he'd never been born."

Judas, his betrayer, answered, *"I* couldn't be the one, could I, master?"

And he says, "You said it!"

Then as they were eating, Jesus took bread, said grace, and gave it to his students saying, "Take and eat this: this is my body." And taking a cup and giving thanks he gave it to them, saying, "Drink from this, all of you: this is my blood, the blood of the testament, poured out for many for the forgiveness of wrongs. I tell you, this is the last I will drink of this vintage from now till that day when I drink it new with you in the kingdom of my Father." And concluding with a hymn, they went out to Mount Olive.

Then Jesus says to them, "All of you will let me down tonight – just like the scripture says, 'I will strike at the shepherd, and the sheep in his herd will scatter.' But after rising up I will go on ahead of you into Galilee."

And Peter answered, "Even if everyone lets you down, I will never let you down."

Jesus said to him, "I promise you, in the night ahead, from now till cockcrow, you will say you don't know me three times."

Peter says to him, "Even if I had to die with you, I would never say I didn't know you," and all his students said the same.

Then Jesus goes with them to the place called Gethsemane and says to the students, "Sit here while I go over there and pray." And taking Peter and the two sons of Zebedee he began to grieve and mourn, then he says to them, "My soul is so full of grief that I could die; wait here and stay awake with me." Then he went off a little ways and fell on his face praying and said, "My Father, if it's possible, let this cup pass me by, but let Your will and not mine be done."

Then he comes over to his students and finds them asleep and says to Simon Peter, "You couldn't stay awake this one hour with me? Keep awake and pray that you don't get put to the test: the spirit may be eager, but the flesh is weak."

A second time he went off and prayed: "My Father, if this can't pass me by without my drinking it, let your will be done." And again he came and found them sleeping, because their eyelids were so heavy.

And again he left them alone and went off and prayed saying the same words a third time. Then he comes back to his students and says to them: "Sleep and get your rest while you can, do you see how near the time is? And the son of humanity will be betrayed into the hands of the godless. . .up now! Come on! Here he comes, my betrayer!"

And even as he spoke, there was Judas, one of the twelve, and with him a large band of people with swords and clubs, sent by the high priests and elders of the people. The betrayer had given them the signal, "Whoever I kiss is the one, take him!" And going right over to Jesus he said, "Good evening, master," and kissed him.

Jesus said to him, "Buddy, what are you here for?" Then they all came up and laid hands on Jesus and took him away. And all of a sudden, one of those with Jesus reached for his sword and hit the high priest's servant, cutting off his ear. Then Jesus says to him, "Put your sword back where it belongs: those who fight swords with swords are lost. You think I can't call on my Father and have him supply me even now with more than twelve

legions of his messengers? But how will the scriptures be fulfilled that say this must happen?"

At that point Jesus said to the mob, "As if in pursuit of a robber you came out to get me with swords and clubs? I used to
sit in the daytime in the temple when I was teaching and you
didn't take me then. This has all happened to fulfill the prophets' writings." Then all his students left him behind and ran.

Next, those holding Jesus led him before Caiaphas the high
priest, where the canon-lawyers and the elders had gathered.
But Peter followed him from a distance as far as the courtyard
of the high priest and went in and was sitting with the servants
in order to see the outcome.

Now the high priests and the whole high court were looking
for some false testimony against Jesus such that they could sentence him to death, but they weren't finding it, even with many
false witnesses coming forward. Finally, two came forward saying, "This guy said, 'I can topple the temple of God and, in
three days, build it again.'"

And the high priest, standing up, said to him, "Don't you
have any answer as to why these people testify against you?" But
Jesus kept silent. And the high priest said to him: "I command
you by the living God to tell us if you are the Anointed, the
son of God."

Jesus says to him, "That's what _you_ say. But I do tell you this:
next time you will see the son of humanity sitting at the right
hand of power and coming on the clouds of the sky."

Then the high priest tore his cloak,* saying, "That's blasphemy!
Why do we need any more witnesses? Didn't you hear that blasphemy just now? What do you say?"

They answered: "This is punishable by death."

Then they spat in his face and boxed his ears, while others
hit him with a stick and said, "Prophesy for us, Mr. Anointed
One: who just hit you?"

*By Jewish custom, ripping your garments expresses your horror at hearing
blasphemy spoken.

Meanwhile Peter was sitting out in the yard, and a girl came over to him and said, "You were with Jesus of Galilee too."

But he denied it and said in front of everybody, "I don't know what you're talking about."

So he went into the outer hallway, where another girl saw him and said to the people there, "This guy was with Jesus of Nazareth."

And again he denied it with an oath, saying "I don't know the fellow."

A little while later those standing there came over and said to Peter, "*Of course* you're one of them; why, even your accent* makes you stand out!"

Then he started to curse and swear up and down, saying "I don't know the fellow," and just then a rooster crowed.

And Peter remembered the words in which Jesus had said, "Before the cock crows you'll say you don't know me three times." And he went outside and cried stinging tears.

27

WHEN it was daylight, all the high priests and elders of the people had a meeting about Jesus and putting him to death. And after tying him up they led him away and gave him over to Pilate the governor.

Then Judas the betrayer, seeing that Jesus had been sentenced, had a change of heart and brought the thirty silverpieces back to the high priests and elders, saying, "I was wrong to betray innocent blood."

But they said, "What's that to us? That's your problem." And he hurled the silverpieces into the temple and stalked out and went off and hanged himself. And the high priests, picking up the silverpieces, said: "It isn't permissible to put this money in the temple coffers, because it's blood-money." So after talking it

*Peter's Galilean accent is as conspicuous in Jerusalem as a Memphis accent would be in New York City.

over they used the money to buy Potter's Field as a burial-place for strangers. (Which is why that field is known as Blood Field to this day. Thus the words of Jeremiah the prophet were fulfilled: "And they took the thirty silverpieces, the price of the prized one whom they had priced, from the sons of Israel, and gave it for the potter's field, as the lord ordered me.")

Meanwhile Jesus stood in front of the governor, and the governor asked him: "So you're the king of the Jews?"

And Jesus said, "That's what _you_ say." And he answered nothing to the denunciations by the high priests and elders.

Then Pilate says to him, "Don't you hear all the things they testify against you?" And he didn't answer him so much as a single word, which surprised the governor very much.

Now at festival time the governor was accustomed to release a prisoner to the crowd, whoever they wanted. At that time they were holding one well-known prisoner named Barabbas. So when they gathered, Pilate said to them, "Who do you want me to release to you: Barabbas? or Jesus, the so-called Anointed?" You see, he knew that they had betrayed him out of envy.

And as he sat on the podium his wife sent word to him saying, "Have nothing to do with that innocent man. I dreamt last night that I suffered horribly because of him."

Now the high priests and the elders had persuaded the crowds to ask for Barabbas and have Jesus be killed. So the governor said to them: "Which of the two do you want me to release to you?" and they said, "Barabbas." Pilate says to them, "Then what do I do with Jesus the so-called Anointed?"

They all said, "Crucify him."

And he said, "But what did he do wrong?"

But they shouted all the louder, "Crucify him."

Pilate, seeing that nothing helped and they only made more and more noise, took water and washed his hands in front of the crowd, saying, "I am innocent of this man's blood, see to it yourselves."

And the whole crowd answered, "Let his blood be on us and our children."

Then he released Barabbas to them, while Jesus he flogged and handed over to them to be crucified.

Then the governor's soldiers took Jesus into the governor's mansion and got the whole platoon together. And they took off his clothes and dressed him in a cloak of royal purple, and wove a crown of thorns and put it on his head, with a stick of cane in his right hand, and they had some fun with him, kneeling before him and saying, "Hail, king of the Jews!" and then spitting in his face and taking the cane and hitting him on the head with it. And when they'd had their fun with him, they took the cloak off and put his clothes back on and led him away to crucify him.

As they came out they found a Cyrenian man named Simon, whom they dragooned into carrying the cross.

And coming out to the place called Golgotha, that is, Skull Place, they gave him wine to drink mixed with wormwood, and after tasting it he wouldn't drink it. And after crucifying him they raffled off his clothes by rolling dice, and sat there keeping an eye on him. And up above his head they put the written charge against him:

THIS IS JESUS, THE KING OF THE JEWS.

Then two thieves were to be crucified with him, one on his right and one on his left. And as they passed by they cursed him, nodding in his direction and saying, "Destroyer of the temple who rebuilds it in three days, save yourself if you're the son of God, come down off the cross."

Likewise, the high priests, with the canon-lawyers and elders, made fun of him, saying, "He saved others, he can't save himself. He's the king of Israel, so let's see him come down off the cross and we'll believe in him. He has placed his trust in God, let God pull him out of this if he wants him. After all, he did say, 'I'm God's son.'"

And the thieves crucified with him insulted him along the same line.

Starting at noon, darkness came over the whole earth till three o'clock, then around three o'clock Jesus cried out with a loud voice: "Eli, Eli, lema sabachthani?" that is, "My God, my God, why did you abandon me?"*

Some of those standing there heard that and said, "He's calling Elijah." And one of them ran right over and took a sponge and filled it with strong wine and put it on the end of a stick so he could drink from it.

The others said, "Let's see if Elijah comes to save him." But Jesus cried out again with a loud voice and breathed his last.

And in that instant the great curtain hanging in front of the temple was sheared in two from top to bottom.** And the earth shook, and the rocks were split, and the graves were opened, and many bodies of the sleeping saints arose, and leaving their graves, after his resurrection, went into the holy city and appeared to many.

But the Roman captain and those with him who were watching Jesus, seeing the tremors and other events, were frightened out of their wits and said, "He really *was* the son of God!"

There were many women there observing from afar, some of whom had followed Jesus from Galilee to serve him; among those, Mary Magdalen, Mary the mother of James and Joseph, and the mother of the sons of Zebedee.

But when it got late, a rich person from Arimathea named Joseph came along, who himself had studied under Jesus. This person went to Pilate and asked for the body of Jesus, at which point Pilate ordered it given to him. And taking the body, Joseph wrapped it in a clean sheet and put it in the tomb that had been newly cut for him in the rock, and rolled a big stone against the door of the tomb and went away, leaving Mary Magdalen and the other Mary sitting there opposite the tomb.

Next morning—that's after Friday night—the high priests and the Pharisees assembled at Pilate's door to say, "Your excellency,

*The first words of the 22nd Psalm.

**The Temple of Jerusalem rips its garments in horror at the blasphemy of Christ's murder.

we can remember how that fraud said while alive, 'I will rise up after three days.' So order the grave to be guarded till the third day, so his students don't come and steal him and say to the people, 'He came back from the dead!' and the fraud ends up worse than before."

Pilate said to them, "You have custody. Go out and guard the grave until you know for sure."

So they went on their way and stationed a guard around the grave and marked the stone with their sign: IN CUSTODY.

28

LATE Saturday night, as it was glimmering toward the first day of the week, came Mary Magdalen and the other Mary to watch the grave. And all of a sudden there was a giant rumbling: it was a messenger of the Lord coming down from the sky, stepping forward, and rolling away the stone, upon which he then sat down. His appearance was like lightning and his clothing white as snow. What with the fear, those watching were shaking all over and as good as dead. Reacting to that, the messenger said to the women: "Don't be afraid, I know you're looking for Jesus who was crucified. He isn't here, he came back just as he said. Look, here's the place where he was lying. So quick, go off and tell his students that he came back from the dead. And remember, he's going on ahead of you to Galilee, where you will see him. Remember I said that to you."

And going away from the tomb quickly, with great fear and great joy, they ran to tell his students. And next thing Jesus himself was there to meet them and said, "Hello!" And they went up and fell at his feet and bowed before him. Then Jesus says to them, "Don't be afraid: Go tell my brothers to go on to Galilee; they'll see me there."

When they had departed, the next thing was, the soldiers went into town and told the high priests everything that happened. And after getting together with the elders and having a meeting, they gave a hefty sum to the soldiers and said, "Say that his students came by night and stole him while you were sleeping. And if word of this reaches the governor, we'll talk to him and make sure you aren't punished." They took the money and did as they were instructed, and that story has been spread among the Jews even to this day.

But the eleven students went on to Galilee, to the mountain Jesus named, and saw him and bowed before him, though some were hesitant. And Jesus came forward and spoke to them, saying, "All authority in the sky and on the earth is given to me. So go out and teach all nations, bathing them in the name of the Father, the son, and the holy spirit, and teaching them to keep everything I commanded you. And do you see? I am with you, every day until the culmination of time."

The Good Word According to
Mark

1

BEGINNING OF THE GOOD WORD OF JESUS THE
ANOINTED, SON OF GOD.

As is written in Isaiah the prophet –

Look, I am sending my messenger before your face,
Who will prepare your road,
The voice of a crier in the desert:
"Make the Lord's road ready,
Straighten his paths" –

so John came along, bathing others in the wilderness and announcing the washing of a changed heart for the forgiveness of
wrongs. And all the country of Judea was coming out to see
him, and all the people of Jerusalem too, and were being bathed
by him in the Jordan River, admitting their mistakes. And John
was dressed in camel hair and a leather belt about his waist, and
eating locusts and wild honey.

And he was proclaiming, "After me comes someone so much
stronger than me, I am not great enough to bend over and untie the thongs of his sandals. I bathed you in water, but he will
bathe you in holy breath."

And it happened in those days that Jesus came from Nazareth, Galilee and was bathed in the Jordan by John. And coming straight out of the water he saw the skies split apart and the
breath like a dove coming down upon him. And a voice came
out of the skies: "You are my son, my beloved son in whom
I am delighted."

And directly the spirit drove him out into the wilderness. And
he was in the wilderness for forty days being tested by Satan,
and he was there among the wild beasts, and heavenly messengers
were taking care of him.

But after John was handed over to the authorities, Jesus went
to Galilee, proclaiming the good word of God and saying, "The

time has come and the kingdom of God is approaching. Repent and trust in the good word."

And going along by the sea of Galilee he saw Simon and Simon's brother Andrew casting their nets into the sea, since they were fishermen. And Jesus said to them, "Come along behind me and I'll make you fishers of humanity." And they put their nets right down and followed him. And going on a little ways he saw James the son of Zebedee and John his brother, both of them in the boat mending their nets. And right away he called to them, and they left their father Zebedee in the boat with the hired hands and followed after him.

And they travel on to Capharnaum. And on the very next Sabbath he went into the synagogue and started teaching. And they were amazed at his teaching, because he was teaching them as if on his own authority, not like their canon-lawyers.

And right there in the synagogue was a fellow with an unclean spirit, and he started shouting, "What have we done to you, Jesus of Nazareth? Did you come to wipe us out? I know who you are, holy man of God!"

And Jesus yelled at him, saying, "Shut up and come out of him." And the unclean spirit, after convulsing him and crying with a loud voice, came out of him.

And everyone was so amazed that they started saying to each other: "What's this? New teaching on his own authority, and then he gives orders to unclean spirits and they obey him!" And word of him immediately went out everywhere, across the whole countryside of Galilee.

And as soon as they came out of the synagogue they went to Simon and Andrew's house with James and John. Now Simon's mother-in-law was in bed with a fever, and they immediately told him about her. And he went in and got her up, taking her by the hand, and the fever left her, and she was at their service.

When it got late and the sun was down they brought him all the people in bad health, and those with demons, and the whole town was gathered by the door. And he healed many people in bad health with various diseases, and threw out many demons, and didn't let the demons talk, because they knew who he was.

And getting up in the early hours of darkness he went outside and went off to a deserted place and prayed there. And Simon and those with him tracked him down and found him. And they say to him, "They're all looking for you."

And he says to them, "Let's go on to another place, into the next villages, so I can proclaim there too, because that's what I came for."

And he came through all of Galilee, proclaiming in their synagogues and throwing out demons. And a leper comes to him, pleading with him and begging on his knees, saying, "If you want to, you can heal me."

And feeling sorry for him, he reached out his hand and touched him and said to him, "I do want to: be healed." And the leprosy went right out of him and he was healed. And Jesus sent him right off, thundering at him and saying, "Careful, say nothing to anyone, just go show yourself to the priest and bring the offering specified by Moses for a purification, as a testimony to them." But he went out and began to proclaim it up and down and spread the word, to the point where he couldn't go openly into town anymore. Instead he stayed out in deserted places, and they came to him from everywhere.

2

AND GOING back to Capharnaum, for days the word went round that he was in that house. And so many gathered together that they couldn't get close to the door, and he was speaking the word to them. And they came bringing him a paralyzed man, carried by four men. And when they couldn't bring him closer to him because of the crowd, they took off the roof over where he was and reached through and let down the cot on which the paralyzed man was lying. And Jesus, seeing their faith, says to the paralyzed man, "Son, your wrongdoing is forgiven."

Now some of the canon-lawyers were sitting there, thinking in their hearts, "Why does this guy talk like that? That's blasphemy! Who can forgive wrongs but God alone?"

And Jesus, immediately sensing in his spirit that they were thinking that way among themselves, says to them, "Why are you thinking those thoughts in your hearts? Which is easier: to say to the paralyzed man, 'Your wrongdoing is forgiven,' or to say, 'Get up and take your cot and walk away'? But so you may see that the son of humanity has authority to forgive wrongs on earth"—he says to the paralyzed man, "I tell you, get up and take your cot and go home."

And he got up and took his cot and went away, in front of everyone, so that everyone was beside themselves and praised God, saying, "We never saw anything like that!"

And he went out by the sea again, and all the crowd was coming toward him, and he was teaching them. And going on he saw Levi the son of Alpheus, sitting at the toll-station, and he says to him, "Follow me," and he stood up and followed him.

And he happened to be sitting down to dinner in his house, and a lot of tax-collectors and godless people were sitting with Jesus and his students—since there were many such that followed him—and the canon-lawyers of the Pharisees, seeing that he ate with godless people and tax-collectors, said to his students, "Tax-collectors and godless people, that's who he eats with?"

And Jesus, hearing that, says to them, "It's not the healthy who need a doctor, it's the sick. I didn't come to call the saints, I came to call the godless people."

And the students of John and the Pharisees were always fasting, and they come and say to him, "Why is it the students of John and the students of the Pharisees fast, but the students you have don't fast?"

And Jesus said to them, "The wedding party can't be fasting while the bridegroom is with them, can they? No, as long as they have the bridegroom with them, they cannot fast. There will come days when the bridegroom will be taken away from them, and then they can fast on that day.

"No one puts a patch of brand-new cloth on an old cloak, because if they do, the new takes away the completeness of the old, and a worse split results. And no one puts new wine into old wineskins, because if they do, the wine bursts the skins, and both wine and skins are lost. Instead, they put new wine in new skins."

And it happened one Sabbath that he was traveling through the grain fields, and his students started making a path for him by breaking off ears of corn. And the Pharisees said to him: "Look at that: why are they doing what isn't allowed on the Sabbath?"

And he says to them, "Didn't you ever read what David did when he was in need and starving, himself and those with him, how he went into the house of God under the high priest Abriathar and ate the sacrificial loaves, which no one was allowed to eat but the priests, and gave them to those with him?" And he said to them, "The Sabbath was made for humanity, not humanity for the Sabbath, so that the son of humanity is superior to the Sabbath."

3

AND HE WENT into the synagogue another time, and there was a fellow there with a withered hand. And they were watching him to see if he was going to heal on the Sabbath, so they could charge him with something. And he says to the fellow with the withered hand, "Come in the middle here." And he says to them, "Which is allowed on the Sabbath: doing good, or doing evil? Saving lives, or killing?" They were silent. And looking round at them in a fury, griefstricken at the stoniness of their hearts, he says to the fellow, "Reach out your hand." And he reached out, and his hand was restored. And the Pharisees, with Herod's men, went right out and had a meeting about him and how to get rid of him.

And Jesus retreated with his students toward the sea, and a great crowd followed from Galilee; and from Judea, Jerusalem, and beyond the Jordan, and round about Tyre and Sidon, a great crowd came toward him, hearing the things he'd done.

And he told his students to have a boat ready for him so they wouldn't crush him. Indeed, he cured many, to the point where everyone who suffered from some scourge was mobbing him, trying to touch him. And the unclean spirits, when they sighted him, fell down before him and cried out loud, "You're the son of God!" And over and over he warned them not to make him famous.

And he goes up the mountain and calls the ones he wanted to him, and they went to him. And he settled on twelve of them to be with him, and to be sent out by him to spread the word, and to have authority to throw out demons. And he gave Simon the name "Rock" ["Peter"]; and he gave James the son of Zebedee and his brother John the name Boanerges, which means "the Thunder Brothers"; plus Andrew, Philip, Bartholomew, Matthew, Thomas, James son of Alpheus, Thaddeus, Simon the Canaanite, and Judas Iscariot, who betrayed him.

And he comes back home, and the crowd gathers again, to the point where they couldn't even eat a meal. Hearing the crowd, those close to Jesus went out to calm them down, because they were saying, "He's gone mad!"

And the canon-lawyers came down from Jerusalem and said, "He serves Beelzebub and has the authority of the demon-king to throw out demons."

And calling them together, he spoke to them in metaphors: "How can Satan throw out Satan? If a country is split in opposition to itself, that country can't stand up; and if a house is split in opposition to itself, that house won't be able to stand up. And if Satan rebels against himself and becomes divided, he can't stand up, that's the end of him. But then, no one can go into a strong man's house and grab his things without first tying up the strong man; only then can he plunder his house.

"I assure you, the sons of humanity will be forgiven for many misdeeds and whatever blasphemies they may have blasphemed. But whoever blasphemes against the sacred breath will find no forgiveness in all eternity; no, he's guilty of eternal sin."

That was because they said, "He has an unclean spirit."

And his mother comes, and his brothers and sisters, and, standing outside, they sent word to him, calling for him. And a crowd was seated around him, and they say to him: "You know, your mother and your brothers and sisters are outside looking for you."

And he answered, "Who _is_ my mother and my sisters and my brothers?" And looking round at those sitting in a circle around him, he says, "Look, here's my mother and my brothers and sisters: whoever does the will of God, that's who my brother and sister and mother is."

4

AND AGAIN he started teaching by the sea. And such a gigantic crowd comes toward him that he had to get into a boat and sit on the waters, with all the crowd by the sea along the shore. And he started teaching them many things in metaphors and said to them in the course of his teaching:

"Listen: once there was a sower who went out sowing. And it happened in the course of his sowing that some of it fell by the roadside, and the birds came and ate it up. And some fell on the rocky ground where there wasn't much soil, and it sprang right up, there being no depth to the soil. And when the sun came up it got scorched and dried out, not having any roots. And some fell into the thorns, and the thorns came up and choked it off, and it bore no fruit. And some fell on good soil and sprang up and grew and bore fruit, here thirty, there sixty, and there a hundred." And he said, "Those with ears to hear, hear!"

And when they were by themselves, those around him, along with the twelve, asked him about the metaphors. And he said to them, "To you the mystery of the kingdom of God is given, but to those people outside it is all done in metaphors,

so that when they look, they look, but do not see;
and when they hear, they hear but do not understand;
lest they should come back, and it should be forgiven them."

And he says to them, "If you don't get this metaphor, how will you get any of them? The sower sows the word. And some of these people are the ones by the wayside: where the word is sown, as soon as they hear it, Satan comes, and takes away the word that was sown. And some of them are the ones sown on the rocky ground: when they hear the word, right away they joyfully seize it, and yet it has no root in them, it's only temporary, so that if there's pressure or persecution because of the word, they fall right down. And others are the ones sown into the thorns: they hear the word, and then the worries of the day and the strategy of moneymaking and the concerns of the future come in and choke off the word, and it becomes unable to bear fruit. And still others are the ones sown on good soil, who hear the word and take it in and bear fruit, here thirty, there sixty, and there a hundred."

And he said to them, "The candle isn't there to be covered with a big basket or put under the bed, is it? Isn't it there to be put up on a tall candlestick? After all, things are hidden only to be revealed, and made secret only to be brought to light. If any have ears to hear, let them hear!" And he said to them, "Watch and listen: by the same measure that you have measured, things will be measured out and put before you. In fact, he who has will be given more, while he who has nothing, even what he has will be taken away from him."

And he said, "The kingdom of God is like a person throwing seeds on the ground, and going to sleep and getting up, by night and by day, while the seed germinates and grows without his knowing it. The earth bears fruit by itself: the first shoots, then the ear, then the grain in the ear. But when it gives ripened grain, he sends the thresher right out, because it's harvest-time."

And he said, "How shall we describe the kingdom of God, or what shall we compare it to? Perhaps to a seed of the mustard plant, which, when it's scattered upon the earth, is the smallest of all the seeds in the world; and yet when it's sown, it comes up and grows bigger than all the vegetables and puts out branches big enough for the birds of the air to be able to camp in its shadow."

And he kept speaking the word to them in metaphors, according as they could hear, and he said nothing to them without metaphors, but privately to his own students he always gave the key.

And he says to them on that day, with evening falling, "Let's go on across." And leaving the crowd behind, they take him along; so that he was in the boat and other boats were with him. And a giant windstorm comes up, and it was hurling the waves into the boat, till the boat was already filling up. And he was in the stern sleeping on a seat-cushion, and they wake him up, saying, "Teacher, you don't care if we get killed?"

And standing up tall he yelled at the wind and told the sea, "Quiet, hush your mouth," and the wind cut down and there was a great calm. And he said to them, "Why are you such cowards? Don't you have any faith?"

And they were as scared as scared could be and said to each other: "Who *is* this guy, that even the wind and the sea obey him?"

5

AND THEY WENT across the sea to the land of the Gerasenes. And as soon as he got out of the boat he was accosted by a fellow with an unclean spirit, coming from the graveyard, who lived among the gravestones, and no one yet had been able to restrain him, even with chains, because every time he was chained and shackled hand and foot, he burst the chains and wore away the shackles, so no one was strong enough to control him. And all the time, night and day, he was there among the gravestones or in the hills, screaming and pounding himself with rocks.

And seeing Jesus from a distance he ran and bowed before him, shouting loudly, "What have I done to you, Jesus son of God the highest? For the love of God, don't torture me" – because he was about to say, "Unclean spirit, go out of this person."

And he asked him, "What is your name?"

And he answered, "My name is Legion: there's many of us." And he pleaded with him over and over not to send them out of the country.

Now there by the mountain there was a big herd of pigs grazing. And they pleaded with him, saying, "Send us to the pigs, let us go into them." And he let them, and the unclean spirits came out and went into the pigs, and the herd of them rushed over the edge of the cliff and into the sea, some two thousand of them, and drowned in the waters.

And their keepers fled and spread the news in town and from field to field, and they came to see what the matter was, and as they come toward Jesus they find the possessed man fully clothed and in his right mind, the one who had the Legion, and they were frightened. And those who saw it explained what happened to the possessed man, and about the pigs. And they started begging him to go away from their neighborhood.

And when he got in the boat, the formerly possessed man begged to go along with him. But he wouldn't allow it, saying instead, "Go home to your own and report to them what the Lord did for you and what mercy he had on you." And he went off and started proclaiming in the Decapolis what Jesus had done for him, and all were amazed.

And when Jesus crossed to the other side again in the boat, a giant crowd gathered toward him, there by the sea. And one of the chief priests of the synagogue, Jairus by name, comes along and when he sees Jesus falls at his feet and begs him over and over, saying, "My daughter's on her deathbed, come and put your hands on her so that she'll be healed and live." And he went with him, and a great crowd followed, pressing him hard.

And a woman who had been hemorrhaging twelve years and who had been treated all sorts of ways by various doctors, spending all she had and getting no relief, indeed, always getting worse, hearing about Jesus, came from behind him through the crowd and touched his cloak, saying to herself, "If I just touch his cloak, I'm saved." And her hemorrhaging dried right up at the source, and she could feel in her body that she was healed from the scourge.

And Jesus, immediately sensing the force being drawn out of him, turned to the crowd and said, "Who touched my cloak?"

And his students said to him, "You see this crowd pressing in from every side? And you say, 'Who touched me?'" And he looked round to see who did it.

So the woman, scared and trembling, knowing what had happened to her, came and fell down in front of him and told him the whole truth. And he said to her, "Daughter, your trust has saved you. Go in peace and be healed of your scourge."

Even as he spoke, they come from the chief priest's house and say, "Your daughter's dead, why are you still bothering the Master?"

But Jesus, overhearing the words spoken, says to the chief priest: "Don't be afraid, just believe." And he allowed no one to follow him but Peter and James and John, James's brother.

And they come into the chief priest's house, and he sees a great pandemonium of weeping and wailing, and comes in and says to them, "Why are you crying and making noise? The child didn't die, she's sleeping." And they were laughing at him. But he, after throwing everybody out, takes along the child's father and mother and those with him and proceeds to the place where the child was. And he takes her hand and says to her, "Talitha kum," which translates as, "Young girl, I tell you, get up." And the girl stood right up and started walking around; after all, she was twelve years old. And they were seized by a great ecstasy. And he commanded them repeatedly that no one should know of this, and said to give her something to eat.

6

ᴀɴᴅ ʜᴇ ᴡᴇɴᴛ away from there; and he comes back to his home town, and his students follow him. And when the Sabbath came round he started teaching in the synagogue, and many people hearing him were stunned and said, "Where does he get all this? What is this wisdom given to him, how can wonders like these be worked through his hands? Isn't this the carpenter, Mary's son and the brother of James, Joseth, Jude, and Simon? And aren't his sisters all here with us?" And they were offended by him.

And Jesus said to them, "A prophet is never dishonored if not in his home town, among his relatives, and in his own house." And he couldn't work any wonders there, except for a few sick people whom he cured by laying his hands on them. And he was amazed at their lack of faith. And he journeyed on, teaching in the villages all around.

And he called the twelve together and started sending them out two by two and giving them authority over the unclean spirits, and he ordered them to take nothing on the road but a walking-stick: "no bread, no knapsack, no coins under your belt, just with sandals under your feet, and don't put on two tunics." And he said to them, "Whatever house you go into, stay there till you leave that place. And whatever place doesn't receive you or listen to you, when you go away from there, shake the dust from underneath your shoes as a testimony to them." And they went out and called on the people to have a change of heart, and threw out many demons and anointed many sick people with oil and cured them.

And King Herod [Archelaus] heard of him, since his name became known, and they said John the Baptist had risen from the dead and that's why these powers work in him. Others said, "It's Elijah"; others, that he was a prophet like one of the prophets. Herod, after listening to them, said, "The one I beheaded, John, that's who has come back from the dead."

(You see, Herod himself had sent his men out and seized John and confined him in jail on account of Herodias his brother Philip's wife, whom he married, because John had told Herod, "You aren't allowed to have your brother's wife." So Herodias had it in for him and wanted to kill him, but couldn't: Herod, it seems, was afraid of John, knowing him to be an innocent and holy man, and so he kept him there, and was often perplexed hearing the many things he said, but liked listening to him.

So when the opportune day came round, when Herod, for his birthday, gave a dinner for his princes and tribunes and the most important men of Galilee, and his daughter Herodias came in and pleased Herod and the guests with her dancing, the king said to the girl, "Ask me whatever you want, and I'll give it to you." And he swore up and down, "Whatever you ask I'll give you, even half my kingdom."

So she went out and said to her mother, "What shall I ask for?"

And she said, "The head of John the Baptist!"

And she came right back in and hastened to the king and asked, "I want you to give me the head of John the Baptist on a tray right now." And the king, most unhappy, didn't want to refuse her because of his oaths and the guests there. So the king sent his guard right out and ordered him to bring the head. And he went off and beheaded him in jail and brought his head on a tray and gave it to the girl, and the girl gave it to her mother. And when his students heard about it they came and took his body away and put it in a tomb.)

And the apostles got together with Jesus, and they reported to him all they'd done and what they had been teaching. And he says to them, "Come along by yourselves to some deserted place and rest a little," because there were many people coming and going, and they couldn't even find time to eat.

And they went off in a boat to a deserted place by themselves. But people saw them going, and many people figured it out and ran there on foot, coming from all different towns, and got there ahead of them.

And as he got out he saw a great crowd, and he felt sorry for them, because they were like sheep that had no shepherd, and he began to teach them many things.

And when many hours had already passed, his students came up to him and said, "This place is in the middle of nowhere and the hour is already late. Let them go, so they can go into the fields and villages around here and buy themselves something to eat."

He answered, "Give them something to eat yourselves."

And they say to him, "You want us to go buy two hundred drachmas' worth of bread and give it to them to eat?"

And he said to them, "How much bread do you have? Go see."

And having found out, they say, "Five loaves, plus two fish." And he told them to sit down, group by group, on the green grass. And they sat down, plot by plot, by hundreds and by fifties. And taking the five loaves and the two fish and looking up to the sky, he blessed and broke the loaves and gave them to his students to hand out to them, and he divided the two fish among them all. And they all ate and had their fill, and they cleared away twelve basketfuls of breadscraps and fish. And those eating were five thousand men.

And next he made his students get in the boat and go on across to Bethesda, until he dismissed the crowd. And after taking leave of them he went up the mountain to pray. And when it got late the boat was in the middle of the sea, and he was alone on land. And seeing that they were having a rough time crossing, because the wind was against them, around the fourth watch of the night he comes toward them walking on the sea and was going to join them. But when they saw him walking on the sea they thought it was a ghost and screamed, because they all saw him and were in consternation. And he spoke right up and said to them: "Courage, it's me, don't be afraid." And he got into the boat with them, and the wind cut down. And they were completely beside themselves, because they didn't understand about the loaves, their hearts were too stony.

And crossing over to the shore they came to Gennesareth and cast anchor. And as soon as they got out of the boat the people, recognizing him, went out all around that country and started bringing sick people on stretchers to the place where they heard he was. And wherever he was traveling into the villages or towns or fields, they set the sick down in the marketplace and begged him to let them touch even just the edge of his cloak, and those who touched it were healed.

7

AND the Pharisees and some of the canon-lawyers come from Jerusalem and assemble in his presence. And seeing some of his students and how they ate their bread with dirty (that is, un-washed) hands—you see, the Pharisees and all the Jews, preserving the tradition of the elders, never eat without washing their hands up to the elbow and never eat what they got at market without washing it, and there is much more that has been handed down to them to keep about washing glasses and pots and copper pans and beds—so the Pharisees and canon-lawyers asked him, "How come your students don't walk according to the tradition of the elders, but rather eat their bread with dirty hands?"

He said to them, "Isaiah prophesied very well about you fakes. As it says,

These people honor me with their lips,
But their heart is far away from me.

Pointlessly they worship me,
Teaching as their doctrine the commandments of the world.

"Leaving aside the commandment of God, you keep the tradition of the world." And he said to them, "You're very good at setting aside the commandment of God to establish your own tradition. After all, Moses said, 'Do right by your father and your mother' and 'Let whoever denounces father or mother end in death.'

"But *you* say, if a person says to his father or mother, 'I'm making a gift (that is, a religious contribution) of whatever you might have gotten from me,' you won't let him do anything further for his father or his mother – thus nullifying the word of God in favor of the tradition you have handed down. And you do lots of things like that."

And calling the crowd toward him again he said to them, "All of you, hear me and understand: there is nothing outside a person that can befoul him going in; it's what comes *out* of a person that befouls him."

And when he had gone home, away from the crowd, his students asked him about that comparison. And he says, "Can you, even, be so uncomprehending? Don't you see that everything coming into a person from outside cannot befoul him because it doesn't go into his heart, but into his belly, and goes out from there into the toilet, purging all that is eaten? Whereas," he said, "what comes out of a person, *that* befouls that person; because from inside the heart come evil designs, whoring, thieving, murdering, adultery, greed, meanness, trickery, brutality, the evil eye, blasphemy, haughtiness, and foolishness. All those evils come from the inside out and befoul a person."

He arose from there and went into the area of Tyre. And going into a house, he didn't want to know anybody but couldn't escape notice. In fact, a woman who had heard about him, whose little daughter had an unclean spirit, came right in and fell at his feet. Now the woman was Greek, Syrophoenician by race, and she asked him to throw out the demon from her daughter.

And he said to her, "First let the children eat their fill, because it isn't good to take the children's bread and throw it to the dogs."

But she answered, "Lord, even the dogs underneath the table get to eat of the children's scraps."

And he said to her, "In that case, go: the demon has gone out of your daughter." And when she went home she found her daughter lying in bed and the demon gone.

And going back out of the area of Tyre, he went through Sidon toward the sea of Galilee, down the middle of the Decapolis area. And they bring him a deaf mute and plead with him to put his hands on him. And taking him aside from the crowd, off by himself, he put his fingers in the other's ears, and spitting, took hold of his tongue, and looking up to heaven groaned and said to him, "Effatha," that is, "Open!" And his ears opened right up, and the restriction of his tongue was released and he could talk correctly.

And he commanded them to tell no one, but however much he commanded them, they only proclaimed it more and more. And they were amazed beyond measure and said, "How well he has done everything: he makes the deaf hear and the speechless speak!"

8

DURING those days, when again there was a great crowd without anything to eat, he calls his students to him and says to them, "I feel sorry for the crowd, because they've been staying with me for three days already and don't have anything to eat. And if I send them home hungry, they'll drop on the road, and some of them have come from far away."

And his students answered, "Where can anyone get bread to satisfy them here in the wilderness?"

And he asked them, "How many loaves do you have?"

They said, "Seven." And he ordered the crowd to sit down on the ground. And taking the seven loaves he gave thanks and broke them and gave them to his students to hand out, and they handed them out to the crowd. And they had a few small fish. And after blessing them he said to hand those out too. And they ate and had their fill, and they cleared away seven basketfuls of leftover scraps. (There were some four thousand people there.) Then he sent them off.

And getting right in the boat with his students he came to the area of Dalmanatha.

And the Pharisees came out and started arguing with him, asking him for a sign from the sky to test him out. And groaning in his spirit he says, "Why do these sorts ask me for a sign? I can tell you for sure whether a sign will be given to these sorts!" And leaving them behind he got in again and crossed to the other shore.

And they forgot to bring bread, and they didn't have even one loaf with them on the boat. And he commanded them, "Watch out, guard against the yeast of the Pharisees and the yeast of Herod." And they remarked to each other that they didn't *have* any bread. And knowing that, he says to them, "Why are you remarking that you have no bread? Do you still not see or understand? Do you have such stony hearts? Though you have eyes, you do not see, and though you have ears, you do not hear? And you don't remember, when I broke the five loaves for the five thousand, how many basketfuls of scraps you cleared away?"

They say to him, "Twelve."

"And when I broke the seven loaves for the four thousand, how many basketfuls of scraps you cleared away?"

And they say, "Seven."

And he said to them, "And you still don't understand?"

And they come to Bethesda. And they bring him a blind man and beg him to touch him. And taking the blind man's hand he brought him outside the village, and after spitting on his eyes and putting his hands on him he asked him, "Do you see anything?"

And looking up he said, "I see people. . .they look to me like trees walking around."

Again he put his hands on the man's eyes, and he looked again and was restored and saw everything perfectly clearly. And he sent him home, saying, "Don't go back into the village."

And Jesus and his students went out to the villages of Philip Caesarea. And on the way he asked his students, "Who do people say I am?"

And they said to him, "John the Baptist, or some say Elijah, or others say one of the prophets."

And he asked them, "And who do *you* say I am?"

Peter answered, "You are the Anointed." And he commanded them to tell no one about him.

And he began to instruct them that the son of humanity would have to undergo many things and be rejected by the elders and high priests and canon-lawyers, and be killed, and rise again after three days. And he said these words in front of everybody, but Peter, taking him aside, began to reproach him. So he, turning round and seeing his students, reproached Peter, saying, "Out of my sight, you Satan, because you're not thinking of God's concerns, you're thinking of human concerns."

And calling the crowd to him, together with his students, he said to them, "If anyone wants to follow after me, let him repudiate himself and pick up his cross and follow me, because whoever tries to save his life will lose it, and whoever loses his life for me and the good word will save it. After all, what does it help a person to gain the whole world and pay for it with his life? What could a person give in exchange for his life? Remember, whoever among this adulterous and sinful race is ashamed of me and my words, the son of humanity will be ashamed of them when he comes in the glory of his Father with his holy messengers."

9

AND HE SAID to them, "I tell you for sure, there are some among those standing here who will never taste death before they see the kingdom of God coming with all its power."

And six days later Jesus takes along Peter and James and John and brings them up a high mountain, alone by themselves, and he was transformed in front of them. And his clothes started shining whiter than white, in a way that no woolspinner on earth could ever whiten them. And Elijah appeared to them with Moses, and they were talking with Jesus. And Peter reacted, saying to Jesus, "Master, it's good that we are here. Let us set up three tabernacles, one for you and one for Moses and one for Elijah." (In fact, he didn't know how to react, they were all so afraid.)

And a cloud came up and overshadowed them, and there was a voice from the cloud: "This is my son, my beloved son: listen to him." And suddenly, looking round they no longer saw anyone, but only Jesus there with them.

And as they came down the mountain he commanded them not to relate what they saw to anyone until the son of humanity should arise from the dead. And they seized upon those words among themselves, debating what "arising from the dead" was.

And they asked him, "Why do the canon-lawyers say, 'First Elijah must come?'"

He said to them, "First Elijah is coming to restore everything. And what does it say about the son of humanity? That he must undergo many things and be treated like nothing. In fact, I tell you, Elijah has arrived, and they did with him whatever they liked, just as the Scripture says concerning him."

And going to rejoin the other students they saw a great crowd around them, with canon-lawyers arguing with them. And right away the whole crowd, seeing him, was overwhelmed and ran up to greet him. And he asked them, "What are you arguing about with each other?"

And a voice from the crowd answered him, "Teacher, I brought my son to see you, stricken mute by a spirit: whenever it takes hold of him, it tears him apart, and he foams at the mouth and gnashes his teeth and becomes dehydrated. And I told your students to throw it out, but they couldn't."

He answered, "You unbelieving race, how long will I be with you? How long will I *put up* with you! Bring him here to me." And they brought him to him. And seeing him the spirit immediately convulsed him, and he fell and rolled on the ground, foaming at the mouth. And he asked his father, "How long has this been happening to him?"

He said, "Since childhood. And it keeps throwing him into the fire and into the water to destroy him. But if you can do something, have mercy on us and help us."

Jesus said to him, "As for whether I 'can do something,' everything is possible for the believer."

And right away the father of the child shouted, "I believe; help me in my lack of faith." Jesus, seeing that the crowd was rapidly surging toward him, yelled at the unclean spirit, "Spirit of muteness and deafness, I command you, go out of him and don't ever go into him again." And with a shout and many convulsions it came out of him. And he became like a corpse, and many people said, He's dead! But Jesus took his hand and pulled him up, and he stood up.

And as he was going home his students asked him privately, "Why couldn't we throw it out?"

And he said to them, "That kind of spirit can't be thrown out by any means but prayer."

And going on from there, they were traveling through Galilee, but he didn't want anyone to know, because he was teaching his students and telling them that the son of humanity would be betrayed into the hands of the world, and they would kill him, and he would rise again three days after being killed. But they didn't get what he was saying and were afraid to ask him.

And they came to Capharnaum. And when he got indoors he asked them, "What were you discussing on the way?" They were silent, because on the way they had been talking among themselves about who was bigger than who. And he sat down and called the twelve and said to them, "If anyone wants to be number one, be the lowest of all and everybody's servant." And taking a child he stood him in their midst and embraced him and said to them, "Whoever receives one of these children in my name receives me, and whoever receives me, receives not me but the one who sent me."

John said to him, "Teacher, we saw someone throwing out demons in your name and told him not to, because he wasn't one of our followers."

But Jesus said, "Don't tell him not to, because no one who works a wonder in my name can speak evil of me soon after: who isn't against us is for us.

"Remember, whoever gives you a glass of water on the grounds that you belong to the Anointed, I assure you that they will not forfeit their reward.

"And whoever trips up one of these little ones who believe in me, better for them to have a giant millstone hung around their neck and be thrown into the sea. And if your hand gets in your way, cut it off; you're lucky if you enter maimed into Life and aren't thrown with both hands into Gehenna, the inextinguishable fire.

"And if your foot gets in your way, cut it off; you're lucky if you enter crippled into Life and aren't thrown with both feet into Gehenna.

"And if your eye gets in your way, pull it out; you're lucky if you enter one-eyed into the kingdom of God and aren't thrown with two eyes into Gehenna, where the worm never dies and the fire is never put out.

"Everything is salted in the fire, and salt is good. But if the salt loses its saltiness, what can you cook it in? So have your seasoning within you and make peace with each other."

10

AND ARISING from there he goes into the area of Judea across the Jordan, and again the crowds assemble before him, and as usual he was teaching them again.

And some Pharisees came up and asked him if a man was allowed to break off with his wife, testing him out. He answered, "What did Moses command you?"

They said, "Moses permitted writing a divorce decree and untying the knot."

Jesus said, "Moses wrote that command in view of the hardness of your hearts. But from the beginning of creation, *male and female he made them, for which reason a man shall leave his father and his mother behind and stick to his wife. And the two shall become one living thing,* so that they aren't two any more, but one living thing. So what God joined, let no person divide."

Back at the house his students asked him about that. And he says to them, "Anyone who breaks off with his wife and marries another is committing adultery against her, and if she divorces her husband and marries another, she's living in adultery."

And they brought him some children so that he could touch them, but his students yelled at them. Jesus was outraged to see that and said to them, "Let the children come to me, don't prevent them, because the kingdom of God belongs to such as these. I assure you, anyone who doesn't receive the kingdom of God like a little child, will never get into it." And he hugged them and blessed them, putting his hands on them.

And as he went on his way someone ran up to him and knelt before him and asked him, "Good teacher, what shall I do to inherit everlasting life?"

Jesus said to him, "Why do you call me good? No one is good, only God. You know the commandments: *You are not to murder, you are not to commit adultery, you are not to steal, you are not to perjure yourself, you are not to defraud, do right by your father and your mother.*"

And he said to him, "Teacher, I have kept all those things since infancy."

Jesus, looking at him, felt love for him and said, "One thing is holding you back: go, sell what you have and give it to the poor, and you will have a treasure in the sky, and come here and follow me." At those words his face fell and he went off in mourning, because he was the owner of many possessions.

And looking around, Jesus says to his students, "How hard it will be for those with money to enter the kingdom of God!" His students were amazed at those words. And Jesus continued, saying again to them, "Children, how hard it is to enter the kingdom of God: it's easier for a camel to squeeze through the eye of a needle than for a rich man to enter the kingdom of God."

They were even more stunned and said to each other, "And who *can* be saved?"

Looking straight at them, Jesus says, "For human beings it's impossible, but not for God: everything is possible for God."

And Peter began speaking to him: "Look at us, we have left everything and followed you."

Said Jesus, "I assure you, no one who has left house or brothers or sisters or mother or father or children or land behind for me and the good word will fail to get back a hundredfold in this time now his houses and brothers and sisters and mothers and children and land, with persecution, and everlasting life in the time to come.* And many of the first will be last and many of the last will be first."

They were now on the road going up to Jerusalem, and Jesus was leading them on; and they were overwhelmed, and those following were frightened, and taking the twelve aside again he started telling them what was going to happen to him: "Here we go up to Jerusalem, and the son of humanity will be handed over to the high priests and canon-lawyers, and they will con-

---

*This is one of very few passages in the Gospels that imply that Christians will prosper in this life as well as the next, and even these words are too obscure and contradictory to be interpreted decisively in that direction or any other. What does it mean to get your mother back a hundredfold? If it means joining the family of Christians, then couldn't getting your house back mean something equally figurative, such as amassing spiritual riches? And would it be a blessing anyway to get your house back "with persecution"? Could that even mean "persecution by the houseful"?

demn him to death and hand him over to the people, and they will make fun of him and spit at him and whip him and kill him, and after three days he will rise again."

And James and John the sons of Zebedee come up to him saying, "Teacher, we want you to do for us what we ask of you."

He said to them, "What do you want me to do for you?"

They said to him, "Grant us that we may sit one on your right and one on your left in your glory."

Jesus said to them, "You don't know what you're asking. Can you drink the cup I drink, or bathe in the bath I am bathed in?"

They said, "We can."

And Jesus said to them, "You will drink the cup I drink and bathe in the bath I am bathed in, but as for sitting on my right or my left, that's not mine to give, it's for whom it has been prepared for."

And when the other ten heard, they were outraged about James and John. And calling them together Jesus says to them, "You know how those who are esteemed the rulers of nations lord it over them, and how big men use their power. Among you it isn't going to be like that: whoever wants to be great among you is to be your servant, and anyone who wants to be number one is to be everyone's slave; because the son of humanity also did not come to be served, but to serve and give his life as a ransom for many."

And they come to Jericho. And as he went out of Jericho with his students and a considerable crowd, Baptimeus the son of Timeus, a blind beggar, was sitting by the roadside. And hearing that Jesus of Nazareth was there he started shouting, "Jesus son of David, have mercy on me." And a lot of people were yelling at him to be quiet, but he only shouted all the more, "Son of David, have mercy on me."

And Jesus stopped and said, "Call him."

So they call to the blind man, saying, "Courage, get up, he's calling you!"

And he, throwing off his cloak, sprang to his feet and went toward Jesus. And Jesus said in answer to him, "What do you want me to do for you?"

The blind man said to him, "Master, let me see again."

And Jesus said to him, "Go, your faith has saved you." And immediately he could see again and followed him on the road.

11

AND AS they approach Jerusalem, Bethphage, and Bethany by Mount Olive, he sends two of his students off, saying to them: "Go into the village across from you, and as soon as you get there you'll find a young donkey tied up, on which no person has ever sat; untie it and bring it. And if anyone says to you, 'Why are you doing that?' say, 'The master needs it,' and they'll send it right back here with you."

And they went and found a young donkey tied outside a door at the intersection, and they untie it. And some of the people standing there said to them, "What are you doing untying the donkey?" But they said what Jesus told them to, and they let them alone. And they bring the donkey to Jesus and throw their cloaks upon it, and he sat down upon it. And many people spread their cloaks on the road, and others cut branches from the fields, and those leading and those following shouted:

Hooray! Bless him who comes in the name of the Lord.
Bless the coming kingdom of our father David!
Hooray to the highest heavens!

And he entered Jerusalem as far as the temple and looking round at everything – the hour being already late – he went out to Bethany with the twelve.

And the next day as they came out of Bethany he got hungry. And spotting a leafy fig tree from a distance, he came to see if in fact he could find anything on it, but when he got to it he found nothing but leaves, because it wasn't fig season. And in response he said to it, "Never again shall anyone eat your fruit," and his students were listening to him.

And they come into Jerusalem. And he went into the temple and started throwing out the sellers and buyers in the temple, and he upended the tables of the money-changers and the chairs of the pigeon-sellers. And he wouldn't let anyone transport goods through the temple. And he started teaching, saying to them, "Doesn't it say,

My house shall be called a house of prayer for all nations?

You have made it a den of robbers."

And the chief priests and canon-lawyers heard that and were looking for a way to get rid of him. The thing was, they were afraid of him, because all the crowd was amazed at his teaching.

And when it got late, they traveled back outside the city.

And in the morning, traveling along they saw the fig tree withered to its roots. And Peter, remembering, says to him, "Master, look, the fig tree you cursed has withered away."

And Jesus answered them, "Have faith in God. I assure you that whoever says to this mountain, 'Get up and throw yourself in the sea,' and doesn't waver in his heart but believes that what he says will happen, it will come true for him. Therefore I tell you, everything you pray for and ask for, believe that you'll get it, and it will come true for you. And when you stand praying, forgive anything you may have against anyone so that your father in the skies may also forgive your transgressions."

And they come back into Jerusalem, and as he was walking around in the temple the high priests and canon-lawyers and elders come toward him and said to him, "What authority do you have to do this? Who gave you any authority to do this?"

Jesus said to them, "I'm going to ask you one question, and when you answer me I'll also tell you what authority I have to do this: Did the washing of John come from heaven or from the world? Answer me."

And they discussed that among themselves, saying, "If we say from heaven, he'll say, 'Then why didn't you believe him?' But if we say from the world" – they were afraid of the crowd, because everyone considered that John was truly a prophet. And they answered Jesus saying, "We don't know."

And Jesus says to them, "I'm not telling you what authority I have to do this either."

12

AND HE started talking to them in metaphors: "Once there was a fellow who planted a vineyard and put a fence around it and dug a wine-cellar and built a tower and let it out to some tenant-farmers and left the country. And in due season he sent a servant to collect part of the produce of the vineyard from the farmers. And they seized him and whipped him soundly and sent him off emptyhanded. And again he sent another servant to them, and they beat him over the head and mistreated him. And he sent another, whom they killed, and many more, some of whom they flayed and some of whom they killed. He still had one beloved son. He sent him to them last of all, saying, 'They will respect my son.'

"But those farmers said to each other, 'It's the heir! Come on, let's kill him, and the inheritance is ours!' And they seized him and killed him and threw him outside the vineyard. So what will the master of the vineyard do? He will come and wipe those farmers out and give the vineyard to others. Didn't you ever read this passage in the scripture:

A stone that the builders rejected,
That one ended up the cornerstone
That was made by the Lord
And is the admiration of our eyes?"

And they were looking to seize him but feared the crowd, because they realized he was making this comparison about them. And they left him behind and went away.

And they send some of the Pharisees and Herod's men to him to trap him in his words. And they come and say to him, "Teacher, we know that you are truthful and no respecter of persons, because you do not look to the face of the world, but teach the way of God based on the truth. Are we allowed to pay taxes to Caesar or not? Should we pay or shouldn't we?"

Seeing through their performance, he said to them, "Why are you testing me? Bring me a drachma and let me see it." And they brought it, and he says to them, "Whose picture and inscription is this?"

They said to him, "Caesar's."

Jesus said to them, "Give Caesar's things to Caesar and God's things to God." And they were astonished by him.

And some Sadducees come to him (who say there is no resurrection) and asked him, "Teacher, Moses wrote, 'If someone's brother dies and leaves a wife behind but leaves no child, his brother should take her to wife and produce offspring for his brother.' Once there were seven brothers, and the first took a wife and left no offspring when he died. And the second took her and also died leaving no offspring. And the third died likewise. And all seven left no offspring, and the wife died last of all. In the resurrection, whose wife will she be when they rise again? After all, all seven had her for a wife."

Said Jesus, "Surely you aren't led astray by that, ignorant of the scriptures and the power of God? Because when they arise from the dead there are no brides and no grooms: they are just like God's messengers in the skies. About the fact that the dead are raised up again, didn't you ever read in the book of Moses and the burning bush how God said to him, 'I am the God of Abraham and the God of Isaac and the God of Jacob'? There is no God of the dead but only of the living. You're wandering far afield."

And one of the canon-lawyers who came up and heard them arguing, seeing how well he had answered them, asked him, "Which commandment is first of all?"

Answered Jesus, "The first is, 'Listen, Israel, the Lord your God is one Lord, and you are to love the Lord your God with all your heart and all your soul and all your thoughts and all your strength.' The second is this: 'You are to love your neighbor as you love yourself.' There is no other commandment greater than these."

And the lawyer said to him, "Teacher, you say well and truly that 'he is one and there is no other besides him,' and that 'loving him with all your heart and all your understanding and all your strength' and 'loving your neighbor as yourself' is greater than all burnt offerings and sacrifices."

And Jesus, seeing with what presence of mind he answered, said to him, "You are not far from the kingdom of God." And after that no one dared to ask him any more questions.

And Jesus continued teaching in the temple, saying, "How can the canon-lawyers say that the Anointed is the son of David? David himself said in the holy spirit,

Said a lord to my lord,
'Sit on my right
While I put your enemies underneath your feet.'

David himself calls him Lord, so how is he his son?"

And a great crowd stood listening to him with delight.

And in the course of his teaching he said, "Watch out for clerics who love walking around in their robes and everyone saying hello to them downtown, and their seats in the front of churches and at the head tables of banquets, who wolf down the houses of widows and make a show of praying at great length. They will receive an extra condemnation."

And as he sat across from the collection-box he saw all the crowd throwing money into the box, and many rich people threw in a lot. And a poor widow came and threw in two small coins, like pennies. And calling his students to him he said to them, "I assure you that this widow put in more than all the other people who put something in the box, because all the others threw in what they had left over, while she threw in the last of all she had to live on."

13

AND AS he was going out of the temple one of his students said to him, "Teacher, look how many stones and how many buildings there are!"

And Jesus said to him, "You see all these great buildings? There isn't one stone upon another here that won't be destroyed."

And as he was sitting on Mount Olive, across from the temple, Peter and James and John and Andrew asked him privately, "Tell us, when will these things be, and what will be the sign when all these things are about to end at once?"

And Jesus started telling them, "Watch out lest anyone delude you: many people will come in my name, saying they are me, and they will fool many people. And when you hear wars, and reports of wars, don't be afraid: it has to happen, but it won't be the end yet. Race will rise up against race, and country against country; there will be earthquakes in places, and famines. These things are the beginning of the death-throes.

"Look to yourselves. They will hand you over to the courts, and you will be whipped in the synagogues and stand before governors and kings on account of me, as a testimony to them. And first the good word must be proclaimed to all peoples. And when they take you away to betray you, don't worry what you will say, because what is given to you in that hour is what you will say: it won't be you talking, but the sacred breath. And brother will hand over brother to his death, and fathers their children, and children will rise up against their parents and kill them. And you will be hated by everyone because of my name. But whoever endures to the end, that's who will be saved.

"So when you see the monster of destruction standing where it shouldn't be, let whoever recognizes it remember: those in Judea, flee into the mountains. Those on the rooftop, don't come down or go in to get anything out of your house. Those in the fields, don't turn back to get your cloak. Woe to those with a child in their bellies, or who are nursing, in those days!

"Pray that it may not happen in winter, because those will be days of oppression such as there has never been from the beginning of creation till now nor ever will be. And if the Lord had not limited those days, no living thing would be saved. But for the sake of those chosen ones whom he has chosen, he has set a limit to those days.

"And then if someone says to you, 'Look here, it's the Anointed,' or 'Look there,' don't believe them, because pseudo-Christs and pseudoprophets will come along and give signs and wonders to the point of fooling, if possible, even the chosen ones. But *you* be on your guard: I have told you everything in advance.

"But in those days, after that oppression,

The sun will darken,
And the moon won't give her beams,
And the stars will be falling out of the sky,
And the powers in the skies will be shaken.

"And then they will see the son of humanity coming on the clouds with great power and glory. And then he will send out his messengers and round up his chosen ones from the four winds, from the top of the earth to the top of the sky.

"Learn from the fig-tree by comparison: when its shoots grow tender and it puts out leaves, you know the harvest-time is near. The same for you: when you see these things happening, you know that he is close by the door.

"I assure you that this generation will not pass away till all these things happen. The sky and the earth will pass away, but my words will never pass away.

"As for the date and the hour, no one knows, not even the messengers in the sky, not even the son, but only the Father.

"Watch out, don't fall asleep, because you don't know when the time is. It's like a fellow going out of the country, who left his house behind, and gave to each of his servants authority to do their job, and commanded the doorkeeper to keep watch. So stay awake, because you don't know when the master of the house is coming, whether evening or midnight or cockcrow or morning; when he comes unexpectedly, don't let him find you sleeping."

14

NOW the Passover and the unleavened bread was two days off, and the high priests and canon-lawyers were looking for a way to seize him by some trick and kill him. They were saying, "Not during the feastdays, there'll be an uproar among the people."

And when he was in Bethany, in the house of Simon Leper, as he was sitting there, a woman with a jar of costly ointment of genuine spikenard broke the jar and poured it over his head. Some of the people there were outraged and said to each other: "What is this waste of perfume for? Why, she could have sold that perfume for three hundred drachmas and given it to the poor." And they were yelling at her.

But Jesus said, "Leave her alone. Why are you giving her grief? She did a fine thing for me. You always have the poor around, and whenever you want you can do them good, but me you do not always have. What she could do, she did: she started in advance to perfume my body for burial. I assure you, wherever the good word is proclaimed in all the world, what she did will also be told in memory of her."

And Judas Iscariot, one of the twelve, went off to the high priests to betray him to them. They were delighted to hear that and promised to give him money. And he was looking for a way to hand him over when the time was right.

And on the first day of unleavened bread, when they were sacrificing for Passover, his students say to him, "Where do you want us to go get ready for you to eat the seder?"

And he sends off two of his students, saying to them, "Go into town, and you'll be met by a fellow carrying a water jug: you're going to follow him, and wherever he goes in, say to the

master of the house, 'Our teacher says, *Where is my banquet hall
where I can eat the seder with my students?* And he himself will
show you a big upstairs room spread out and ready, where you
can make preparations for yourselves."

And the students went out and went into town, and found
it as he had told them and got the seder ready.

And when it gets late he comes with the twelve. And as they
were sitting and eating Jesus said, "I tell you for sure, one of
you is going to hand me over, one of you here eating with me."

And they started agonizing and saying to him one by one:
"It couldn't be me, could it?"

He said to them, "One of the twelve, dipping his bread in
the gravy-boat with me. Yes, the son of humanity is going just
as it is written about him, but woe to that person by whom
the son of humanity is betrayed. Better for that person if he'd
never been born."

And as they were eating he took bread, blessed it and broke
it and gave it to them saying, "Take this, this is my body." And
taking a cup and giving thanks he gave it to them, and they all
drank of it. And he said to them, "This is my blood, the blood
of the covenant, poured out for many. I tell you for sure, I will
drink no more of the produce of the vineyard till that day when
I drink it new in the kingdom of God."

And concluding with a hymn they went out to Mount Olive.
And Jesus says to them, "All of you will let me down. After
all, what does it say?

I will strike the shepherd, and the sheep will scatter.

"But after arising I will go ahead of you to Galilee."

Peter said to him, "Even if everyone lets you down, I still
won't."

Says Jesus, "I'm telling you the truth: this very night, before
the cock crows twice, three times you'll say you don't know me."

But he kept saying over and over, "Even if I have to die with
you, I'll never say I don't know you." And they all said the same.

And they come to the place whose name is Gethsemane, and he says to his students, "Sit here till I've finished praying." And he takes Peter and James and John with him and he started wailing and mourning and said to them, "My soul is so sick with grief that I could die. Wait here and stay awake." And going a little ways off he fell on the ground and prayed that, if possible, his hour might pass him by, and said, "Papa, Father, everything is possible for you. Take this cup away from me. But not what _I_ want, what you want." And he comes and finds them sleeping and says to Peter: "Simon, are you sleeping? You couldn't stay awake one hour? Stay awake, and pray that you don't get put to the test: the spirit may be eager, but the flesh is weak." And he went off and prayed again, saying the same words. And he came again and found them sleeping – their eyes were just so heavy, they didn't know what to say. And he comes a third time and says to them: "From here on you can sleep and take your rest, that's all right, the hour has come: watch the son of humanity being betrayed into the hands of criminals. Get up, come on! See there? My betrayer has arrived!"

And even as he spoke, Judas, one of the twelve, shows up, and with him a crowd with swords and clubs, sent by the high priests and canon-lawyers and elders. His betrayer had given them the signal, "Whoever I kiss, that's the one, make sure to seize him and drag him away." And when he came he went right over to him and called him "Master" and kissed him. And they laid hands on him and seized him. One of those standing there drew his sword and struck the high priest's slave and took off his ear.

And Jesus answered them: "As if you were going after a robber, you came out here with swords and clubs to arrest me? During the day I was there among you in the temple teaching and you didn't take me then – but let the scriptures be fulfilled."

And they all left him behind and turned and ran. And one guy, a teenager, was following him, wrapped in a sheet and nothing else. And they seized him, but he jumped out of the sheet and ran off naked.

And they took Jesus away and brought him to the high priest, and all the high priests and canon-lawyers and elders assembled. And Peter was following from a distance as far as the high priest's courtyard and was sitting there with the servants, warming up by the fire.

Now the high priests and the whole high court were looking for evidence against Jesus on the basis of which they could execute him, and they weren't finding it, because there were many people perjuring themselves against him, but their stories were never the same. And some stood up and started lying about him under oath, saying, "We heard him say, 'I will destroy this man-made temple and in three days build another one not made by man,'" but even so the story didn't come out the same.

And the high priest stood up in front of everyone and asked Jesus, "Don't you have any answer as to why these people testify this way against you?" But he was silent and made no answer. Again the high priest asked him: "Are you the Anointed, the Son of the Most Blessed?"

Jesus said, "Yes I am, and you will see the son of humanity sitting on the right hand of power and trailing the clouds of the sky."

Tearing his garments, the high priest says, "What do we need witnesses for any more? You heard that blasphemy! How does it look to you?" They all judged that it was punishable by death.

And some of them started spitting at him, and covering his face, and punching him and saying, "Prophesy!" and the servants hit him blows with canes.

And Peter being down in the courtyard, one of the high priest's girls comes and sees Peter warming himself and looks at him and says: "You were with the Nazarene too—you know: Jesus."

But he denied it, saying, "I don't know or understand what you're talking about." And he went out on the porch, and a cock crowed.

And the girl, seeing him again, started telling the people who were standing there, "This guy is one of them." And he denied it again.

And a little later the people who were standing around started saying to Peter, "Of course you're one of them: after all, you *are* a Galilean."

And he started cursing and swearing, "I don't know this fellow you're talking about." Just then the rooster crowed for the second time. And Peter remembered the words Jesus had spoken to him about how "Before the cock crows twice, three times you'll say you don't know me," and he rushed out and started crying.

15

AND AS SOON as it was daylight the high priests, after calling a meeting with the elders and canon-lawyers and the whole high court, tied Jesus up and led him away and gave him over to Pilate.

And Pilate asked him, "You're the king of the Jews?"

He answers, "That's what *you* say."

And the high priests charged him with all sorts of things, and again Pilate asked him, "Don't you have anything to answer? See all these things they're charging you with?" But Jesus still answered nothing at all, much to Pilate's amazement.

Now at festival time he always released to them one prisoner that they asked for. So there was one called Barabbas, chained among the rebels who had committed murder in the recent uprisings. And the crowd surged toward him and started asking what he would do for them. And Pilate answered, "Do you want me to let the king of the Jews go?" You see, he knew the high priests had delivered him up out of envy.

But the high priests stirred up the crowd to say, "No, let Barabbas go instead."

And Pilate answered again, "What do you want me to do with the so-called king of the Jews?"

And they shouted back, "Crucify him."

And Pilate said to them, "But what has he done wrong?"

But they just kept shouting over and over, "Crucify him."

So Pilate, wishing to do as much as possible for the masses, let Barabbas go for them, and handed over Jesus – whipping him soundly first – to be crucified.

The soldiers took him away to the hall, that is, the courthouse, and they call together the whole platoon. And they put him in a robe of royal purple and put a crown on him that they wove out of thorns. And they started paying him homage and saying, "Good day your majesty, king of the Jews," and hitting him on the head with a cane and spitting on him, and they were on their knees bowing down in front of him.

And after they'd had their fun with him, they took the royal purple off him and put his own clothes back on.

And they're leading him out to crucify him, and there's a certain Simon Cyrenean, Alexander and Rufus's father, passing by on his way from the country, and they dragoon him into carrying the cross.

And they bring him up to the place Golgotha, which translates to Skull Place. And they tried giving him myrrh-laden wine, which he wouldn't take.

And they put him on the cross, and they're dividing up his clothes and rolling dice to see who'd get them. It was about nine o'clock, they crucified him then. And the name of his crime was written overhead:

THE KING OF THE JEWS.

And along with him they crucify two robbers, one on his right and one on his left.

And the people passing by yelled curses at him, shaking their heads and saying, "Bah! Destroyer of the temple and rebuilder in three days, save yourself by coming down off the cross."

Along the same line the high priests were joking with each other and the canon-lawyers, saying, "He saved others, but he can't save himself. Hey, Anointed King of Israel, come down now off the cross, so we can see and believe!" And even the others crucified with him were insulting him.

And when it got to be noon, darkness came over the whole land, from then till three o'clock. And at three o'clock, Jesus cried out in a loud voice, "Eloi, Eloi, lema sabachthani," which translates to "My God, my God, why did you desert me?"

And some of the people standing there heard him and said, "Look at that, he's calling on Elijah." And somebody ran and filled a sponge with the sour wine and put it on the end of a cane for him to drink out of, saying, "Let's see if Elijah comes to get him down." But Jesus let out a loud cry and breathed his last.

And the great curtain hanging in front of the temple was sheared in two from top to bottom. When the Roman captain who had been standing in front of him saw the way he had died, he said, "This person really *was* the son of God!"

There were also some women watching from a distance, among them Mary Magdalen and Mary mother of James and Joseth, and Salome, who had followed him and served him when he was in Galilee, and many others who had come up to Jerusalem with him.

And since it was already getting late and it was Friday, meaning the day before the Sabbath, Joseph of Arimathea, an upstanding member of the high court who himself lived in expectation of the kingdom of God, went boldly to Pilate and asked for the body of Jesus. Pilate was amazed that he was dead already and called the captain over and asked him if he just died, and when he found out from the captain, he made Joseph a present of the body. And first he bought a sheet, and then took him down and wrapped him in the sheet and put him in a tomb that had been cut out of the rockface, and rolled a stone up against the doorway of the tomb. Mary Magdalen and Mary, Joseth's mother, saw where they put him.

16

AND WHEN the Sabbath was over, Mary Magdalen and Mary, James's mother, and Salome brought perfumes so they could go embalm him. And going at the crack of dawn on the first day of the week, they get to the tomb just after sunrise. And they were saying to each other, "Who's going to roll the stone away from the doorway of the tomb for us?" And then they look again and see that the stone *is* rolled away – and it was a very big stone indeed.

And going into the tomb they saw a young man sitting on their right in a white robe, and they were dumbfounded. And he said to them, "Don't be astonished. You're looking for Jesus of Nazareth, the one who was crucified. He rose up, he isn't here. See? There's the place where they laid him. Now go tell his students and Peter that he's going on ahead of you to Galilee, where you will see him, just as he told you."

And they ran out of the tomb in the grip of terror and ecstasy and said nothing to anybody, they were so afraid.

After he arose early on the first day of the week, he appeared first of all to Mary Magdalen, from whom he had thrown out seven demons. She went and told those who had been with him as they were mourning and wailing. And when they heard he was alive and had been seen by her, they didn't believe it.

After that he appeared in another form to two of them walking, as they were going to the fields, and they also went and reported to the others, and they didn't believe them either.

Finally, as the eleven were sitting at a meal, he appeared and castigated them for their lack of faith and hardness of heart in not believing those who had seen him risen. And he said to them, "Travel through the whole world and spread the good word to all creation. Whoever has faith and is washed will be saved, and whoever has no faith will be condemned. The faithful will be attended by the following signs: in my name they will throw out demons; they will speak new languages; they will take snakes in their hands, and even if they drink the poison it won't hurt them; and they'll put their hands on sick people, and they'll be well again."

And so then, Lord Jesus, after talking to them, was taken up into the sky and sits at the right hand of God. But they went out and spread the word everywhere, while the Lord worked with them, underscoring their words with accompanying miracles.

The Good Word According to
LUKE

1

MOST HONORABLE THEOPHILUS,

Since indeed many people have tried to draw up an account of the things fulfilled in our midst as transmitted to us by those who were eyewitnesses from the beginning and became servants of the word, I thought that I also, having followed it all from the first, would write it down for you correctly in order so that you may know the solid truth about the things that have reached your ears.

There was, in the days of Herod king of the Jews, a priest named Zachariah, from the line of Abijah, and he had a wife, one of the daughters of Aaron, and her name was Elizabeth. They were both innocent in the sight of God, walking in the ways of all the commands and judgments of the Lord, without a fault. But they had no child, seeing as how Elizabeth was sterile and both of them were advanced in years.

Now it happened that in the course of his priestly duties before God in the order of the day, according to the custom of the priesthood he drew the assignment of going in and incensing the temple of the Lord, while all the multitude of the people were outside praying during the hour of incensation. And a messenger of the Lord appeared to him, to the right of the incensing altar. And Zachariah was disturbed by the sight, and fear came over him. But the messenger said to him:

"Don't be afraid, Zachariah;
Because your prayer has been heard,
And your wife Elizabeth will have a son,
And you will call his name John.
And he will be a joy and a delight to you,
And many will rejoice in his birth,
Because he will be great in the sight of God
And will drink no wine and no liquor,

And will already be full of the sacred breath
In his mother's womb.
And he will bring many of Jerusalem's sons
Back to the Lord their God.
And he will go before God's face in the breath and power of
  Elijah,
To bring the hearts of fathers back to their children,
And reestablish unbelievers in the consciousness of the just,
And prepare for the Lord a reformed race."

And Zachariah said to the messenger, "How am I to understand this? Remember, I'm an old man, and my wife is getting on in years."

And the messenger answered, "I am Gabriel, who stands before the face of God, and I was sent to talk with you and give you this good news. But now look, you will be silent and unable to talk from now till the day when all this happens, on account of your not believing my words, words that will be fulfilled in their time."

And the people were waiting for Zachariah and were surprised he was taking so long in the temple. Then when he came out, he couldn't talk to them, and they could tell he'd seen a vision in the temple, and he just kept nodding at them and remained mute. And as it happened, when his days on duty were finished, he went home. After those days, his wife Elizabeth conceived, and she kept out of sight five months, saying, "This is what the Lord has done for me on the day when He saw fit to lift my shame from before the world."

During her sixth month, Gabriel the messenger was sent from God to a town in Galilee named Nazareth to see a girl engaged to a man named Joseph, from the family of David; and the girl's name was Mary. And he came in saying, "Hello, favorite of God, the Lord is with you!" She was confused at those words and wondered what kind of greeting that was. And the messenger said to her:

"Don't be afraid, Mary: you found favor with God.
Watch: you're about to conceive in your belly and bear a son,
 and you will call his name Jesus.
He will be great and called son of the Most High.
And the Lord your God will give him the throne of David
 your father,
And he will be king of the family of Jacob for all time,
And his reign will have no end."

Said Mary to the messenger, "How will this happen if I haven't
been with a man?"
And the messenger answered,

"The sacred breath will come over you,
And the power of the Most High will overshadow you.

"Because of his being sacredly born, he will be called God's
son. And look: your relative Elizabeth? She's conceived a child,
at her age, and that child is six months along, after they called
her sterile. Because nothing you can name is impossible for God."
 Said Mary, "Here I am, the slave of the Lord: let it happen
to me the way that you have said." And the messenger went away.
 One day soon after, Mary hastened into the highlands to the
town of Juda and stopped at Zachariah's house and said hello
to Elizabeth. And what happened was, that when Elizabeth
heard Mary's "Hello," the baby gave a jump inside of her, and
Elizabeth, filling up with the sacred breath, raised her voice in
a great shout and said,

"Blessings upon you of all women,
And blessings on the fruit of your womb.

And how do I come to have the mother of my Lord coming
to see me? Did you see? As the sound of your greeting reached
my ears, the baby inside of me jumped for joy. And good luck
to the woman who believes that there will be a fulfillment for
these words of the Lord to her."

Said Mary,

"My soul magnifies the Lord,
And the breath within me has been delighted by God my
    savior,
That He should look down upon the lowness of His slave.
Why, look! from now on, all races will call me the lucky one,
Because the All-Powerful did great things with me.
His name is holy, and His mercy is for generations and
    generations toward those who fear Him.
He summoned strength to His arm,
He scattered the proud with the thoughts in their heart;
He pulled dynasties off thrones
And put peasants on high.
He loaded starving people with goods
And sent rich people away emptyhanded.
Israel has claimed its child
As a reminder of mercy,
As He said to our fathers, to Abraham and his seed forever."

Mary stayed with her some three days and returned home.
Then Elizabeth's time to give birth came round, and she bore
a son. And her neighbors and relatives heard that the Lord had
lavished his mercy on her, and they were happy with her. And
as it happened, they went a week later to circumcise the baby,
and they were going to call him by his father's name, Zachariah. And his mother answered, "No, he's supposed to be called
John." And they said to her, "But there's no one in your family
by that name."

Then they signaled his father as to what he wanted him called.
And motioning for a tablet, he wrote, "John is his name," which
astonished everybody. And instantly his mouth and tongue were
reopened, and he started talking, praising God.

And fear came over all those who lived in the area, and in all
the highlands of Judea these words were spoken and respoken.
And all who heard them took them to heart saying, "Who will
this child be? Because the Lord's hand was certainly with him."

And Zachariah his father was filled with the sacred breath and prophesied, saying,

"Blessed is the Lord God of Israel,
That He should look down and pay the ransom on His people,
And extend to us the brimming horn of salvation,
Here in the house of David His child.
As He spoke through the mouth of the holy prophets of ages
    ago:
About safety from our enemies, from the hands of everyone
    who hates us,
About being merciful with our fathers
And remembering the holy covenant,
The oath He swore to Abraham our father,
To grant that we, fearlessly snatched from the enemy's clutches,
Might serve Him in holiness and innocence,
There before Him, all the days of our lives.
And you, child, you will be called prophet of the Most High,
Because you will walk in front of the Lord to clear his path,
So as to give the knowledge of salvation to his people
For the forgiveness of their wrongs
Through the merciful senses of our God,
Which will make Him look down on us as a sunrise from on
    high,
To shine for those in darkness and sitting in the shadow of
    death,
To correct our steps back to the road of peace."

So the baby grew and got stronger in spirit, and he was out in the wilderness until the day of his presentation to Israel.

2

IT HAPPENED during those days that a decree went out from Caesar Augustus to register the whole world. This first census happened when Syrias Cyrenius was governor. So everyone was going to get registered, each to their own home town. And

Joseph came up from Galilee, from the town of Nazareth, into Judea, to a city of David which is called Bethlehem – he being of the family and descent of David – to be registered with Mary his fiancee, who was pregnant. As it happened, during their stay there her days of childbirth came round, and she bore her son, her firstborn, and wrapped him up and made his bed in a grain-crib, because there was no room for them in the living-quarters.

Now shepherds were in that area, staying up late and taking turns through the night watching out for their sheep. And a messenger of the Lord stood in front of them, and the Lord's glory surrounded them, and they felt the fear of fears. And the messenger said to them, "Don't be afraid, I hereby give you the good news of a great joy which will be for all the people, namely that a savior was born for you today who is an anointed lord in a city of David. And this is your sign: you'll find the baby wrapped up and lying in a grain-crib."

And all of a sudden beside that messenger there was a mass of the heavenly army praising God and saying,

"Glory in the highest to God,
And on earth, peace among people in his good favor."

And it happened, as off into the sky went the messengers, that the shepherds were saying to each other, "Now let's get on to Bethlehem and see this word fulfilled that the Lord revealed to us." And they went off as fast as they could and came upon Mary and Joseph and the baby lying in the grain-crib. When they saw that, they understood what had been told them concerning this child. And everyone was amazed to hear what the shepherds said to them, but Mary preserved all these things that were said, turning them over in her heart. And the shepherds returned, glorifying and praising God to all who heard and saw how they were being spoken to.

And when a week was up, the time to circumcise him, his name was indeed called Jesus, the name he was called by the messenger of God before he was conceived inside his mother.

And when the purification days came round according to the law of Moses, they brought him up to Jerusalem to present him to the Lord (as it says in the law of the Lord: "Every male child that comes out of the womb shall be called sacred to the Lord") and also to give sacrifice as it says in the law of the Lord: "A brace of turtledoves, and two fledgling pigeons."

And there was this man in Jerusalem named Simeon, and this fellow lived innocently and correctly while he waited for the consolation of Israel, and the sacred breath was upon him. And he had been promised by the sacred breath not to see death without first seeing the Anointed of the Lord.

And in this spirit he went to the temple. And while the parents of Jesus were bringing him in so they could do the usual with him according to the law, this same Simeon was there to greet him, and took him in his arms and blessed God and said,

> "Here you are letting Your slave go, Master,
> In peace, according to Your promise,
> Now that my eyes saw the salvation
> You prepared with all races watching,
> A light for the revealing of nations
> And a glory to his people Israel."

And his father and his mother stood wondering at the things said about him. And Simeon blessed them and said to Mary his mother, "Here he lies, the fall and rising up again of many in Israel, and the sign, much disputed – yes, the sword will run your heart right through – by which the thoughts of many hearts will be revealed."

And there was a prophet, Anna, Thanuel's daughter from the line of Aser, she being very advanced in years, having lived with a husband for seven years after her girlhood and by herself as a widow up to her eighty-fourth year; she never left the temple, devoting herself night and day to fasting and prayer. And coming on the scene at the same time, she started thanking God in advance and talking about him to all who waited for the rescue of Israel.

And when they'd done everything according to the law of the Lord, they went back to their own town, Nazareth; the child grew and gained strength as he filled with wisdom, and God's grace was upon him.

And his parents used to make an annual trip to Jerusalem for the feast of Passover. And when he was twelve, after they came up as usual for the festival and finished out the day, as the rest of them were going back, the boy Jesus stayed behind in Jerusalem, and his parents didn't know that. Thinking he was somewhere in the caravan they went several days' journey and kept looking for him among their relatives and family friends, and after they didn't find him they came back to Jerusalem to look for him. And it turned out that after three days they found him in the temple, sitting among the scholars and listening to them and asking questions. All those who heard him were overwhelmed by his understanding and his answers. And when they saw him they were amazed, and his mother said to him: "Son, why did you do this to us? See how your father and I have been looking for you in agony?"

And he said to them, "For me? Why were you looking for me? Didn't you know I have to be immersed in the things of my father?" And they didn't understand the words he was saying to them. And he left the city with them and went back to Nazareth and was obedient to them. And his mother preserved all these words in her heart. And Jesus kept forging ahead in wisdom, maturity, and favor with God and the world.

3

IN THE fifteenth year of Tiberius Caesar's rule, with Pontius Pilate governing Judea; and Herod being governor of Galilee, Philip his brother governor of the countries Ituria and Trachonitis, and Lysanius governor of Abilena; during the high priesthood of Annas and Caiphas the words of God came to John, Zachariah's son, there in the wilds.

And he went through all the country round the Jordan, announcing the washing of a changed heart for the forgiveness of wrongs. As is written in the book of the words of Isaiah the prophet,

The voice of a crier in the desert,
Get the Lord's road ready,
Straighten his paths.
Every gully will be filled in,
And every mountain and hill worn down,
And the twists will come out straight,
And rough will be on its way to smooth,
And every living thing will see the savior of God –

so he said to the crowds traveling out to be washed by him, "Children of vipers, who tipped you off to run from the coming fury? Bear fruit worthy of a changed heart and don't start saying to each other, '*We* have Abraham for our father!' because I'm telling you, God can raise children for Abraham out of these stones. The ax is already poised at the root of the trees, so any tree not bearing good fruit gets cut down and thrown into the fire."

And the crowds were asking him, "So what do we do?"

He answered, "Whoever has two robes, share with someone who has none; whoever has food, do likewise."

And some tax collectors came to be washed and said to him, "Teacher, what do we do?"

And he said to them, "Don't do anything beyond what you're assigned to."

And some Army men asked him, "What about us, what do we do?"

And he said to them, "No harassing anybody, no backbiting, and be content with your wages."

Since the nation was waiting, and since in their hearts all were considering about John, whether *he* might not be the Anointed, John answered, saying to everybody, "I'm washing you in water, but someone is coming who is so much stronger than me, I'm not great enough to untie the thongs of his sandals: *he* will wash you in holy breath and fire, whose winnowing-fan is in his hand to clean up his threshing-floor, collecting the wheat into his silo, while he burns the chaff in a never-extinguished fire."

With many and various exhortations he brought the good word to the people. But Herod the governor, when he got told off by him on account of Herodias, his brother's wife – and all the bad things Herod had done – putting that on top of all the other offenses, he clapped John in jail.

In the course of the whole country being washed, when Jesus had also been washed and was praying, the sky happened to open, and the holy breath to alight in the physical form of a dove upon him, and a voice to come from the sky: "You are my son, my beloved son, in you I am delighted."

And Jesus himself was getting to be some thirty years old, the son, so he was considered, of Joseph son of Eli son of Matthat son of Levi son of Melchi son of Jannae son of Joseph son of Mattathias son of Amos son of Nahum son of Esli son of Naggae son of Maath son of Mattathias son of Semein son of Josech son of Joda son of Johanan son of Resa son of Zorobabel son of Salathiel son of Neri son of Melchi son of Addi son of Kosam son of Elmadam son of Er son of Jesu son of Eliezer son of Jorim son of Matthat son of Levi son of Symeon son of Juda son of Joseph son of Jonam son of Eliakim son of Melea son of Menna son of Mattatha son of Nathan son of David son of Jesse son of Jobed son of Booz son of Salmon son of Naasson son of Aminadab son of Admin son of Arni son of Esrom son of Phares son of Juda son of Jacob son of Isaac son of Abraham son of Thara son of Nachor son of Serouch son of Ragau son of Phalek son of Eber son of Sala son of Cainan son of Arphaxad son of Shem son of Noah son of Lamech son of Methuselah son of Enoch son of Jared son of Maleleel son of Cainan son of Enos son of Seth son of Adam son of God.

4

NOW Jesus returned from the Jordan full of holy spirit and was led in that spirit into the wilds for forty days, being tested by the devil. And he didn't eat a thing during those days, and at the end of them he was starving. So the devil said to him, "If you're God's son, tell this stone to become bread."

And Jesus answered him, "It is written, 'A person is not to live only on bread.'"

And taking him up high, he showed him – in an instant of time – all the kingdoms of the world. And the devil said to him, "I will give you every bit of that power, and the glory of them all; it's been given to me, and I can give it to whomever I like. Just bow down in front of me, and it will all be yours."

And Jesus answered, "It says, 'The Lord your God is whom you shall adore, and you shall serve only Him.'"

So he took him into Jerusalem and set him up on top one wing of the temple and said to him, "If you're God's son, throw yourself down from there. After all, it says,

His messengers have been instructed about you, to guard you,

and

They will take you in their hands,
So you don't stub your foot against a stone."

And Jesus answered, "It says, 'You are not to experiment with the Lord your God.'"

And after exhausting all his tests the devil retired from him awaiting a better time.

And Jesus returned in the power of the spirit to Galilee, and the word went out across the whole neighborhood about him. And he was teaching in their synagogues, acclaimed by all.

And he came to Nazareth, where he had grown up, and, as his custom was, went to the synagogue on the day of the Sabbath and stood up to read. And he was given a book of the prophet Isaiah, and opening the book up he found the place where it says,

A spirit of the Lord is upon me,
The one for which he anointed me
To bring the good word to the poor.
He has sent me out
To proclaim release for prisoners
And sight for the blind,
To send the bone-crushed away with a cure
And proclaim the official Year of the Lord.

And closing the book he gave it to the acolyte and sat down. And all eyes in the synagogue were staring at him, as he began saying to them, "Today this scripture is fulfilled in your ears."

And they all witnessed him and were amazed at the words of grace coming out of his mouth and said, "Isn't this Joseph's son?" And he said to them, "From all sides you're going to use the expression, 'Physician, heal thyself: what we heard of, happening in Capharnaum, do that here in your own home town.'

"But," said he, "I tell you for sure, no prophet is accepted in his home town. I assure you, there were plenty of widows in Israel in the days of Elijah, when the sky was sealed for three years and six months so that there was a great famine over all the earth, but Elijah wasn't sent to any of them, but rather to Sarepta, in Sidonia, to see a widowed woman there. And there were plenty of lepers in Israel in the time of Eliseus the prophet, but none of them were cleansed, only Naman the Syrian." And it filled everybody with anger to hear him say those things in the synagogue, and they got up and threw him out of town and took him right up to the edge of the cliff on which the town was built, to throw him down. But he slipped through their midst and went his way.

And he went down to Capharnaum, a town in Galilee. And he was teaching them on the Sabbath. And they were stunned at his teaching, because his words were on his own authority.

And in the synagogue there was a fellow with the spirit of an unclean demon, and it raised its voice in a loud cry: "Stop, what have we done to you, Jesus of Nazareth? Did you come to wipe us out? I know who you are, holy one of God."

And Jesus yelled at it, saying, "Shut up and come out of him." And after throwing him down in the middle of the floor, the demon came out without injuring him in the least.

And awe came over everyone, and they said to each other, "What words does he use so that by his own power and authority he commands unclean spirits and they come out?" And the clamor about him traveled out to every place in the surrounding countryside.

But after getting up and leaving the synagogue, he went to Simon's house. Now Simon's mother-in-law was suffering from a great fever, and they asked him about her. And he stood over her and yelled at the fever, and it left her. Standing suddenly upright, she was at their service.

As the sun was setting, everyone who had someone sick with various diseases brought them to him, and he put his hands on every one of them and cured them. And demons came out of many people shouting, "You're the son of God!"

And he yelled at them and forbade them to speak; *they* knew he was the Anointed.

When it was daylight, he went out traveling to a deserted place. And the crowds were looking for him and came to him and hindered him from leaving them. But he said, "I have to spread the good word of the kingdom of God in the other cities too, that's what I was sent for." And he was spreading the word in the synagogues of Judea.

5

As IT HAPPENED, while the crowd was hanging on him and hearing the words of God, he was standing by Lake Gennesareth. And he saw two boats sitting by the lake. The fishermen had gotten out of them and were washing their nets. So getting into one of the boats, which was Simon's, he asked him to shove off from shore a ways, and sitting in the boat, he was teaching the crowds.

Then when he finished talking, he said to Simon, "Head out for deep water and lower your nets for the catch." And Simon answered, "Chief, we didn't catch anything, sweating away all night long, but on your word I'll let the nets down." And when they did, they closed their nets on a great mass of many fish, their nets were bursting with them. And they signaled their mates in the other ship to come help them take hold of it. And they came and filled both boats till they were riding low in the water. Seeing that, Simon Peter fell at the knees of Jesus and said, "Get away from me, I'm an evil man, Lord"; astonishment overwhelmed him and all who had joined him in pursuit of the fish they'd caught, including James and John the sons of Zebedee, who were associates of Simon's.

And Jesus said to Simon, "Don't be afraid: from now on you will be fishers of humanity." And after bringing their boats in to shore they left everything and followed him.

And it happened while he was in one of the towns, there was this man with full-blown leprosy. Seeing Jesus, he fell on his face and begged him, "Lord, if you want to, you can heal me."

And he reached out his hand and touched him, saying, "I *do* want to. Be healed." And the leprosy went right out of him. And he instructed him to say nothing to anybody: "Just go show yourself to the priest and contribute what Moses commanded in thanks for your purification, as a testimony to them." More and more the word got out about him, and great crowds assembled to listen and be healed from their illnesses, but he was retreating to the wilds and praying.

And it happened on one of those days that he was teaching, and there were Pharisees and teachers of the law sitting there who had come from every village in Galilee and Judea, and from Jerusalem. And the power of the Lord was on him to heal. And these men came bringing a man on a bed who was paralyzed, and they were looking for a way to bring him inside and put him in front of him. And finding no way to bring him in, what with the crowd, they climbed up on the roof and let him down, with his cot, between the shingles onto the floor in front of Jesus. And seeing their faith, he said, "Fellow, your wrongs are forgiven you."

And the canon-lawyers and Pharisees started mulling that over and saying, "Who is this guy who speaks such blasphemies? Who can forgive wrongs but God alone?"

But Jesus, observing their thoughts, answered them, "Why are you muttering in your hearts? Which is easier: to say, 'Your wrongs are forgiven,' or to say, 'Get up and walk'? But so you see that the son of humanity has authority to forgive wrongs on earth" – he said to the paralyzed man – "I tell you, get up, pick up your cot, and go on home."

And he stood up suddenly in front of them, picked up the cot he'd been lying on, and went home praising God. And everyone was gripped by an ecstasy and praised God, and they filled with fear, saying, "We saw the impossible today."

And after that he came out and spotted a tax-collector named Levi sitting at the toll-station and said to him, "Follow me." And he left everything behind and stood up and followed him. And Levi gave him a grand reception at his house, and there was a big crowd of tax-collectors and other people who were sitting with them. And the Pharisees and their canon-lawyers started grumbling at his students, saying, "What do you eat with tax-collectors and godless people for?" And Jesus answered them, "It's not the healthy who need a doctor, it's the sick. I am not here to call the virtuous to a change of heart, I'm here to call the godless people."

Then they said to him, "John's students fast heavily and make petitions to God, and so do those of the Pharisees, but yours eat and drink away."

Jesus said to them, "You can't make the wedding party fast while the bridegroom is with them, can you? There will come days when the bridegroom will be taken away from them; then they will fast, on those days."

Then he made them a comparison about how no one cuts a patch from a new garment and patches an old garment with it, because if they do, it cuts the new garment up, besides which the patch from the new garment doesn't match the old. And no one pours new wine into old skins, because if they do, the new wine bursts the skins, and it itself pours out, while the skins are destroyed. Instead, new wine should be poured into new skins. And no one drinking old wine wants new wine instead; they say, "The old stuff is nice."

6

ONCE on the Sabbath he happened to be traveling through the grain fields, and his students were picking the ears of grain and eating them, cleaning them by hand. Some of the Pharisees said, "Why are you doing what isn't allowed on the Sabbath?"

In answer to them Jesus said, "Haven't you even read what David did when he and those with him were starving: how he went into the house of God and took and ate the sacramental loaves and gave them to those with him, bread which no one was allowed to eat except the priests?" And he said to them, "The son of humanity is superior to the Sabbath."

On another Sabbath he happened to go into the synagogue and teach, and there was a fellow there, and his right hand was withered. Now the canon-lawyers and Pharisees were watching him to see if he would heal on the Sabbath, so they could find something to charge him with. But he knew their thoughts, so he said to the man with the withered hand, "Get up and stand here in the middle." And he got up and stood there. Jesus said to them, "I ask you, which is permissible on the Sabbath: doing good, or doing evil – saving a life or destroying it?" And looking round at them all he said to him, "Reach out your hand." He did, and his hand was restored. But they were filled with mindlessness and started talking with each other about what they were going to do to Jesus.

It happened in those days that he went up the mountain to pray and was spending the night in prayer to God. And when the day came, he called his students to him, and picking twelve of them, named them emissaries ["apostles"]: Simon, whom he named the Rock ["Peter"], and Andrew his brother, and James and John and Philip and Bartholomew and Matthew and Thomas and James Alpheus and Simon "the Revolutionary" and Judas Jacobson and Judas Iscariot, who turned traitor.

And after coming down with them he stood on level ground, and with him a great crowd of his students, and a giant mass of the people from all Judea and Jerusalem and the shores of Tyre and Sidon, who came to hear him and be healed from their diseases; and those afflicted by unclean spirits were healed, and all the crowd were trying to touch him, because a force was coming out of him and healing everybody.

And raising his eyes toward his students, he said,

"You the poor are in luck, because the kingdom of God is yours.
You who are starving now are in luck,
Because you will have your fill.
You who are crying now are in luck,
Because you will laugh.

You are in luck when the world hates you and excludes you and defames you and casts your name out like something evil, because of the son of humanity. Be happy on that day and jump for joy; because look, your reward will be great in the sky. After all, that's the same way their forefathers treated the prophets.

But woe to you the rich,
Because you have had your consolation.
Woe to you who are satisfied now,
Because you will starve.
Woe to those who are laughing now,
Because you will grieve and mourn.
Woe to you when all the world speaks well of you:
After all, that's the same way their forefathers treated the pseudoprophets.

"But I speak to you who are listening: love your enemies, treat well those who hate you, bless those who curse you, pray for those who rail against you. If someone slaps you on one side of your jaw, give him the other side, and if someone takes your coat, don't begrudge him your shirt either. To all those who ask of you, give; and from those who take what is yours, don't ask to have it back.

"And just as you want people to treat you, treat them the same: if you love those who love you, what grace do you get? After all, even the evildoers love those who love them. And if you do good to those who do good to you, what grace do you get? Even wrongdoers do the same. And if you lend to those from whom you hope to get something, what grace do you get? Even wrongdoers lend to wrongdoers in order to receive in kind. But rather love your enemies, and do good and make loans expecting nothing back, and your reward will be great, and you will be sons and daughters of the Most High, because He too is kind to the ungrateful and the evil.

"Be merciful just as your Father is merciful. And don't judge, and you won't be judged. And don't condemn, and you won't be condemned. Let others off, and you'll let off. Give, and you'll be given to—they'll put it in your pocket in good measure, shaken and pushed down and overflowing the top, because by the same measure you use, things will be measured for you."

And he made this comparison for them: "A blind man can't lead a blind man around, can he? Won't they both fall into the ditch? No pupil is above his teacher; when perfected, in every case he will be like his teacher.

"Why do you look at the splinter in your brother's eye, but don't notice the log in your own eye? How can you say to your brother, 'Brother, let me get that splinter out of your eye,' not seeing the log in your own eye? You fake, first get the log out of your eye, and then you can see about getting the splinter out of your brother's eye.

"You see, there is no good tree that gives rotten fruit, nor, on the other hand, any rotten tree that gives good fruit. Indeed, each tree is known by its own fruit. After all, they don't gather figs from thorn-trees, nor do they dry out grapes gotten from a bramble-bush. The good person brings forth good from his heart's good treasury, and the bad person, from his bad treasury, brings forth bad, because his mouth speaks out what his heart is brimming over with.

"Why do you call me 'Lord, Lord,' and don't do what I tell you? Everyone who comes to me and hears my words and does them, I'll give you a glimpse of what he's like: he's like a person building a house who dug a hole and made it deep and set a foundation on the rock. So when there was a flood, the river came up to that house and couldn't shake it because of its being well grounded. But whoever hears, and doesn't act, he's like a person building a house on the ground with no foundation, which, when the river came up to it, fell right down, and the smashing-up of that house was tremendous."

7

WHEN he had filled the ears of the people with all his words, he went to Capharnaum.

Now a certain Roman captain's slave was sick and going to die, one who was dear to him. So when he heard about Jesus, he sent some of the elders of Judea to him to ask him to come save his slave. When they got to where Jesus was, they begged him earnestly, saying, "He deserves that you should do him this service: he loves our people and built our synagogue for us." So Jesus went along with them.

But when he was already not far from the house, the captain sent friends to him saying, "Lord, don't trouble yourself, because I'm not important enough for you to come under my roof, which is why I also didn't consider myself worthy to come see you; just say the word, and let my child be healed. After all, I'm a person placed under authority, with soldiers under me, and I tell this guy 'Go,' and he goes, and another guy 'Come,' and he comes, and I tell my slave 'Do this,' and he does it."

Hearing that, Jesus was amazed by him and turned to the crowd following him and said, "Even in Israel I never found so much trust." And the ones sent out returned to the house and found the slave healthy.

And it happened next that he traveled to a town called Nain, and his students and a great crowd were traveling with him. But as they got near the gate of the city, there was this dead man being carried out, his mother's only son, and she was a widow; and a sizable crowd from the town was with her. And seeing her, the Lord was sorry for her and said to her, "Don't cry." And he came up and touched the coffin, and the pallbearers stopped, and he said, "Young man, I tell you, get up!" And the dead man sat up and started talking, and he gave him back to his mother.

But fear gripped everyone, and they praised God, saying, "A great prophet has arisen among us," and "God looked down upon his people." And this story about him went out among all of Judea and all the country round.

And his students went and reported to John about all these things, and John, calling two of his students to him, sent them to the Lord, saying, "Are you the one who's coming, or should we look for another?" When they got to him, the men said,

"John the Baptist sent us to you saying, 'Are you the one who's coming, or should we look for another?'"

In the same hour he cured many people of diseases and afflictions and evil spirits, and bestowed sight on many of the blind. And he answered them, "Go report to John what you see and hear: the blind see, the lame walk, lepers are cleansed, the deaf hear, the dead arise, the poor are given the good word, and the person is in luck who doesn't let me down."

When John's messengers had left, he started speaking to the crowds about John: "What did you go out into the wilds to see? A reed shaken by the wind? No, what did you go out to see? A person dressed in nice soft clothes? See here, the people in splendid clothing and living in luxury are in the royal houses. Come on, what did you go out to see? A prophet? Yes, I tell you, a prophet and more: he is the one about whom it is written,

Look, I am sending my messenger before your face,
To prepare your way before you.

I'm telling you, among all those born of women there is no greater than John – but the lowest person in the kingdom of God is greater than him.

"And all the people who heard, and all the tax-collectors, did justice to God by being bathed in the bath of John. But the Pharisees and lawyers rejected God's will toward them when they were not bathed by him.

"What shall I compare the people of this generation to, and what are they like? They're like little kids sitting in the marketplace and hollering at the others, as they say,

We-played-the-flute-and-you-wouldn't-dance,
We-beat-our-breasts-and-you-wouldn't mourn!

After all, John the Baptist has come along eating no bread and drinking no wine, and you say, 'He's possessed!' The son of humanity has come along eating and drinking, and you say,

'Look at this wine-drinking gourmand, the friend of tax-collectors and godless people.' But wisdom always was vindicated by all of its offspring."

Now one of the Pharisees asked him to eat with him, and he went into the house of the Pharisee and reclined at table. And the next thing was, a fallen woman who was in the town and who had found out that he was having dinner at the Pharisee's house brought in a vial of perfume and stood behind him crying, and started wetting his feet with her tears and drying them off with the hair of her head; and she was kissing his feet and applying the perfume to them. Seeing that, the Pharisee who had invited him said to himself, "If this guy was a prophet, he'd know what kind of woman was touching him, that she's a fallen woman."

And Jesus reacted, saying to him, "Simon, I have something to say to you."

"Speak, Master," he said.

"Once there was a lender who had two debtors: one owed five hundred drachmas and the other fifty. Since they had no way to pay him back he absolved them both. So which of them will love him more?"

Answered Simon, "I presume, the one who was absolved of more."

And he said to him, "You guessed right." And turning to the woman he said to Simon, "See this woman here? I came into your house and you didn't bring me water for my feet, but she watered my feet with her tears and dried them with her hair. You didn't give me a kiss, but she, since I came in here, hasn't stopped kissing my feet. You didn't anoint my head with olive oil, but she anointed my feet with perfume; by grace of which, I tell you, her wrongs shall be forgiven, many as they are, because she showed so much love. Who is forgiven less, loves less." Then he said to her, "Let your wrongs be forgiven."

And the others sitting there started saying to themselves, "Who is this guy who even forgives wrongdoing?"

But he said to the woman, "Your trust has saved you; go in peace."

8

AND IT HAPPENED afterwards that he himself journeyed through town and village, proclaiming and bringing the good word of the kingdom of God, with the twelve coming along, and also certain women who had been cured of evil spirits and sicknesses – Mary known as Magdalen, from whom seven demons had come out, and Joanna, wife of Chuza the trustee of Herod, and Susanna and many others – who took care of them with what possessions they had.

With a great crowd assembling and people of this town and that traveling out to see him, he said by way of comparison: "Once the sower went out to sow his seed. And in the course of his sowing, some fell by the roadside and was trampled, and the birds of the sky ate it up. And some fell upon stone, and when it came up it withered away from having no moisture. And some fell in the middle of thorns, and the thorns growing with it choked it off. And some fell on the good soil and came up and yielded fruit a hundredfold." Saying these things, he cried, "Whoever has ears to hear, let them hear."

But his students asked him what the comparison was about. He said, "To you it is given to know the mysteries of the kingdom of God, but to the rest of them it is only given in metaphors, so that 'seeing they may not see, and hearing they may not understand.'

"This is the comparison: the seed is the word of God. Those by the roadside are those who hear, but the devil comes and takes the word from their heart, so they won't believe and be saved. The ones upon stone are those who, when they hear the word, receive it with joy; but they have no roots, those who believe for a time but in trying times fall away. Those who fell into the thorns, those are the ones who hear, but as they travel on with their worries, and their wealth, and the pleasures of life, they get choked off and never yield anything. The seed on good soil, those are the ones who hear and preserve the word in a good and clean heart and bear fruit by perseverance.

"No one who lights a candle covers it with a pot or puts it under the bed; they put it up on a tall candlestick so those who come in can see the light. After all, there is no secret thing that won't be made public, nor anything hidden away that won't be made known and come to light.

"So watch how you listen, because he who has will be given more, and he who doesn't have, even what he thought he had will be taken away from him."

Then his mother showed up to see him, with his brothers and sisters, and they couldn't get at him because of the crowd. And he was given the message, "Your mother and your brothers and sisters are standing out there and want to see you."

And he answered them, "My mother and my brothers and my sisters are those who hear the word of God and do it."

It happened on one of those days also that he got into a boat along with his students and said to them, "Let's cross to the other side of the lake," and they sailed off.

As they were sailing, he dozed off; and a windstorm descended on the lake, and they were taking on water, and in danger. They went up to him and roused him, saying, "Chief, chief, we'll be killed!"

And he got up and yelled at the wind and the surging waters, and they stopped short, and it became calm. And he said to them, "Where is your faith?"

But they were frightened and amazed and said to each other, "Who *is* this guy that he even gives orders to the winds and the water and they obey him?"

And they landed at the country of the Gerasenes, which is on the shore opposite Galilee. As he got out on shore he was met by a certain man with a demon, who for quite some time had worn no clothes, nor lived in a house, but in the graveyard instead. Seeing Jesus, he gave a shout and fell down in front of him and said in a loud voice, "What have I done to you, Jesus son of God the highest? I beg you, don't torment me," because he was about to order the unclean spirit to go out of the fellow. It seems that for many seasons they had tried seizing him, and he had been bound with chains and kept shackled, but he always broke free of the bonds and was driven by the demon into the wilds. So Jesus asked him, "What is your name?"

He said, "Legion," because many demons had entered into him. And they pleaded with him not to order them into the abyss. Now there was a sizable herd of pigs grazing on the mountain. And they asked him to let them go into those, and he agreed. So the demons came out of the fellow and went into the pigs, and the herd rushed over the edge of the cliff into the lake and drowned.

When the herdsmen saw what happened they ran off and reported it in town and in the fields. They came out to see what had happened and came toward Jesus and saw the fellow that the demons had gone out of, sitting there fully dressed and in his right mind, by the feet of Jesus, and they were terrified. Those who had seen it explained to them how the possessed man had been saved. And they asked him, that whole crowd of people from the environs of the Gerasenes, to go away from them, because they were seized by a great fear. So he got in the boat and went back. And the man from whom the demons had come out asked to go with him. But Jesus left him, saying, "Go back home and tell the story of what God did for you." And he went all through town spreading the word of what Jesus had done for him.

Upon the return of Jesus, the crowd was glad to see him: they had all been expecting him. And along came a man named Jairus, and he was the chief of the synagogue, and falling at the feet of Jesus, he begged him to come to his house, because he had an only daughter, some twelve years old, and she was dying. And as he went off with him the crowds pressed him hard. And a woman who had been hemorrhaging for twelve years, who had spent her whole life's savings on doctors but couldn't be cured by any of them, came up to him from behind and touched the edge of his cloak, and suddenly her hemorrhaging stopped. And Jesus said, "Who was that touching me?"

When everyone denied it, Peter said, "Chief, the crowds are pressing in on you and rubbing against you."

But Jesus said, "Somebody touched me, because I felt the force going out of me." Seeing that she hadn't gotten away with it, the trembling woman came and fell before him* and explained in front of all the people the reason she had touched him and how all of a sudden she had been cured. And he said to her, "Daughter, your trust has saved you, go in peace."

Just as he says that, someone comes from the chief of the synagogue's house saying, "Your daughter's dead, don't bother the teacher any further."

But Jesus heard that and said to him, "Don't be afraid, just have faith, and she'll be saved."

Going into the house, he wouldn't let anyone come in with him except Peter, James, John, and the father and mother of the child. Everyone was wailing and beating their breasts, but he said, "Don't cry: she didn't die, she's only sleeping." And they were laughing at him, because they knew she had died. But he, taking her hand, cried, "Child, get up!" And the breath came back into her, and she stood up suddenly, and he ordered that she be given something to eat. And her parents were ecstatic, but he commanded them not to tell anybody what happened.

9

THEN calling the twelve together, he gave them power and authority over all demons and for the healing of diseases and

---

*She isn't afraid because she stole a cure, but because her bloody sickness was considered unclean and she wasn't supposed to be touching anybody.

sent them out to spread the word of the kingdom of God and cure the sick. And he said to them, "Take nothing on the road, no walking stick, no knapsack, no bread, no silver, nor two tunics on your back. And whatever house you go into, stay there till you leave that place. And wherever they don't receive you, when you leave that town shake the dust from your feet as a testimony to them." And they went out and started going through the villages, bringing the good word and curing people everywhere.

Now Governor Herod heard about all that had happened and was at a loss, because it was said by some that John had risen from the dead, by others that Elijah had appeared, and by still others that one of the ancient prophets had arisen. But Herod said, "John? I beheaded him. So who is this guy I keep hearing these things about?" And he was anxious to see him.

And the apostles came back and recounted to him what they had done. And taking them along he retreated privately to a town called Bethesda. But the crowds found out and followed him. And he, glad to see them, talked to them about the kingdom of God, and cured those who had need of a healing.

Now the sun was beginning to set, and the twelve came up to him and said, "Let the crowd go, so they can head for the villages and farms around here to find lodging and food, since we're here in the middle of nowhere."

He said to them, "Give them something to eat yourselves."

They said, "We have no more than five loaves of bread and two fish, unless we're supposed to go buy food for this whole population" – there were some five thousand men there.

But he said to his students, "Have them sit down in groups of fifty or so." And they did, and got them all seated. Then taking the five loaves and the two fish he looked up to the sky and blessed them and broke them and gave them to his students to put before the crowd. And they ate, and everybody ate their fill, and what they had left over was cleared away, twelve basketfuls of scraps.

And it happened while he was praying privately that his students were with him, and he asked them, "Who do the crowds say I am?"

They answered, "John the Baptist. . .others say Elijah, others say one of the ancient prophets risen again."

Then he said to them, "And you, who do you say I am?"

Peter answered, "The Anointed of God." But he strictly ordered them not to tell that to anyone, saying that the son of humanity would have to undergo many things and be rejected by the elders and high priests and canon-lawyers, and be killed, and rise up on the third day.

He said to them all, "If anyone wants to follow after me, let him repudiate himself and take up his cross day by day and follow me, because whoever wants to save his life will lose it, but whoever loses his life because of me, that's who will save it. After all, what does it help a person to gain the whole world if he loses himself or pays himself as the price? Because whoever is ashamed of me and my words, the son of humanity will be ashamed of him too when he comes in his glory and the glory of his Father and the holy messengers. I tell you truly, there are some of those standing right here who will never taste death before they see the kingdom of God."

It happened a week or so after he said these words that taking Peter and John and James along, he went up the mountain to pray. And in praying, his face took on a different appearance, and his clothing turned lightning white. And look, two men were talking with him: it was Moses and Elijah, appearing in glory, who were telling about the expedition he was going to make to Jerusalem. Peter and those who were with him were dragging with sleep, but they stayed awake and saw his glory and the two men standing there with him. And it happened while the others were taking leave of him that Peter said to Jesus, "Chief, it's good for us to be here, and let's make three tabernacles, one for you and one for Moses and one for Elijah"—he didn't know what he was saying. As he said that, a cloud came down and overshadowed them. They got scared, going into the cloud. And a voice came out of the cloud, saying, "This is my son, my chosen son: listen to him!" And as the voice came, Jesus was found alone. But they kept silent and told no one at the time of any of the things they'd seen.

It happened on the next day, as they were going down the mountain, that he was met by a great crowd. And this man came out of the crowd shouting, "Teacher, I beg you to have a look at my son, who is my only child, because one minute the spirit takes him and all of a sudden it screams, and it convulses him, with foaming at the mouth, and keeps wearing him down, hardly ever receding from him. And I asked your students to throw it out and they couldn't."

And Jesus answered, "Oh perverse and faithless crew, how long will I be with you and put up with you? Bring your son up here." Even as he came forward the demon made him break into convulsions, but Jesus yelled at the unclean spirit and healed the boy and gave him back to his father. And everyone was thunderstruck by the greatness of God.

As everyone was marveling at all the things he'd done, he said to his students, "Store these words in your ears: the son of humanity is going to be betrayed into the hands of the world." But they didn't know what he was saying, it was hidden from them so they wouldn't perceive it, and they were afraid to ask him about what he'd said.

And a dispute arose in their ranks about who was greater than who. And Jesus, knowing the thoughts in their hearts, went over to a little child and stood the child near him and said to them, "Whoever accepts this child in my name, accepts me. And whoever accepts me accepts the one who sent me. The lowest person among you, that's someone great."

At that, John said, "Chief, we saw someone throwing out demons in your name and stopped him, because he isn't one of our followers."

Jesus said to him, "Don't stop him: whoever isn't against us is for us."

It happened as the days of his exaltation were coming closer that he set his sights on journeying to Jerusalem. And he sent messengers before his face, and going their way they went into the village of the Samaritans so as to prepare things for him; and they wouldn't receive him, because his sights were set on journeying to Jerusalem. When his students saw that, James and John said, "Lord, do you want us to tell the fire to come down from the sky and burn them to ashes?" But he turned to them and told them off. And they traveled on to another village.

And with them traveling on the road, someone said to him, "I will follow you anywhere you go."

Said Jesus, "Foxes have dens, and the birds of the sky have places to camp, but the son of humanity has nowhere to lay his head."

He said to another, "Follow me."

And he said, "Let me first go bury my father."

But he said to him, "Let the dead bury their own dead, but you go off and tell about the kingdom of God."

Another one said, "I'll follow you, Lord, but first let me say goodbye to the people at home."

Jesus said to him, "No one who looks behind him when he puts his hand on the plow is cut out for the kingdom of God."

10

AFTER THAT the Lord designated seventy-two others and sent them out by twos before his face to every town and place where he himself was going to come. And he said to them, "An ample harvest, and few workers! So ask the harvestmaster to send out workers to help with the harvesting. Go: I hereby send you out like lambs in the midst of wolves. Don't take a wallet or a knapsack or sandals, and don't pause to greet anyone along the way.

"Whatever house you go into, first say, 'Peace to this house.' And if a son of peace is there, your peace will alight on him; if not, it will turn round and come back to you. Stay in that place, eating and drinking with them, because the worker is worth his wages; don't move around from house to house. And whatever city you go into and they receive you, eat what's put before you, and cure the sick, and tell them, 'The kingdom of God is close upon you.' But whatever city you go into and they don't receive you, go out on the main streets and say, 'Even the dust of your town that clings to our feet we are wiping off in your face; but know this much, that the kingdom of God is approaching.' I'm telling you, Sodom will be better off than that city on that day.

"The worse for you, Chorazin! The worse for you, Bethesda! Because if the wonders had occurred in Tyre and Sidon that have occurred in you, *they* would long since have repented, sitting in sackcloth and ashes. But Tyre and Sidon will be better off on the judgment day than you. And you, Capharnaum, won't *you* be exalted to the skies? You'll sink into hell!

"Whoever listens to you, listens to me, and whoever rejects you, rejects me; but whoever rejects me, rejects the one who sent me."

The seventy-two came back saying joyfully, "Lord, even the demons are subject to us in your name."

And he said to them, "I saw Satan falling like lightning from the sky. Here, I have now given you authority to step on snakes and scorpions and all the power of the enemy, and none of it shall ever hurt you. But don't be glad that the spirits are subject to you, be glad that your names are inscribed in the skies."

In that hour he was delighted by the holy spirit and said, "I praise you, Father, lord of the sky and earth, that you hid these things from scholars and wits and opened them up to babies – yes, Father, because that's how your good pleasure could be manifested before you. Everything was given me by my Father, and no one knows who the son is but the Father, and no one knows who the Father is but the son and those to whom the son chooses to reveal Him."

And turning privately to his students, he said, "How lucky your eyes are to see what you see, because I'm telling you, many prophets and kings wanted to see what you see and never saw it, and wanted to hear what you hear and never heard it."

And this lawyer stood up to test him saying, "Teacher, what do I do to inherit everlasting life?"

He said to him, "What does it say in the law? What do you read there?"

He answered, "You are to love the Lord your God with all your heart and all your soul and all your strength and all your thoughts, and love your neighbor as yourself."

He said to him, "You answered right. Do that and you'll live."

He, trying to defend himself, said to Jesus, "But who *is* my neighbor?"

By way of answer Jesus said, "Once there was a fellow coming back from Jerusalem to Jericho, and he fell among thieves, who stripped him, gave him a beating, and went off leaving him half dead. Now by chance a priest was coming down the same road, and seeing him, he walked the other way. Likewise a Levite who happened on the spot saw him and walked the other way. But a certain Samaritan who was on the road came upon him and felt sorry for him, and went up and bandaged his wounds, poured oil and wine on them, and seating him on his own mount, brought him to the inn and looked after him. The next day he pulled out two drachmas and gave them to the innkeeper saying, 'Look after him, and whatever you lay out I will repay you on my way back.' Which of these three would you say turned out to be the neighbor of the one who fell among thieves?"

He said, "The one who had mercy on him."

Said Jesus, "Go and do likewise."

In the course of their traveling he went into a certain village, and a woman named Martha received him. And she had a sister called Mary, who sat at the Lord's feet and listened to his words. Martha, meanwhile, was busy with all the work. So she got up and said, "Lord, you don't care that my sister left me here to work alone? Tell her to share the work with me."

But the Lord answered, "Martha, Martha, you're worrying and making noise about many things, when only one thing is needed. Mary chose the better half, and it won't be taken away from her."

11

AND IT HAPPENED when he was in a certain place praying, that when he stopped, one of his students said to him, "Lord, teach us to pray, the same as John taught his students."

And he said to them, "When you pray, say:

Father,
Let Your name be sanctified,
May Your kingdom come.
Give us day by day the next day's bread,
And absolve us of our wrongs,
For we too absolve all those indebted to us.
And do not expose us to temptation."

And he said to them, "Which of you has a friend and if you went to him at midnight saying, 'Friend, lend me three loaves of bread, because a friend of mine just showed up from the road to see me and I have nothing to give him,' he would answer from within, 'Don't bother me! My door is locked already, my children are with me in bed, I can't get up and give you anything'? I'm telling you, if he doesn't get up and give it to you on account of your friendship, on account of your sheer effrontery he will get up and give you what you need. So I say to you, ask and you will be given to, look and you will find, knock and they will open for you. Because every asker receives, every seeker finds, and whoever knocks is always admitted. Which of you, if your son asked you for a fish, would give him a snake instead of a fish? Or if he asked for an egg, you'd give him a scorpion? Well then, if you, villains that you are, know enough to give good gifts to your children, how much more will your Father send the sacred breath down from the sky to all who ask Him."

And he was throwing out a demon of muteness. And as it happened, when the demon was out, the mute man started talking, and the crowds were amazed. But some of them said, "By the power of Beelzebub, the demon ruler, he throws out demons." Others, testing him, asked him for a sign from the sky.

But he, knowing their thoughts, said to them: "Any kingdom split against itself gets wiped out, with one house falling on another. And if Satan is divided against himself, how will his kingdom stand up? – since you say I'm throwing out demons by Beelzebub's power. But if I'm throwing out demons in Beelzebub's name, by whose power are *your* children throwing them out, and won't they have reason to condemn you on that account? But if I throw out demons by the finger of God, truly the kingdom of God has caught up with you.

"When the strong man stands guarding his front yard in full armor, his possessions are at peace; but if someone stronger than him comes and overpowers him, he takes the armor in which the other had trusted and divides up the loot. Whoever isn't with me is against me, and whoever doesn't come herding with me scatters the herd.

"When the unclean spirit goes out of a person, it wanders through arid regions looking for a rest and not finding it. Then it says, 'I'll go back home where I came from.' And arriving it finds everything swept and tidied up. Then it goes and brings in seven spirits worse than itself, and they all go in and settle down there, and the person ends up worse off than before."

It happened as he was saying these things that a woman raised her voice from the crowd and said to him, "How lucky the womb that carried you and the breasts that nursed you!"

But he said, "More to the point, how lucky those who hear the word of God and keep it!"

As the crowds were collecting, he started talking: "This generation is an evil generation. It looks for a sign, and won't be given any sign but the sign of Jonah, because just as Jonah became a sign to the Ninevites, so will the son of humanity be a sign to this generation. The Queen of the South will stand up on judgment day among the men of this generation and will condemn them, because *she* came from the ends of the earth to hear the wisdom of Solomon, and here's more than Solomon right here. The men of Nineveh will stand up on judgment day among this generation and condemn it, because *they* had a change of heart in the face of Jonah's message, and here's more than Jonah right here.

"No one lights a candle and hides it away or puts it under a big basket; no, they put it up on a tall candlestick, so the people coming in can see the light.

"The candle of the body is the eye. If your eye is in one piece, your whole body is also lighted. If your eye goes bad, your body is likewise in darkness. So make sure the light within you isn't dark. If your whole body is lighted, with no part dark, everything will be as shining as when the candle illumines you in a flash."

As he was talking, a Pharisee asked him to have lunch with him, and he went in and sat down. The Pharisee was surprised to see that he didn't wash up first before lunch. But the Lord said to him, "Now as for you Pharisees, you clean off the outside of your cup and your platter, but the insides of you are full of greed and dishonesty. Fools, didn't the same maker who made the outside make the inside too? Instead, show the tenderest concern for the vessel's contents, and watch how everything comes clean for you.

"But woe to you Pharisees for getting your ten percent of the mint, parsley, and mixed vegetables and ignoring justice and the love of God: *those* are the things you should have done, and then the others shouldn't be omitted.

"Woe to you Pharisees for being in love with your seats in front of the church and the way everyone says hello to you downtown.

"Woe to you for being like obscure graves that people walk on without even knowing it."

Replied one of the lawyers, "Teacher, when you say that you're insulting us too."

And he said, "And woe to you lawyers for burdening the people with unbearable taxes, while you let no taxes come within arm's length of *you*.

"Woe to you for building monuments to the prophets, when it was your forefathers that killed them. You bear witness and give your approval to the deeds of your fathers: they killed them, you build the monuments. That's why the wisdom of God also said, 'I will send them prophets and emissaries, whom they will kill and persecute, so that all the prophets' blood shed from the beginning of the world will be taken out on them, from the blood of Abel to the blood of Zachariah, who was killed halfway between the altar and his house. Yes, I tell you, that will all be taken out on this generation.

"Woe to you lawyers for holding the key to knowledge: you don't go in yourselves, and you stop the others from going in."

And by the time he left that place, the canon-lawyers and Pharisees had begun to be fiercely against him, and they started firing questions at him about various things, waiting in ambush for him to trap him with his own mouth.

12

MEANWHILE with a crowd in the tens of thousands gathered, so many they were trampling each other, he started telling his students, "First of all, keep away from the yeast – that is, the hypocrisy – of the Pharisees.

"There is nothing hidden that won't be discovered, and no secret that will never be known; which means that what you said in the darkness will be heard in the light, and what you whispered in someone's ear inside a vault will be proclaimed from the housetops.

"But I tell you, my friends, don't be afraid of those who kill the body but after that have nothing more they can do. I'll tell you who to be afraid of: be afraid of Him who after your death has power to throw you into Gehenna. Yes, I tell you, fear Him! Aren't five sparrows sold for fifty cents? And not one of them is overlooked by the sight of God. No, even the hairs on your head are all accounted for. Don't be afraid. You matter more than a heap of sparrows.

"Let me tell you, everyone who stands behind me in front of the world, the son of humanity will stand behind them in front of the messengers of God. But whoever ignores me in front of the world will also be ignored in front of the messengers of God.

"And everyone who says something against the son of humanity, that will be forgiven them, but whoever speaks blasphemies against the sacred breath won't be forgiven.

"When they haul you into the synagogues and before the powers and authorities, don't worry about what defense you'll make or what you'll say. The sacred breath will tell you at the proper time what you must say."

Said someone from the crowd, "Teacher, tell my brother to share his inheritance with me."

But he said to him, "Fellow, who made me judge or executor between you?" Then he said to them all, "Watch and guard against having to have it all, because though you may be in the midst of plenty, real life doesn't come from possessions."

He made a comparison for them, saying: "Once there was a rich fellow whose land yielded a bumper crop. And he thought to himself, 'What shall I do? I don't have anywhere to store my crops.' And he said, 'This is what I'll do: I'll tear down my old silos and build bigger ones and store all my grain and goods there, and then I will say to my soul, *Soul, you have enough goods stored up for many years: relax; eat, drink, be merry.*"'

"But God said to him, 'Fool, this very night you must give up your life. The things you got together, who are they for?' That's how it is with a person who stores up treasures for himself instead of being enriched in God."

And he said to his students, "That's why I tell you not to trouble your heart about what you'll eat or what you'll put on your back, because the breath of life is greater than food, and the body is greater than its clothing. Look at the crows: they don't sow, don't harvest, and don't have store-rooms or silos, and God still feeds them. And you matter so much more than birds. Which of you, by worrying about it, can add a foot to his height? Well then, if you can't do even the smallest things, why worry about the others? Look how the lilies grow: they don't toil and don't spin, but I'm telling you, not even Solomon in all his glory was ever dressed like one of them. And if that's how God clothes the wild grass in the field, there today and thrown into the furnace tomorrow, how much more will He clothe you, unbelievers. And don't wonder what you'll eat and what you'll drink, and avoid stargazing: all the nations of the world ask for these things, but your Father knows that you need these things. Just ask for his kingdom, and those other things will be put before you. Don't be afraid, little flock, because your Father saw fit to give you the kingdom.

"Sell your possessions and give to charity. Make yourselves wallets that don't wear through, an inexhaustible treasure in the skies, where no thief comes near and no moth eats away. After all, where your treasure is, that's where your heart will also be.

"Let your waist be belted and your lanterns lighted, and be like people waiting for their master when he breaks away from the wedding, so that when he comes and knocks they can open right up for him. Lucky for those slaves if the master comes and finds them awake. I tell you for sure, he will put on an apron and have them sit down and come serve them dinner. And if he comes in the second watch of the night, or the third, and finds them that way, lucky for them. You know this much: if the owner of the house knew what time the thief was coming, he would not let his house be tunneled into. And you be ready, because the son of humanity is coming at a time when you don't expect it."

Said Peter, "Are you making this comparison for our benefit or for everyone's?"

Said the Lord, "Who is the good and faithful steward whom the master appointed for his staff to give them their rations on schedule? Lucky for that slave if the master comes and finds him doing just that. I tell you truly, he will put him in charge of everything he owns. But if that slave says in his heart, 'My master is a long time coming' and starts beating up on the other serving-boys and -girls and eating and drinking and getting drunk, that slave's master will come on a day he isn't expecting and at a time he doesn't know, and will tear him apart and rank him among the infidels.

"That slave who knows the will of his master and doesn't get anything finished or do anything in line with his will, will receive many lashes, while the one who does something that deserves a beating without knowing it will receive few lashes: from the one to whom much was given, much will also be asked, and from the one to whom they entrusted much, they will ask even more.

"I came to set the earth on fire, and what do I wish? That it were already ablaze! I have a bath to be bathed, and how can I rest easy till that is carried out? Do you think I came to bring peace on earth? No, I tell you, I came to bring division: from now on there will be five in one house split three against two or two against three. Father will be turned against son and son against father, mother against daughter and daughter against mother, mother-in-law against daughter-in-law and daughter-in-law against mother-in-law."

Then he said to the crowds: "As soon as you see the clouds rising in the west, you say, 'It's going to be overcast'; and so it turns out. And when the south wind blows you say, 'It's going to be blazing hot,' and so it is. You fakes, you know how to read the face of the earth and sky, how come you don't know how to read the signs of these times?

"Why don't you discern, even by yourselves, what justice is? Because if you're going with your adversary before the governor, while you're on the road make an effort to settle with him, so he doesn't hale you before the judge, and the judge hands you over to the jailer, and the jailer throws you in jail. I'm telling you, you won't get out of there till you've paid off every last penny."

13

THERE WERE some people there at that time reporting to him about the Galileans whose blood Pilate had mixed with his sacrifices. And he answered them, "Do you think those Galileans were any greater criminals than all the other Galileans? I say no, but if you don't all have a change of heart you'll die the same way. Or how about those eighteen people on whom the tower fell at Siloam, killing them all: do you think they deserved to have that happen more than all the other people inhabiting Jerusalem? I say no, but if you don't all have a change of heart you'll die the same way."

Then he made this comparison: "Once there was someone who had a fig tree planted in his orchard and came looking for the fruit and found none. So he said to the gardener, 'This is three years now I've been coming to look for some fruit on this fig-tree and not finding any. Cut it down: why should it even take up space?'

"But he answered, 'Master, leave it alone this one year more, while I dig around the roots and give it manure, to see if it bears fruit in the future; if not, you can cut it down.'"

He was teaching in one of the synagogues on the Sabbath. And there was this woman who had had a spirit weakening her for eighteen years, and she was bent over and unable to lift her head all the way up. Jesus saw her and called to her, "Madam, you are delivered from your weakness," and he put his hands on her, and she suddenly straightened up and glorified God.

But the chief of the synagogue, outraged at Jesus for healing on the Sabbath, said to the crowd: "You have six days on which work is to be done, you can come on one of those days and heal, and not on the Sabbath-day."

But the Lord answered him, "You fakes, which of you, when it's the Sabbath, doesn't let his ox or his ass out of the stall and give it water? But this daughter of Abraham, whom Satan bound these eighteen years, wasn't supposed to be released from those chains because it was the Sabbath?" And when he said that all his opponents were put to shame, and all the crowd rejoiced at all the glorious things done by him.

So he said, "What is the kingdom of God like, and what shall I compare it to? It's like a seed of the mustard-plant which a person took and threw into their garden, and it grew and turned into a tree, and the birds of the sky settled among its branches."

And again he said, "What shall I compare the kingdom of God to? It's like yeast, which a woman took and mixed in with three sacks of flour till it all rose."

And he went on through towns and villages, teaching and making his way to Jerusalem.

Said someone to him once, "Lord, are only a few saved?"

And he said to them, "Struggle to get in through the narrow door, because many people, I'm telling you, try to get in and don't make it. And at the point when the master of the house gets up and bars the door, and you start standing outside and beating on the door, saying, 'Lord, let us in,' he will answer you, 'I don't know where you come from: away from me, all workers of iniquity!' That's where the wailing and gnashing of teeth will be, when you see Abraham, Isaac, Jacob, and all the prophets in the kingdom of God, and you thrown outside. And they will come in from east and west and from north and south and sit down to dinner in the kingdom of God. And watch how many of the last will be first and how many of the first will be last."

At that hour some Pharisees came up to him saying, "Go on your way and get out of here, because Herod's looking to kill you."

And he said to them, "Go tell the old fox, 'Look, I'm throwing out demons and completing cures today and tomorrow, and day after tomorrow I'll be done. But for today and tomorrow and the day after, I have to go free—because it's against the rules for a prophet to be killed anywhere outside Jerusalem.'

"Jerusalem, Jerusalem, killer of prophets, stoner of ambassadors to the city, how often I have wished to gather your children together the way a bird gathers her nestlings under her wing—and you didn't want to! And now look, your house is taken away from you. But I tell you, you will see me no more until you say, 'Bless him who comes in the name of the Lord.'"

14

AND IT HAPPENED once when he came to the home of one of the leaders of the Pharisees to take bread on the Sabbath, that the others were also watching him.

And there was this fellow with dropsy there in front of him. And Jesus reacted by saying to the lawyers and Pharisees, "Is it all right to heal on the Sabbath or not?" They were silent. And taking hold of the man he cured him and sent him off. Then he said to them: "Which of you would let your son—or your cow—fall into a ditch and not immediately reach out your hand, because it was the Sabbath-day?" And they had no answer for that.

And he made this comparison for the guests, noticing how they picked out the choicest seats for themselves: "When you sit down to the banquet at someone's wedding, don't sit at the head table, in case some more honored guest than you has been invited, and the one who invited both him and you comes and says, 'Give this person your seat,' and then you have to get up red-faced and go to the very back. But when you're invited some-place, go sit down in the back, so that when your host comes he'll say to you, 'Dear friend! Please come up front!' That way it will be an honor for you in front of all your fellow-guests, because the one who exalts himself will be humbled and the one who humbles himself will be exalted."

Then he said to his host, "When you give a luncheon or dinner, don't invite your brothers and sisters or your relatives, or your rich neighbors, because then they'll return the invitation and you'll be paid back. But when you give a party, invite the poor, the sick, the crippled, the blind; and you'll be in luck, because they have nothing to pay you back with: you'll be paid back in the resurrection of the just."

One of the guests, on hearing that, said to him, "How lucky the person who eats bread in the kingdom of God!"

And he said to him, "Once there was a fellow who gave a big dinner party and invited a lot of people and sent his slave at dinner time to tell the guests, 'Come on, everything's all ready.'

"And they started begging off one after the other. The first one said, 'I just bought a field, and it's vital that I go out and see it.' And another said, 'I just bought five yokes of oxen and I'm going just now to look them over; please consider me excused.' And another said, 'I just got married, that's why I can't come.' And when the slave got back he told all that to his master.

Then the master of the house said to his slave in a fury, 'Go through the main streets and side-alleys of the city and bring the poor here and the maimed and the blind and the lame.'

"And the slave said, 'Lord, what you ordered is done, and there's still room.'

"And the master said to the slave, 'Go out into the streets and yards and make them come, till my house is full, because I'm telling you, none of those men who were invited will ever taste my dinner.'"

Now giant crowds were gathering around him, and he turned and said to them, "If anyone comes to me and cares about his father or his mother or his wife or his children or his brother or his sisters or even his own life, he can't be my student. Whoever doesn't pick up the cross and walk behind me, can't be my student.

"After all, which of you planning to build a tower would not first sit down and weigh the expenses to see if there would be enough to finish it? – so you don't end up laying the foundation and then being unable to finish it off and everyone who sees it starts making fun of you and saying, 'Look at this fellow who started building and couldn't finish!' And what king marching forth against another king to engage him in war does not first sit down and take stock as to whether with his ten thousand he can take on the one coming against him with twenty thousand? Because if not, before the other even gets close he will send his emissaries to ask terms of peace. Well, in the same way, anyone of you who doesn't say goodbye to all your possessions can't be my student.

"Salt is certainly a good thing, but if it goes tasteless, what will you spice it with? It's no good for the soil, nor even for the dungheap, you just throw it out. Whoever has ears to hear, hear!"

15

NOW all the tax-collectors and crooks were coming close to hear him. And the Pharisees and canon-lawyers were grumbling, "This guy gives godless people a warm welcome and eats with them."

But he made this comparison for them, saying, "What person among you who had a hundred sheep and lost one of them would not leave the ninety-nine there in the wilds and go look for the lost one till he finds it? And when he finds it won't he happily put it on his shoulders and go home and call his friends and neighbors in, saying, 'Be happy with me: I found my sheep that was lost'? Likewise, I tell you, there will be joy in the sky over one evildoer's change of heart more so than over ninety-nine of the just who have no need of a change of heart.

"Or what woman who has ten drachmas and loses one wouldn't light a lantern and sweep the house and carefully look till she finds it, and on finding it wouldn't call her friends and neighbors in, saying, 'Be happy with me, because I found the drachma I had lost'? Likewise, I tell you, there is joy among the messengers of God over one evildoer's change of heart."

And he said, "Once there was a fellow who had two sons. And the younger of them said to the father, 'Father, give me the part of your property coming to me.' So he divided his property between them. And not many days later, the younger son collected all his things and took off for a faraway country where he squandered his fortune with dissolute living. After he'd spent it all, an intense famine came over that country, and he started to run short. So he went and attached himself to one of the citizens of that country, who sent him into his fields to keep the pigs. And he was dying to eat some of the carob pods that the pigs were eating, but no one gave him any. And coming to himself he said, 'Think of all the hired hands in my father's house who have plenty of bread, and here I am dying of hunger. I'll get up and go to my father and say to him, *Father, I did wrong against heaven and in your eyes. I don't deserve to be called your son any more, treat me like one of your hired hands.*' And he got up and went to his father. While he was still at a distance, his father saw him and was moved, and ran and threw his arms around him and kissed him. The son said to him, 'Father, I did wrong against heaven and in your eyes. I don't deserve to be called your son any more.'

"But the father said to his slaves, 'Quick, bring the finest robe and put it on him, and put a ring on his finger and shoes on his feet. And bring the fattened steer and slaughter it, and let's eat and be happy, because this son of mine was dead and came to life again, he was lost and was found again.' And they started making merry.

"Now his older son was in the fields, and as he came near the house, he heard the music-making and singing, and he called one of the boys over and inquired what that was all about. He said to him, 'Your brother came back, and your father slaughtered the fattened steer, because he got him back safe and sound.' But he got mad and wouldn't go inside.

"So his father came out and pleaded with him, but he answered his father: 'How many years is this that I have slaved away for you and never sidestepped any command of yours? And you never let *me* have a goat so I could have a good time with my friends. But when this son of yours who frittered away your fortune on whores came back, for him you slaughtered the fattened steer!'

"But he said to him, 'Child, you're always with me, and everything that's mine is yours. But we had to make merry and rejoice, because this brother of yours was dead and came alive again, and was lost and was found again.'"

16

AND HE SAID to his students further: "Once there was a rich fellow who had an estate manager who was reported to him as squandering his goods. And calling him in he said to him, 'What's this I hear about you? Hand in the manager's books, you can't be my manager any more.'

"The manager said to himself, 'What will I do now that my master is taking my manager's job away from me? I'm not strong enough to dig and I'm ashamed to beg. I know what I'll do, so that when I move out of my manager's position I'll be welcome in their houses.'

"And calling each one of his master's creditors in he said to the first, 'How much do you owe my master?'

"And he said, 'A hundred tubs of olive oil.'

"He said to him, 'Here's your certificate, sit right down and make it fifty.'

"Then he said to another, 'And how much do you owe?'

"He said, 'Four hundred bushels of wheat.'

"He says to him, 'Here's your certificate, make it three hundred.'

"And the master commended the manager for the felony insofar as he had acted prudently: 'The children of the here and now are so much more prudent in dealing with their own kind than the children of the light!' And I say to you, use your ill-gotten wealth to make friends for yourselves, so that when it runs out you will always be welcome in their eternal lodgings.*

"Whoever is trustworthy in the smallest matter is also trustworthy in something larger, and whoever is dishonest in the smallest matter is also dishonest in something larger. So if you couldn't be trusted with ill-gotten gains, who will credit you with your legitimate earnings? And if you couldn't be trusted with other people's things, who will give you what is yours?

"No servant can serve two masters. Either he'll hate the one and love the other, or he'll put up with one and despise the other. You can't serve God *and* the Almighty Dollar."**

Some of the Pharisees who were moneygrubbers heard all that and started sneering at him. And he said to them, "You're the kind who justify yourselves in the eyes of the world. But God knows your hearts: what is sublime to the world is a horror in the eyes of God.

"The Law and the Prophets go up to John; from that point on the good word of the kingdom of God has been spread, while everyone does violence against it. But it is easier for the sky and the earth to go away than for a single comma to fall out of the law.

"Anyone who puts away his wife and marries another is living in adultery, and anyone who marries a divorced woman is living in adultery.

---

*On the whole this parable is understandable as an example of "being forgiven our debts as we forgave our debtors," but why will the debtors who were let off easy welcome the dishonest manager into their "eternal" lodgings? Perhaps because they will be his defenders on Judgment Day? Or is the word an exaggeration: "they will welcome you into their lodgings forever"?

**See the note on page 13.

"Once there was a rich fellow, and he was dressed in royal purple and fine linen and spent every day feasting in splendor. And there was a beggar named Lazarus lying outside his gates, full of ulcers and dying to satisfy his hunger with the crumbs dropping from the rich man's table. But the dogs even came and licked his wounds. Finally the beggar died and was carried by God's messengers to the bosom of Abraham. The rich man died too and was buried.

"And lifting up his eyes in hell, where he was in torment, he sees Abraham from afar and Lazarus in his lap. And he called out, 'Father Abraham, have pity on me and send Lazarus to dip the tip of his finger in water and cool off my tongue, because I'm tormented by these flames.'

"Said Abraham, 'Child, remember that during your life you had all the good things, and Lazarus likewise all the bad. But now here he is consoled, while you are tormented. And all through here there is fixed a great gulf, so that those who want to cross from here to you can't do so, nor can they cross from there toward us.'

"So he said, 'Then father, I beg you, send him to my father's house – you see, I have five brothers – so he can bear witness to them, so that they don't end up in this place of torment too.'

"Says Abraham, 'They have Moses and the prophets, let them listen to them.'

"But he said, 'No, father Abraham, but if one of the dead goes to them they will change their minds.'

"He said to him, 'If they won't listen to Moses and the prophets, even if someone arises from the dead they won't be persuaded.'"

17

HE SAID to his students, "It's unavoidable that scandals should come along, but woe to him through whom they come. It would be a good thing for him to have a millstone tied around his neck and be thrown into the sea, rather than mislead one of these little ones: watch yourselves!

"If your brother does you wrong, have it out with him, and if he changes his mind, forgive him. And if seven times a day he does you wrong and seven times comes back and says, I'm sorry, you shall forgive him."

And the apostles said to the lord, "Give us more faith!"

Said the Lord, "If you have a mustard-seed's worth of faith, if you said to this mulberry tree, 'Pull up your roots and plant yourself in the sea,' it would obey you. Which of you who has a slave plowing or herding would say to him as he comes in from the fields, 'Go right on in and have dinner' instead of saying to him, 'Make dinner for me and serve me with your apron on till I've finished eating and drinking, and then you can eat and drink'? And do you feel obliged to the slave because he carried out your orders? No. The same goes for you, then: when you've carried out all the commandments, say, 'We're just good-for-nothing slaves who've done our job.'"

And it happened as he was journeying to Jerusalem that he passed through the middle of Samaria and Galilee.

And as he was entering a certain village he was met by ten men with leprosy, who stood at a distance and raised their voices, saying, "Master Jesus, have pity on us."

And seeing them he said, "Go show yourselves to the priests." And what happened was that as they went their way, they were cleansed. One of them, though, seeing he had been healed, came back glorifying God with a loud voice and fell on his face at his feet thanking him – he was a Samaritan. Jesus responded, "Weren't all ten cleansed? Where are the other nine? Was nobody seen returning to give glory to God but this one foreigner?" And he said to him, "Get up and go your way, your trust has saved you."

Asked by the Pharisees when the kingdom of God was coming he answered: "The kingdom of God doesn't come with watching like a hawk, and they won't say, Here it is, or There it is, because, you know what? the kingdom of God is inside you."

Then he said to his students, "There will come days when you will be dying to see one of the days of the son of humanity, but you won't see it. And they will say to you, Look there, or Look here, but don't go there and don't go hunting. Because as the lightning flashes from underside to underside of the sky, that's what the son of humanity will be like when his day comes. First, though, he must undergo many things and be rejected by this generation. And just as it happened in Noah's day, so will it be in the son of humanity's day: they were eating, drinking, and taking wives and husbands up to the day when Noah went into the ark and the cataclysm came and destroyed them all. Likewise, just as it happened in the days of Lot, they were eating, drinking, buying, selling, planting, building; then on the day Lot went out of Sodom, it rained fire and sulfur from the skies and destroyed them all. It will be along the same lines on the day the son of humanity is revealed. On that day whoever is up on the roof with their things down in the house, don't go down to get them, and whoever is in the fields, likewise, don't turn back: remember Lot's wife. Whoever tries to keep their life safe will lose it, whereas whoever loses their life will engender it. I'm telling you, that night there will be two in one bed: one will be taken along and the other left behind. Two women will be grinding corn together: one will be taken along and the other left behind."

And they said, "Where will that be, Lord?"

He said to them, "Where the body is, the vultures also gather."

18

HE SPOKE to them making a comparison about how necessary it is always to pray and never to lose heart, saying, "There was a certain judge in a certain city who neither feared God nor respected humanity. Now there was a widow in that city, and she came to him saying, 'Take on my case against my adversary,' and for a long time he wouldn't.

"But finally he said to himself, 'Even if I don't fear God nor respect humanity, because of the grief this widow is giving me I'll take on her case, so that she doesn't end up giving me a black eye.'"

Said the Lord, "Hear what that dishonest judge says? Now won't God take the side of His chosen ones crying to Him night and day, and have patience with them? I tell you He will take their side at once. The real question is, will the son of humanity when he comes find any faith upon the earth?"

He spoke further to some people who were convinced of their own innocence and inclined to regard the others as nothing, making this comparison: "Once there were two fellows who went up to the temple to pray, one a Pharisee and the other a tax-collector. The Pharisee stood and prayed to himself as follows: 'God, I thank you that I'm not like the rest of the world – greedy, unjust, unchaste – nor indeed like this tax-collector here. I fast twice a week, I give ten percent of everything I own.'

"Whereas the tax collector stood way in the back, wouldn't even raise his eyes skyward, just beat his breast and said, 'God, be kind to a loser like me.' I'm telling you, he went home cleared of his guilt – more so than the other one, because all who exalt themselves will be humbled, and all who humble themselves will be exalted."

Now they were even bringing the little kids to him so he could put his hands on them; when they saw that, his students yelled at them. But Jesus called them to him, saying, "Let the kids come to me and don't hold them back: the kingdom of God belongs to such as these. I tell you for sure, anyone who does not accept the kingdom of God like a little child will never get into it."

And a certain prince asked him, "Good teacher, what shall I do to inherit everlasting life?"

Said Jesus, "Why do you call me good? No one is good but God alone. You know the commandments: 'You are not to commit adultery, you are not to murder, you are not to steal, you are not to perjure yourself, do right by your father and your mother.'"

He said, "I have kept all those since childhood."

Hearing that, Jesus said to him, "One thing is still missing in you: sell everything you have and give it out to the poor, and you will have a treasure in the skies, and come here and follow me." Hearing that, he was most unhappy, because he was very rich indeed.

Seeing how unhappy he had become, Jesus said, "How difficult it is for those with money to enter the kingdom of God. Indeed, it's easier for a camel to squeeze through the eye of a needle than for a rich man to get into the kingdom of God."

Those who heard him said, "Then who *can* be saved?"

He said, "What's impossible for human beings is possible for God."

Said Peter, "Look at us: we have left behind what was ours and followed you."

He said to them, "I assure you, no one who has left house or wife or brothers or parents or children for the kingdom of God will fail to get it back many times over in this life, along with everlasting life in the time to come."

Taking the twelve along he said to them: "Here we go up to Jerusalem, and all the writings of the prophets will be fulfilled for the son of humanity: he will be handed over to the people and made fun of and mistreated and spat upon, and after whipping him they will kill him, and on the third day he will rise again." And they didn't understand any of that; his words were hidden from them and they didn't know what he was saying.

It happened as he was nearing Jericho that a certain blind man was sitting by the road begging. Hearing the crowd passing through he inquired what was going on. They told him Jesus of Nazareth was passing by. And he cried out, "Jesus, son of David, have mercy on me." And the people in the front of the crowd yelled at him to be quiet, but he shouted all the more, "Son of David, have mercy on me."

Stopping in his tracks, Jesus ordered him to be brought to him. When he got closer, he asked him, "What do you want me to do for you?"

He said, "Lord, let me see again."

And Jesus said, "See again! Your trust has saved you." And suddenly he could see again and followed him, praising God. And all the people, seeing that, gave praise to God.

19

AND AFTER entering Jericho he passed on through. And there was this man, Zacchaeus by name, and he was the chief tax-collector and a very rich man. And he wanted to see who this Jesus was and couldn't because of the crowd, since he was too short. And running up front he climbed up a mulberry tree to see him, because he was about to pass by it.

And as he reached the spot, Jesus looked up and said to him, "Zacchaeus, come down as fast as you can, I'm going to stay at your house today." And he came down as fast as he could and joyfully received him.

And seeing that, everyone started grumbling, "He went to stay with that evil man."

But Zacchaeus, stopping in place, said to the Lord, "I hereby give half my possessions to the poor, and if I have strongarmed anybody out of anything, I'll give it back quadruple."

Jesus said to him, "Today salvation came to this house, which is indeed descended from Abraham; after all, the son of humanity came to look for and recover what was lost."

While they were listening to these things he made a further comparison having to do with his being near to Jerusalem and their belief that the kingdom of God would appear any second. He said, then: "Once there was a nobleman who went to a far-away land to take possession of a kingdom and return. Calling ten of his underlings he gave them a thousand drachmas and said to them, 'Do business while I'm gone.'

"But his subjects hated him and sent messengers after him, saying, 'We don't want this person ruling us.' And as it happened, upon his return after taking possession of the kingdom he also had these underlings called in to whom he had given the money, to find out how they'd handled it.

"The first came along saying, 'Master, your hundred drachmas brought in a thousand.'

"And he said to him, 'Well done, good servant! Since you proved trustworthy in the smallest matter, receive authority over ten cities.'

"And the second came and said, 'Your hundred drachmas, master, made five hundred.'

"And he said to him, 'So take over five cities.'

"And another came and said, 'Master, here's your hundred drachmas back which I kept hidden in a handkerchief. Thing is, I was afraid of you, you being the hard fellow that you are, who picks up what he didn't drop and reaps what he didn't sow.'

"He says to him, 'Your own mouth convicts you, you terrible servant! You knew I was a hard fellow, did you, picking up what I didn't drop and reaping what I didn't sow? Then how come you didn't put my money in the bank, where I could have gone and gotten it back with interest?' And he said to those assembled, 'Take the hundred drachmas from him and give it to the one with a thousand.'

"And they said, "But master, he already *has* a thousand!'

"'I'm telling you,' he said, 'he who has will be given more, from him who has nothing even what he has will be taken away. But as for those enemies of mine that didn't want me ruling over them, bring them here and slaughter them in front of me.'"

And after saying all that he journeyed onward, going up to Jerusalem.

And it happened as he got near to Bethphage and Bethany, by the mountain called Mount Olive, that he sent off two of his students saying, "Go into that village over there, where upon entering you'll find a young donkey tied up which no person has ever sat upon: untie it and bring it here. And if anyone asks you, 'What are you untying it for?' just say, 'Its master needs it.'

The ones dispatched went off and found it as he had told them. As they were untying the donkey its keepers said to them, "What are you doing untying that donkey?"

So they said, "Its master needs it."

And they brought it to Jesus, and after throwing their cloaks over it they seated Jesus upon it. And as he rode on, they were throwing their cloaks along the road. By the time he was close to coming down Mount Olive the whole mass of his students had already started the jubilee, loudly praising God for all the wonders they had seen and saying, "Bless him who comes there, the king in the name of the Lord! Peace in the sky! Glory to the highest heavens!"

And some of the Pharisees came out of the crowd and said to him, "Teacher, restrain these students of yours."

And he answered, "I tell you, if they fell silent, the rocks would scream out."

And as they neared the city he saw it and wept for it saying, "If you only knew on this day which way leads to peace – but now it is hidden from your eyes; because there will come upon you days when your enemies corner you in a hollow and surround you and press in on you from every side, and hurl you and your children to the ground, and leave no stone upon another amongst you all, because you didn't know when the time of your inspection was."

And going into the temple he started throwing out the dealers, saying to them, "It says,

My house shall be a house of prayer,

but you've made it a den of thieves."

And he was teaching in the temple daily, and the high priests and canon-lawyers wanted to get rid of him and so did the leaders among the people, but they couldn't figure out what to do, because the people were all listening to him, hanging on his every word.

20

AND IT HAPPENED on one of the days when he was teaching the people in the temple and spreading the good word that the high priests and canon-lawyers, along with the elders, finally said to him, "Tell us what authority you have to do this. Who gave you any such authority?"

He answered them, "I also want to ask you a question: Tell me, did the washing of John come from heaven or from the world?"

They discussed that among themselves, saying, "If we say from heaven, he'll say, 'Then why didn't you believe him?' But if we say from the world, the entire mob will pelt us with rocks, they're so convinced that John was a prophet." So they answered, "We don't know where it came from."

And Jesus said to them, "I won't tell you what authority I have to do this either."

He began to make this comparison for the people: "Once there was a fellow who planted a vineyard and leased it to some tenant-farmers and left the country for quite a while. In time he sent his slave to the farmers to get the produce of the vineyard from them, but the farmers whipped him soundly and sent him off emptyhanded. He sent an additional slave, whom they also flayed and brutalized and sent off emptyhanded. And he went on sending a third, whom they wounded and threw out. Said the owner of the vineyard, 'What shall I do? I will send my beloved son: maybe they will respect *him*.'

"But when they saw him, the farmers said to each other, 'Look, it's the heir! Let's kill him, and the inheritance is ours.' And they dragged him outside the vineyard and killed him. So what will the owner of the vineyard do? He'll come and wipe those farmers out and give the vineyard to others."

When they heard that they said, "Let's hope it never happens."

Looking straight at them he said, "What does it say there:

A stone that the builders rejected,
That one ended up the cornerstone?

Anyone who falls on that stone will be smashed to bits. And anyone it falls upon will be crushed."

And the canon-lawyers and high priests wanted to put their hands on him at that point, except that they were afraid of the people; they knew he was making that comparison about _them_.

And as they looked on, their henchmen were sent forth, acting innocent, to get some word out of him such that they could hand him over to the government and the authority of the governor. And they asked him, "Teacher, we know you talk and teach straightforwardly and are no respecter of persons, but rather teach God's way based on truth: Is it all right to pay taxes to Caesar or not?"

Sensing their plot he said, "Show me a denarius. Whose picture and inscription does it have on it?"

They said, "Caesar's."

So he said to them, "Well, then, give Caesar's things to Caesar and God's things to God." And they weren't able to catch him in his words in front of the people and were dumbfounded at his answer.

Some Sadducees came forward, the ones who said there was no resurrection, and asked him this question: "Teacher, Moses prescribed for us that 'If someone's brother dies who had a wife, but was childless, let the brother take his wife and raise up offspring for his brother.' So: once there were seven brothers, and the first took a wife and died childless. And the second took her, and the third, and in this manner finally all seven died without leaving children; last of all the wife died. So, in the resurrection, whose wife will that woman be? After all, all seven had her for a wife."

And Jesus said to them, "The sons and daughters of the here and now take wives and husbands, but those who have proven worthy to receive that other Life and be resurrected from the dead take no wives and no husbands, because they can't die any more: they're equal to the angels and are sons and daughters of God, being sons and daughters of the resurrection. That the dead rise again was mentioned even by Moses before the burning bush, when he talks about 'the Lord, God of Abraham and the God of Isaac and the God of Jacob.' There is no God of the dead, only of the living: to him, everyone is alive."

Some of the canon-lawyers answered, "Teacher, you spoke well." After that they didn't dare ask him any more questions.

Then he said to them, "How can they say the Anointed is David's son? Why, David himself says in the book of Psalms,

A Lord said to my Lord,
Sit on my right
Till I've finished making your enemies
Into a footstool for your feet.

David, then, called him 'Lord,' so how can he be his son?"

Then with all the people listening he said to his students, "Watch out for clerics who want to walk around in fine robes and who like everybody saying hello to them downtown and their seats in the front of churches and at the head tables of banquets, who wolf down the houses of widows and make a show of praying at great length. They will receive an extra condemnation."

21

THEN HE LOOKED round and saw the rich people throwing their contributions into the collection-box, and he saw a poor widow throwing in a couple of dimes. And he said, "I'm telling you the truth, that poor widow put in more than all the others. Because all the others put in what they had left over as their contributions while she in her extremity put in all she had to live on."

And as some were talking about the temple, what fine masonry and what fine artworks it was decorated with, he said, "As for what you see here, there will come days when not a stone of it will rest upon another without being toppled."

And they asked him, "Teacher, when will that be, and what will be the sign that it's going to happen?"

He said, "Watch out, don't be fooled, because many will come along in my name saying, Here I am, and The time has come. Don't follow after them. And when you hear of wars and revolutions, don't go into shock. Those things have to happen first, but that's not quite the end."

Then he said to them, "Nation will rise against nation, country against country. There will be giant earthquakes, famines and plagues in places, terrors and mighty signs from the sky.

"But before all that they will lay their hands upon you and persecute you, handing you over to synagogues and jails; you'll be haled before kings and governors because of my name. It will happen to you as a testimony. So put in your hearts that you're not going to worry about speaking in your defense: I will give you a mouth and wisdom such as all your adversaries together cannot withstand or gainsay. You will also be betrayed by parents, sisters, brothers, relatives, and friends; they will kill some of you, and you will be despised by everyone because of my name. And not a hair of your head will be lost; your perseverance will gain you your souls.

"When you see Jerusalem surrounded by armies, then you know its destruction is approaching. Then those in Judea, flee into the mountains, and those in the central region, get out, and those in the other countries, don't come in; because those will be days of settling scores, of fulfilling all the scriptures. Woe to those with a child in their belly or nursing in those days! There will be great need upon the earth and anger toward this people, and they will fall by the tooth of the sword and be enslaved to all the nations, and Jerusalem will be stamped on by pagans, till the pagans' time is up.

"And there will be signs in the sun and moon and stars, and on earth an anxious mass of people in confusion over the roar of the sea and the tides, with people dying of fear and apprehension about what's coming over the world. Yes, the powers of heaven will be shaken. And then they will see the son of humanity coming on a cloud with power and great glory. When these things start to happen, look up and raise your heads, because your redemption is approaching."

And he made a comparison for them: "You see the fig tree – indeed, all the trees? When they're already bearing fruit, you can tell from looking at them that the harvest time is already close. In the same way, when you see these things happening, you know the kingdom of God is close. I assure you that this generation will not pass away till it all happens. The sky and the earth will pass away, but these words of mine will never pass away.

"Watch yourselves now; don't let your hearts get sluggish with debauchery and drinking and the worries of life, and then all of a sudden that day comes upon you, because it will spring like a trap on all those who inhabit the face of all the earth.

"So stay awake, begging at all times that you will be able to escape from all these things that are going to happen and stand before the son of humanity."

He was teaching in the temple by day and going out by night and camping on the mountain called Mount Olive. And all the people were getting up early to go hear him in the temple.

22

THE FEAST of the unleavened bread was getting close, the one called Passover. And the high priests and canon-lawyers were searching for the way to get rid of him, except that they were afraid of the people.

Then Satan entered Judas, known as Judas Iscariot, who was numbered among the twelve, and he went off and talked with the priests and generals about the way for him to hand him over to them. And they were delighted and promised to give him money. And he gave them his word and started looking for the right time to hand him over to them without a crowd around.

So came the day of the unleavened bread, when it was time to sacrifice for Passover. And he sent off Peter and John saying "Go get the seder ready for us to eat."

They said to him, "Where do you want us to get it ready?"

He said to them, "Just as you're getting into town you'll be met by a fellow carrying a water jug. Follow him into the house he enters and say to the owner of the house, 'Our teacher says, *Where are the quarters where I can eat the seder with my students?*' And he'll show you a big furnished room on the second floor. That's where you'll get it ready." They went and found things as he had told them and got the seder ready.

And when the time came, he sat down, and the apostles with him. And he said to them: "I wanted with all my heart to eat the seder with you before my suffering begins, because I'm telling you, I'll never eat it again until it is fulfilled in the kingdom of God." And being handed a cup he gave thanks and said, "Take this and share it among you, because I'm telling you, I'll never drink again of the produce of the vineyard till the kingdom of God comes." And taking bread he gave thanks and broke it and gave it to them saying, "This is my body given for you: do this in my memory." And he did the same with the cup after dinner, saying, "This cup is the new contract, sealed in my blood poured out for you.

"But what's this? The hand of my betrayer is with me on the table! Yes, the son of humanity is going to meet his destiny, but woe to that person by whom he is betrayed." And they started arguing with each other about which of them it could possibly be who was going to do such a thing.

And finally rivalry broke out among them about who was greater than who. And he said to them, "The kings of nations lord it over them and those who throw their weight around are called patriots. But you're different: whoever is greatest among you, act like the youngest person there; whoever is the leader, act like the servant. After all, who is higher up: the guest or the servant? The guest, right? But here I am in your midst like a servant.

"You are the ones who have stayed with me through all my trials, and I am putting a kingdom in your hands as my Father put it in mine, that you may eat and drink at my table in my kingdom and sit upon your thrones judging the twelve tribes of Israel.

"Simon, Simon, look there! Satan asked for you to be given up, for him to winnow his wheat with. But I pleaded for you that your faith might not give out. And you will return the favor someday by shoring up your brothers."

And he said to him, "Lord, with you at my side I'm ready to go to jail or even to my death."

He said, "I'm telling you, Peter, the cock won't crow tomorrow morning before you have said three times that you don't know me."

And he said to them: "When I sent you off with no wallet or knapsack or shoes, you didn't run short of anything, did you?"

They said, "No, nothing."

He said to them: "But now, whoever has a wallet, take it along, and your knapsack likewise; and whoever doesn't have a sword, you'd better sell your cloak and buy one, because I'm telling you that the scriptures will be fulfilled through me, the part about 'And he was numbered among the outlaws' – in fact, its words about me are coming to fulfillment."

And they said, "Lord, we have two swords here."

And he said, "That's enough."

And going outside he walked as usual up Mount Olive, with his students also following him. Reaching the spot, he said to them, "Pray not to be put to the test." And he excused himself, going about a stone's throw away from them, and went down on his knees and prayed: "Father, if you can, take this cup away from me, but let your will be done, not mine." A messenger appeared to him from the sky to give him strength. And sinking into agony he prayed even harder, and his sweat came like drops of blood raining down on the ground. And when he stood up from praying and came back to his students he found them sleeping off their pain and said to them, "Why are you sleeping? Get up and pray that you may not be put to the test."

Even as he spoke, there was the crowd, and the one of the twelve called Judas was leading them, and he came close to Jesus to kiss him. And Jesus said to him, "Judas, are you going to betray the son of humanity with a kiss?"

Those around him, seeing what was coming, said "Master, shall we strike them with the sword?" And one of them struck the high priest's slave and took his right ear off.

But Jesus answered, "Let's stop short of that," and picked up the ear and restored it.

Said Jesus to the high priests and generals of the temple and elders who had come out after him, "As if to catch a robber you came out with swords and clubs? When I was there in the temple with you in broad daylight you didn't put your hands on me, but this is your hour and your authority is the authority of darkness."

Seizing him they led him away and brought him to the high priest's house.

Now Peter was following him from a distance. They'd made a fire in the middle of the courtyard and were sitting around it, and Peter sat down in their midst. One of the serving-girls, when she saw him sitting there by firelight, stared at him and said, "This guy was with him too."

But he denied it saying, "I don't know him, lady."

And after a while someone else saw him and said, "You're one of them too."

But Peter said, "No, man, I'm not."

And after the space of about an hour someone else said emphatically, "Of course this guy was with him too: after all, he *is* a Galilean."

But Peter said, "Fellow, I don't know what you're talking about." And suddenly, before he even finished speaking, a rooster crowed, and the Lord turned round and looked at Peter, and Peter was reminded of the words in which the Lord said to him:

"Before the cock crows tomorrow morning you'll say three times that you don't know me." And going outside he cried stinging tears.

And the men holding him had some fun with him, beating him black and blue, blindfolding him and saying, "Prophesy for us –who just hit you?" And they made all sorts of blasphemous remarks about him.

And when day came, the elders of the people, the high priests, and the canon-lawyers met and haled him before their bench, saying, "Are you the Anointed? Tell us."

And he said to them, "If I tell you, you won't believe me. And if I ask you a question, you won't answer. From now on the son of humanity will be seated at the right hand of God's power."

And they all said, "So you're the Son of God!"

And he said to them, "You said it yourselves, that's what I am."

So they said, "What do we need witnesses for any more? We heard it from his own mouth."

23

AND STANDING up en masse they led him off to Pilate.

They started accusing him, saying, "We caught this guy undermining our society and keeping people from paying taxes to Caesar and saying he had been anointed the king."

So Pilate asked him, "Are you the king of the Jews?"

He answered, "That's what *you* say."

Pilate said to the high priests and the crowds, "I don't see any charge against this person."

But they were carrying on and saying, "He's inciting the populace, teaching all through Judea, starting with Galilee and ending here."

When he heard that, Pilate asked if the fellow was a Galilean. And confirming that he was under Herod's jurisdiction, he sent him to Herod, who happened to be in Jerusalem at the time.

Herod was simply delighted to see Jesus. For quite a while now he'd wanted to see him because he'd heard so much about him and he was hoping to see some miracle performed. So he asked him questions at great length, but he didn't answer at all, while the high priests and canon-lawyers were standing there stridently denouncing him. After Herod and his armies had once again treated him with contempt and made a joke of him, he put a shining white robe* on him and sent him back to Pilate. From that day on Herod and Pilate became friends with each other; they had been at odds with each other before.

Then Pilate, calling together the high priests and rulers and the people, said to them: "You brought me this person on the grounds that he was undermining society, and you see how I examined him in front of you and found no charge against the fellow of the kind you accused him of.

"Nor could Herod. That's why he sent him back to us: he just hasn't done anything worthy of death. So we'll whip him to teach him a lesson and let him go."

But they shouted in chorus, "Keep him and release Barabbas" – who had been thrown in jail on account of some uprising in the city and charged with murder. Again Pilate called to them, trying to let Jesus go. But they were shouting out, "Crucify, crucify him!"

A third time he said to them, "But what did he do wrong? I couldn't find any capital charge against him. So I'll whip him soundly and let him go." But they persisted, loudly demanding that he be crucified, and their voices grew more and more insistent.

Finally Pilate decided to let their request be granted. He released the man thrown into jail for rioting and murder whom they had asked for and handed Jesus over to them to do as they wished with.

And as they led him away, picking out a certain Simon the Cyrenian who was coming from the country, they imposed on him to carry the cross behind Jesus.

*A "royal" robe for "the king of the Jews": Herod has the same sense of humor as Pilate's soldiers.

Following behind him was a great crowd of the people, with many women too, beating their breasts and mourning him. Turning to them, Jesus said, "Daughters of Jerusalem, don't cry for me, cry for yourselves and your children, because watch, there will come days when they will say, 'Lucky for those who were sterile, for the wombs that never bore and the breasts that never nursed.' Then they will start saying to the mountains, 'Fall upon us,' and to the hills, 'Cover us up,' and if they do that when the wood is still green, what will they do by the time it dries?"

Now they were also bringing out two criminals to be executed with him.

And when they reached the spot they called The Skull, they crucified him there, and the criminals, too, one on his right and one on his left. And Jesus said, "Father, forgive them: they don't know what they're doing." And they rolled dice and divided up his clothes.

And the people were standing around watching, and the rulers were sneering at him, saying "He saved others, let him save himself, if he's the Anointed chosen by God."

Even the soldiers watching him were making fun of him, bringing him the sour wine and saying, "If you're the king of the Jews, save yourself." And there was a sign over his head: THIS IS THE KING OF THE JEWS.

One of the criminals hanging there started cursing him saying, "Aren't you the Anointed? Save yourself and us."

The other barked at him and said, "Do you have no fear of God, just because your sentence is the same? We're rightly getting what's coming to us for what we did, but he did nothing unlawful." Then he said, "Jesus, remember me when you get to your kingdom."

And he said to him, "I promise you, today you will be with me in Paradise."

And it was already about noon when darkness came over the whole land, from then till three o'clock, during which time there was no sun. And the great curtain hanging in front of the temple was sheared down the middle. And after crying out in a loud voice, Jesus said, "Father, I put my spirit in your hands"; having said that, he breathed his last.

When the Roman captain saw what had happened, he praised God saying, "This person really was innocent." And all the crowds who had collected in front of the spectacle, when they saw what had happened, went home beating their breasts.

Everyone who saw him was standing at a distance, including the women who had followed him there from Galilee and were now watching all this.

And this man named Joseph, who was a member of the high court, a good and innocent man – he hadn't gone along with the high court and its actions – who came from Arimathea, a Judean city, and lived in expectation of the kingdom of God, this man went to Pilate and asked for the body of Jesus. And after taking it down he wrapped it up in a sheet and put it in a carved-out tomb where no one had ever lain. And the day was Friday, with the Sabbath dawning.

Following along, the women who had come with him from Galilee observed the tomb and how his body was laid to rest, then they went back and prepared spices and perfumes, and since it was the Sabbath, kept quiet according to the command.

24

ON THE FIRST day of the week, at the crack of dawn, they came to the tomb bringing their prepared spices. But they found the stone rolled away from the tomb. Going inside, they couldn't find the body of Lord Jesus. And it happened, as they were looking around, all of a sudden these two men were standing in front of them in lightning-white clothing. As they fell into a panic and sank their faces down against the ground they said to them, "Why are you looking for the living among the dead? He isn't here, he rose up. Remember how he told you when he was still in Galilee that the son of humanity would have to be betrayed into the hands of evil people and be crucified and rise again on the third day?" And they remembered what he had said.

And returning from the tomb they reported all this to the eleven and all the rest. There was Mary Magdalen, and Joanna, and Mary, James's mother, and the others with them. They said these things to the apostles, but to them it seemed like delirium what they were saying, and they didn't believe them.

But Peter got up and ran to the tomb and bent down and saw the shroud and nothing more, and went back to his place amazed at what had happened.

And then next thing was, two of them were traveling that same day to a village by the name of Emmaus, seven or eight miles from Jerusalem, and they were conversing with each other. And it happened while they were conversing and arguing that Jesus himself approached and started walking on with them, but their eyes were overpowered so as not to recognize him. And he said to them, "What are these words you're trading as you walk along?" and they stood there looking grim.

Then one of them—his name was Cleopas—said to him, "You must be the only inhabitant of Jerusalem who doesn't know what has happened there in the last few days."

And he said to them, "Like what?"

They said, "All about Jesus of Nazareth, the man who had become a powerful prophet in word and action before God and all the people, and how our high priests and rulers handed him over to his death sentence and they crucified him. And we were hoping he was the one who would ransom Israel. But what with one thing and another it's going on the third day since it happened. Actually, some of our women gave us a shock, because they were at the grave at dawn and when they couldn't find his body they came back saying they'd seen a vision of holy messengers saying he was alive. And some of the people there with us went to the grave and found it as the women had said, but they didn't see him."

And he said to them, "Mindless and slow in your hearts to believe all the things that were said by the prophets! Didn't the Anointed have to die and enter into his glory?" And starting with Moses and all the prophets he interpreted for them all the passages in all the scriptures that were about him.

And they were getting close to the village where they were going, and he acted as if he was going to travel on. And they pressured him, saying, "Stay with us: it's getting toward evening, the daylight is already sinking away." And he went inside to stay with them. And it happened as he sat down with them to eat that he took bread and blessed it and broke it and gave it to them, and their eyes opened and they recognized him, and he vanished from their sight. And they said to each other, "Weren't our hearts blazing within us when he talked to us on the road and disclosed the scriptures to us!"

And at that point they got up and returned to Jerusalem and found the eleven gathered together and those who were with them, saying the Lord really did rise up, and appeared to Simon. And they explained what happened on the road and how he made himself known to them in the breaking of the bread.

As they were saying all this he himself stood in front of them and says to them, "Peace to you!" Electrified and panic stricken, they thought they were seeing a ghost. And he said to them, "Why are you so confused and what are these questions rising in your hearts? You can see from my hands and feet that it's me in person. Feel me, and see that a ghost doesn't have flesh and bones, as you will observe I have." And saying that he showed them his hands and his feet. When they were still incredulous with joy and amazement he said to them, "Do you have anything to eat here?" and they gave him a piece of roast fish. And he took it and ate it in front of them.

And he said to them, "Those were the words I said to you when I was still among you, that everything written about me in the law of Moses and the prophets and the Psalms had to be fulfilled." And he disclosed to them the sense in which to understand the scriptures. And he said to them, "That's what it says, that the Anointed suffered and rose again from the dead on the third day, and to announce to all nations in his name a change of heart for the forgiveness of wrongs, starting from Jerusalem. You are witnesses of all this. I hereby devolve the mission of my Father upon you. But stay in the city till you are clothed in power from on high."

He led them out to Bethany, and lifting his hands he blessed them. And as it happened, during his blessing he moved away from them and was carried up into the sky.

And they, after bowing down before him, returned to Jerusalem with great joy, and were always in the temple blessing God.

The Good Word According to
JOHN

1

IN THE BEGINNING was the Word, and the Word was toward God, and God was what the Word was. It was with God in the beginning. All things happened through it, and not one thing that has happened, happened without it. Within it there was Life, and the Life was the light of the world. And in the darkness the light is shining, and the darkness never got hold of it.

There was a person sent from God, and he had the name John. He came as a witness to testify about the light, so that all would have faith through him. He wasn't the light himself, he was to testify about the light.

The light was the true light that comes into the world and shines for every human being. He was in the world, and the world was created by him, and the world didn't know him. He came to his own kind, and his own kind wouldn't accept him. But to those who did accept him he gave the right to become children of God if they had faith in his name, they who were born not of blood, nor the flesh's will, nor a man's will, but of God.

And the Word turned flesh and lodged among us, and we witnessed his glory, the kind of glory a father gives his only son, full of grace and truth. John testifies about him, and has been heard crying, "This is the one of whom I said that the one coming after me has come ahead of me, because he *is* ahead of me," because from his abundance we all received grace for grace; since the law was given through Moses, but grace and truth came through Jesus the Anointed. No one has seen God ever; God's only son who has been on his father's lap, he himself explained that to us.

And such was the testimony of John when the Jews sent priests and Levites from Jerusalem to ask him, "Who are you?" And he admitted it and didn't try to deny it, he admitted, "I am not the Anointed."

And they asked him, "Are you Elijah?"
And he says, "No, I'm not."
"Are you the Prophet?"
And he answered, "No."
So they said to him, "Who *are* you? So we can give some kind of answer to the people who sent us. What do you have to say about yourself?"
He said, "I am

The voice of a crier in the wilderness:
Make the Lord's way straight!

as Isaiah the prophet said."
And the envoys were of the Pharisee party. And they questioned him, saying, "Why are you bathing these people if you aren't the Anointed, nor Elijah, nor the Prophet?"
John answered, "I bathe in water, but someone is standing in your midst whom you do not know, who is coming after me and whose sandals I am not worthy to untie." That happened in Bethany, beside the Jordan, where John was washing.
The next day he sees Jesus coming to him and says, "Look here, it's the lamb of God who takes upon himself the wrongdoing of the world. This is the one about whom I said, 'Behind me is a man who has come ahead of me, because he *is* ahead of me.' Even I didn't know him, but it was to proclaim him to Israel that I came along bathing in water." And John has testified, saying, "I saw the breath descending like a dove from the sky, how it alighted upon him. And I didn't know him, but it was the one who sent me to bathe in water who said, 'Whoever you see the breath descending and alighting upon, that's the one who will bathe them in the sacred breath.' And I have seen and certified that this is the son of God."
The next day John was standing there again with two of his students and, with his eyes on Jesus as he walked by, he says, "Look there, it's the lamb of God." And his two students heard him talking and followed Jesus.

Turning and noticing that they were following, Jesus says to them, "What do you want?"

They said to him, "Rabbi" – which would be translated as "Teacher" – "where are you staying?"

He says to them, "Come and see." So they came and saw where he was staying and stayed with him that day till it got to be about four o'clock.

Andrew the brother of Simon Rock ["Peter"] was one of the two who followed him after hearing of him from John.

He went first and found his brother Simon and said to him, "We have found the Messiah," which translates as "Anointed."

He brought him to Jesus. Jesus looked straight at him and said, "You are Simon, the son of John: you will be called Kephas" – which translates as "Rock."

The next day he decided to go out to Galilee. And he comes across Philip, and Jesus says to him, "Follow me."

Now Philip was from Bethesda, the same town as Andrew and Peter. Philip finds Nathaniel and says to him, "We have found the one written about by Moses in the Law and the Prophets: Jesus son of Joseph, from Nazareth."

Said Nathaniel, "Can anything from *Nazareth* be any good?"

Says Philip, "Come and see."

Jesus saw Nathaniel coming toward him and said about him, "Here is truly an Israelite without guile."

Nathaniel says to him, "Where do you know me from?"

Jesus answered him, "Before Philip called you, I saw you under the fig tree."

Nathaniel answered him, "Rabbi, you are the son of God, you are the king of Israel."

Jesus answered him, "Because I said I saw you underneath the fig tree, now you believe? You'll see more than that." And he says to him: "Truly, truly I tell you, you will see an opening in the sky and the messengers of God ascending from and alighting upon the son of humanity."

2

TWO DAYS after that there was a wedding in Cana, Galilee, and Jesus's mother was there. Also, Jesus and his students were invited to the wedding. And when the wine ran out, Jesus's mother said to him, "They don't have any wine."

Says Jesus, "What is that to you and me, madam? My time hasn't come."

Says his mother to the servants, "Whatever he tells you, do it."

Now there were six stone jars which were there for the Jewish purification, holding twenty or thirty gallons apiece. Jesus says to them, "Fill the jars with water," and they filled them up to the top. And he says to them, "Scoop it out and bring it to the headwaiter," and they did so.

But when the headwaiter tasted the water-turned-wine, not knowing where it came from – only the servants who had scooped the water out knew – the headwaiter called to the bridegroom and said to him, "Everyone else in the world puts out the fine wine first, and then the cheaper stuff when they're soused. But you've kept the fine wine till now."

Thus Jesus marked the beginning of his miracles in Cana, Galilee, and manifested his glory; and his students put their faith in him.

Afterwards he went down to Capharnaum, and so did his mother, his brothers and sisters, and his students, and they stayed there a few days.

And it was close to the Jewish Passover, so Jesus went up to Jerusalem.

And he found people in the temple selling cattle and sheep and doves, and the moneychangers sitting there; and he made a whip of ropes and threw them out of the temple – sheep, cows and all – and scattered the coins and upended the tables of the moneychangers. And to the pigeon-sellers he said, "Get that stuff out of here, don't make my father's house a house of merchandise." His students recalled how scripture says, "The zeal for your house consumes me."

So the Jews responded, saying to him, "What sign can you show us as to why you're doing this?"

Jesus answered them, "Destroy this temple, and in three days I will raise it up."

So the Jews said, "This temple was forty-six years in the building, and you'll raise it up in three days?" But he was talking about the temple of his body. So when he rose from the dead, his students remembered that he'd said that, and believed in the scripture and the words that Jesus said.

While he was in Jerusalem for the feast of Passover, many came to believe in his name after witnessing the wonders he performed. But Jesus didn't confide in them, because they all knew him, and because he didn't need anyone to give him evidence about people, he already knew what was inside people.

3

NOW THERE WAS a fellow named Nicodemus, one of the Pharisees, a leader among the Jews. He came to him by night and said to him, "Master, we know you have come from God to be our teacher. After all, no one could work the wonders you work if God wasn't with him."

Jesus responded by saying to him, "Anyone who is not born again will never see the kingdom of God."

Says Nicodemus, "How can a person be born in old age? Can he climb into his mother's belly a second time and be born?"

Answered Jesus, "Truly, truly I tell you: anyone who isn't born of water and breath can never get into the kingdom of God. What's born of the flesh is flesh, and what's born of the breath is breath. Don't be amazed because I told you you have to be born again. The wind blows where it will and you hear the sound of it, but you don't know where it comes from or where it goes; it's the same with everyone born of the breath."

Nicodemus answered him, "How can all this happen?"

Jesus answered him, "You are the teacher of Israel and you don't know? Truly, truly I tell you that we are talking of what we know and testifying what we have seen and you don't accept our testimony. If I told you earthly things and you don't believe, how, when I tell you heavenly things, will you ever believe? And no one has ascended into the sky but the one who came down from the sky, the son of humanity. And as Moses held the serpent on high in the desert, so the son of humanity must be held on high, so that everyone who believes in him can have everlasting life. You see, God loved the world so much He gave His only son, so that everyone who believes in him would not be lost but instead have everlasting life. God didn't send His son into the world to condemn the world, but so the world could be saved by him. Whoever believes in him is not condemned, while the unbeliever is already condemned for not believing in the name of God's only son. This is the world's condemnation: that the light came into the world and the people liked the darkness better than the light, because their deeds were so foul. Naturally, anyone who's up to no good hates light and doesn't come near the light, so his doings won't be scrutinized. Somebody who is carrying out the truth comes toward the light, so that their deeds will be known as having been done in the spirit of God."

After that Jesus came with his students to the land of Judea and stayed there with them for some time and continued bathing people.

John was also bathing his followers in Enon, near Salem, where there was a lot of water, and people were showing up to be bathed. (At this point John hadn't been thrown in jail.)

So an argument arose between the students of John and a Jew about purification. And they came to John and said to him, "Master, the one who was with you on the other side of the Jordan, about whom you testified, guess what! he's bathing the people and they're all coming to him now."

John answered, "No one on earth can receive a single thing beyond what is given them from the sky. You yourselves are my witnesses that I said I was not the Anointed, but that I was sent on before him. The possessor of the bride is the bridegroom. The bridegroom's best man, who stands and listens, finding the joy of joys in the voice of the bridegroom – that pleasure, which has been my own, is done. He is to be augmented, I am to be diminished."

The one who comes from above is above everything. Whoever comes from the earth is of the earth and talks of the earth; he who comes from the sky is above everything. What he has seen and heard is what he testifies, yet no one accepts his testimony. But whoever accepts his testimony has signed his name to the reality of God. Because the one whom God sent tells what God said; there's no limit to the spirit he gives forth. The Father loves the son and has put everything in his hands. Whoever believes in the son has everlasting life, but whoever isn't convinced by the son will never see Life; no, the wrath of God rests upon him.

4

WHEN Jesus found out that the Pharisees had heard that Jesus was gathering more students and bathing more people than John – though to be sure Jesus himself didn't bathe them, his students did – he left Judea and went back to Galilee.

Now he had to go through Samaria. So he went into a Samaritan town called Sicher near the spot that Jacob gave to Joseph his son. There was a "Well of Jacob" there. So Jesus, worn out from traveling, sat down there at the well – it was about noon. A Samaritan woman comes to draw water. Jesus says to her, "Give me a drink." (His students had gone into town to buy food.) So the Samaritan woman says to him, "How can you as a Jew ask for something to drink from a Samaritan woman like me? Jews don't associate with Samaritans."

Jesus answered her, "If you knew what a gift from God this is and who is saying 'Give me a drink' to you, you would ask him for a live spring of water and he would give it to you."

Says the woman, "Sir, you don't have a bucket and the well is deep: where are you going to get a live spring of water? Are you greater than our father Jacob, who gave us the bucket and drank from it himself, as did his sons and daughters and their offspring?"

Jesus answered her, "Everyone who drinks that water will get thirsty again, but whoever drinks the water I give him will never thirst again for all eternity; no, the water I give him will become a spring of water rushing toward everlasting life."

Said the woman, "Sir, give me that water, so I'll never thirst again and won't have to keep coming down here to draw water."

He says, "Go call your husband and come back here."

The woman answered, "I don't have a husband."

He says to her, "That's a good way to put it: 'I don't have a husband'! You've had five husbands and the man you have now is not your husband, so you told the truth."

Says the woman, "Sir, I see you are a prophet. Our fathers worshipped on this mountain, but your people say Jerusalem is the place where one must worship."

Says Jesus, "Believe me, madam, the time is coming when you will worship the Father neither on this mountain nor in Jerusalem. You worship you know not what; we worship something we know, because salvation comes from the Jews. But the time is coming, indeed is here already, when the real worshipers will worship the Father in truth and spirit. And in fact that's the kind of worshipers the Father wants. God is spirit, and his worshipers must worship in spirit and truth."*

*With these words, the idea of worshiping in a holy place is superseded by the idea of worshiping in a holy state—an enormous change when you consider how much the Jewish worship of the time was centered in, indeed confined to, the Temple of Jerusalem: imagine that Mass isn't supposed to be said in New Jersey; you're supposed to come into New York and hear it at Saint Patrick's Cathedral, where it can be said properly.

Says the woman, "I know the Messiah is coming, the so-called Anointed. When _he_ comes, he'll tell us everything."

Jesus says to her, "That's who I am, here speaking to you."

And at that his students came back and were surprised to see him talking with a woman, but no one said, "What do you want with her?" or "Why are you talking with her?" So the woman put her pitcher down and went into town, where she said to the people, "Come see this fellow who told me everything I'd ever done. He couldn't be the Anointed, could he?" And they came from the town and went out to see him.

In the meantime his students were asking him, "Master, please eat."

But he said to them, "I have food to eat that you don't know about."

So his students said to each other, "Nobody brought him anything to eat, did they?"

Jesus says to them, "My food is to do the will of the one who sent me and complete His work.

"Don't you say yourselves, 'We're four months into the season, the harvest is coming'? Well, look now! raise your eyes and see how the lands are golden with the harvest. Already the reaper pockets his wage and gathers the produce in to eternal life, so that the sower can be just as happy as the reaper. I have sent you reaping what you didn't labor over: others labored over it and now you ride upon their labor."

In that town many of the Samaritans believed in him because of the words of the woman who testified, "He told me everything I'd ever done." So when the Samaritans came to see him, they asked him to stay with them, and he stayed there two days. And many others were convinced by his words and said to the woman, "We no longer believe because of what you said: we've heard him and know for ourselves that this is really the savior of the world."

After the two days he left that place for Galilee. Jesus himself testified, in fact, that a prophet in his home town goes without respect. So when he went to Galilee, the Galileans accepted him on the basis of having seen all the things he did during the festival at Jerusalem, since they'd been to the festival themselves.

So he came back to Cana, Galilee, where he'd made the water wine.

And there was a royal person whose son was sick in Capharnaum. Hearing that Jesus was coming from Judea to Galilee, he went to him and asked him to come down and cure his son, because he was about to die. So Jesus said to him, "If you don't see signs and wonders, you refuse to believe."

The royal person says, "Lord, come down with me before my child dies."

Jesus says, "Go your way, your son's going to live." The fellow believed the words Jesus said to him and went his way. As he started downhill his slaves were already there to meet him saying, "Your boy's going to live." So he asked them what time it was when he started having it easier. So they told him, "Yesterday afternoon at one o'clock the fever left him." Then the father knew that that was the hour when Jesus said to him, "Your son's going to live," and he was convinced and so was his wife and his whole household. This, then, was the second wonder that Jesus worked while coming out of Judea into Galilee.

5

AFTER THAT there was a Jewish festival, and Jesus went up to Jerusalem.

Now in Jerusalem, at the Sheep Gate, there is a pool called, in Hebrew, Bethesda, with five porticos, in which a great mass of the sick, the blind, the lame, and those with withered limbs used to lie. Now there was one fellow there who had lived thirty-eight years with his sickness. When Jesus saw him lying there and realized he'd been there a long time already, he says to him, "Do you want to be well?"

"Sir," answered the sick man, "I don't have anyone to push me into the pool after the water's been stirred up. While I'm coming along, someone else steps in before me."*

Jesus says, "Get up, take your cot and walk away." And the fellow was suddenly well, and picked up his cot and walked away.

Now it was the Sabbath that day, so the Jews said to the cured man, "This is the Sabbath, you aren't allowed to carry your cot around."

And he answered them, "The person who made me well, he told me, 'Pick up your cot and walk away.'"

They asked him, "Who was the fellow who told you, 'Pick it up and walk'?"

But the cured man didn't know who it was, because Jesus had slipped off, there being a crowd of people in the place. Later Jesus comes across him in the temple, and he said to him, "See, now you're well again: do no more wrong, lest something worse should happen to you." The fellow went and reported to the Jews that Jesus was the one who made him well. And the Jews went after Jesus for that, because he did it on the Sabbath.

But Jesus answered them, "My Father has been working up to this point and now I am working." For that, the Jews wanted to kill him more than ever, because he didn't just break the Sabbath, he called God his own father, making himself equal to God.

So Jesus answered them, "Truly, truly I tell you, the son cannot do anything by himself, only what he sees his Father doing; whatever He does, the son does likewise. You see, the Father likes the son and shows him everything He does, and shows him how to do greater things than this, so that you will be amazed: because just as the Father raises the dead and makes them live, so the son gives life to whomever he wants. You see, the Father doesn't even judge anyone, He has left all judging to the son, so that all will honor the son as they honor the Father. Whoever doesn't honor the son, doesn't honor the Father who sent him.

*To be cured, you have to be the first one in after the pool has been stirred up by an angel.

"Truly, truly I tell you, whoever hears my words and believes in the one who sent me has everlasting life and doesn't come to judgment, but instead has turned away from death toward life. Truly, truly I tell you, that time is coming and indeed is here when the dead will hear the voice of the son of God and having heard will live. Because just as the Father has life within Him, so He has given it to the son to have life within him. And He gave him the authority to make judgments, because he is the son of humanity.

"Don't be surprised at that, because the time is coming when all those who are in their graves will hear his voice and come out: those who did good, to a resurrection of life; those who did no good, to a resurrection of punishment.

"I can do nothing by myself. As I hear, so I judge, and my judgment is just, because I don't seek my own way but the way of the one who sent me.

"If I testify about myself, my testimony isn't valid. There is someone else testifying about me, and I know the testimony is valid that he gives about me. You have sent to John, and he has testified to the truth. Now I'm not going on the word of a human witness myself, I'm saying these things for you, so you will be saved.

"He was the lantern, blazing and conspicuous, but you didn't want to rejoice in his light at the time.

"But I have a more important testimony than that of John: the deeds my Father gave me to complete, those deeds I do testify about me, saying that the Father has sent me. And the Father who sent me has also testified about me Himself. You've never heard His voice ever, nor have you seen His face. And you don't have His words lodged within you, either, because the one He sent to you, you won't believe. Pore over the scriptures, if you think that within them there's everlasting life to be had: they are the very witnesses about me. And *still* you don't want to come to me and receive true life!

"I don't look for glory from the human kind, but I have noticed about you that you have no love of God within you. I have come in the name of my Father, and you won't accept me. If someone else came in his own name, him you'd accept. How can you believe you're giving each other glory and want none of the glory that comes from the only God there is?

"Don't think that I will file charges against you with my Father. Your accuser is Moses, in whom you place your hopes; because if you believed in Moses, you'd believe in me –after all, he wrote about me. If you don't believe his written word, how will you believe my spoken word?"

6

AFTER THAT Jesus went across the sea of Galilee, by Tiberias. He was followed by a great crowd, because they observed the wonders he worked with the sick. He went up the mountain and sat there with his students. It was near Passover, the festival of the Jews.

So Jesus, raising his eyes and noticing that a great crowd was coming toward him, says to Philip, "Where can we buy bread for them to eat?" (He said that to him as a test: he knew what he was going to do.)

Answered Philip, "Two hundred drachmas worth of bread wouldn't be enough for each of them to get a little piece."

One of his students, Andrew the brother of Simon Peter, says, "There's a kid here who has five loaves of barley-bread and two small fish, but what's that among all these people?"

Said Jesus, "Tell the people to sit down." There was a lot of grass in the place. So the men sat down, numbering about five thousand. So Jesus took the bread and gave thanks and gave them out to the seated crowd, and gave them the fish too, as much as they wanted. When they were full, he says to his students, "Collect the leftover scraps so nothing goes to waste";

they collected it all and filled twelve baskets with the scraps of the five loaves of barley-bread that were left over after they'd eaten.

So the people, seeing what a miracle he had performed, said, "This is truly the Prophet, coming into the world." Jesus, therefore, realizing that they were about to come and take him away and make him a king, slipped away again to the mountain, all by himself.

Then as evening came his students went down to the sea, boarded a boat, and went across the sea to Capharnaum. And it had already gotten dark and Jesus hadn't come to them yet. The sea was stirred up with a great wind blowing. So, after getting some three or four miles out they sighted Jesus walking on the sea and getting close to the boat, and they got scared. But he said to them, "It's me, don't be afraid." So they readily took him into the boat, and in no time the boat was on the shore where they were going.

The next day the crowd standing on the other shore saw that there was no other boat but just that one and that Jesus hadn't gotten into the boat with his students, his students had gone off by themselves.

But some boats came by from Tiberia near the spot where they ate the bread after the Lord gave thanks. So when the crowd saw that Jesus wasn't there, nor his students, they boarded the boats and went to Capharnaum looking for Jesus. And on finding him on the other side of the sea, they said to him, "Rabbi, when did you get here?"

Jesus answered them, "Truly, truly I tell you, don't look for me because you saw miracles, or because you ate the bread and were full. Provide yourself, not with perishable food, but with the food leading to everlasting life that the son of humanity will give you, because he bears the stamp of God the Father."

So they said to him, "What do we do to perform the works of God?"

Answered Jesus, "This is the work of God: to believe in the one he sent."

So they said to him: "Then what sign will you perform so we can see it and trust in you? What works will *you* perform? Our fathers ate the manna in the wilderness, just as it says: 'Bread from the sky he gave them to eat.'"

So Jesus said to them, "Truly, truly, I tell you, Moses didn't give you the bread from the sky, but my Father is giving you bread from the sky for real, because the bread of God is the one who descends from the sky and gives his life for the world."

So they said to him, "Lord give us this bread for good."

Said Jesus to them, "I am the bread of life: whoever comes to me will never starve, and whoever trusts in me will never thirst again.

"But I told you that you've even seen me and you still don't believe. Everything my Father gives to me, comes to me, and whoever comes to me is never thrown out, because I have not come down from the sky to do my own will but the will of the one who sent me. And this is the will of the one who sent me: that I shouldn't lose any of all He has given me, but raise it all up on the last day. You see, it is the will of God that everyone who beholds the son and believes in him shall have everlasting life, and I will raise him up on the last day."

So the Jews were grumbling about him, because he said, "I am the bread come down from heaven," and they said, "Isn't this the son of Joseph, don't we know who his father and his mother are? So now how does he say, 'I have come down from heaven'?"

Answered Jesus, "Don't grumble among yourselves. No one can come to me unless the Father who sent me draws him, and I raise him up on the last day. It says in the books of the prophets, 'And they will all be pupils of God.' Whoever hears from the Father and learns, comes to me. Not that anyone has seen the Father except the one who is from God: *he* has seen the Father. Truly, truly I tell you, whoever believes has everlasting life.

"I am the bread of life. Your fathers ate the manna in the wilderness and they died. This is the bread that comes down from heaven so that a person can eat of it and *not* die. I am the living bread that has come down from heaven. If someone eats of this bread they will live forever, and the bread I will give is my flesh, given for the life of the world."

So the Jews started arguing with each other, saying, "How can this guy give us his flesh to eat?"

So Jesus said to them, "Truly, truly I tell you, if you don't eat the flesh of the son of humanity and drink his blood, you have no life within you. The one who eats my flesh and drinks of my blood has life everlasting, and I will raise him up on the last day. You see, my flesh is true food and my blood is true drink. The one who eats my flesh and drinks my blood remains in me and I in him. Just as the living Father sent me and I live through the Father, so the one who eats me also lives through me. This is the bread come down from the sky, not like your fathers ate and died: the one who eats this bread will live forever."

He said all that while teaching in a synagogue at Capharnaum. As a result, many of his students after listening said, "These are hard words! Who can listen to him?"

Jesus, though, knowing inside that his students were grumbling about that, said to them: "Does that throw you? Then what if you see the son of humanity ascending where he was before? Breath is the lifegiver, flesh serves for nothing. The words I have said to you are breath and life. But there are some of you who don't believe" – you see, Jesus knew from the beginning who the unbelievers were and who his future betrayer was. And he said, "That's why I have told you that no one can come to me unless that is given to him by the Father."

From that point on, many of his students went back where they came from and stopped traveling around with him. So Jesus said to the twelve, "You don't want to go too, do you?"

Answered Simon Peter, "Lord, who should we go to? You have words of everlasting life, and we are convinced and certain that you are the holy one of God."

Jesus answered them, "Didn't I pick you twelve? And yet one of you is a devil." (He meant Judas, son of Simon Iscariot, because he, one of the twelve, was going to betray him.)

7

AND AFTER THAT Jesus started walking around Galilee: he didn't want to walk around Judea, because the Judeans were looking to kill him.

It was close to Succoth, the Jewish "festival of the tents." So his brothers and sisters said to him: "Leave that place and come back to Judea so that even your students can witness the deeds you do. After all, no one does something in secret who himself wishes to be in the public eye. If you're doing these things, show yourself to the world" –even his own brothers and sisters didn't believe in him.

So Jesus says to them, "My time isn't here yet, whereas your time is always at hand. The world can't hate you; but it hates me because I testify about it, saying that its deeds are evil. You go on up to the festival, I'm not going up to the festival this time, because my time isn't fulfilled yet." Saying that, he remained in Galilee.

But when his brothers and sisters had gone up to the festival, then he went too, not openly but more or less incognito. So the Jews were looking for him at the festival and said, "Where is that guy?" And there was a lot of murmuring about him among the crowds, with some saying, "He's a good man," and others saying, "No, he misleads the masses." No one, however, talked publicly of him for fear of the Jews.

Then with the festival already in full swing, Jesus went up to the temple and started teaching. So the Jews were amazed and said, "How does this guy know how to read without ever going to school?"

So Jesus answered them, "My teaching isn't my own, but that of the one who sent me. If anyone desires to do His will, he will find out about this teaching as to whether it comes from God or whether I'm speaking for myself. Someone who speaks for himself seeks his own glory. But someone who seeks the glory of the one who sent him, that's an honest person, and there's nothing crooked about him.

"Didn't Moses give you the law? Yet none of you follows the law. Why are you looking to kill me?"

The crowd answered, "You're crazy, who's looking to kill you?"

Jesus answered them, "I did one deed and you're all amazed. This is what Moses gave you circumcision for—not that it comes from Moses, it comes from your forefathers—and yet you circumcise a man on the Sabbath. If a man can get circumcised on the Sabbath without the law of Moses being broken, why are you angry with me for making a whole man healthy on the Sabbath? Don't judge by appearance, render true judgment."

So some of the people of Jerusalem said to him: "Isn't this the one they're looking to kill? And look at that, he's talking in public and they aren't saying anything to him. You don't suppose the rulers actually found out that he's the Anointed? But no, we know where he's from. When the Anointed comes, no one knows where he's from."

So Jesus raised his voice while he taught, saying, "So you know me and know where I'm from. Yet I am not here on my own; no, the one who sent me is real, the one whom you don't know. I know Him because I am from Him and that is who sent me."

So they tried to seize him, but no one got their hands on him, because his time hadn't come yet.

But many in the crowd believed in him and said, "When the Anointed comes, could he ever work greater wonders than this man worked?"

The Pharisees heard the crowd murmuring these things, and the high priests and the Pharisees sent their assistants to seize him. So Jesus said, "I am with you for only a little while more, then I go to the one who sent me. You will look for me and not find me, and where I go you cannot follow."

So the Jews said to each other: "Where is this guy going to travel that we won't be able to find him? Could he be planning to go among the Jews of the Greek diaspora and bring his teaching to the Greeks? What are the words he said about that: 'You'll look for me and find me,' and 'Where I go you cannot follow'?"

On the last big day of the festival Jesus was standing and shouting, "If any are thirsty let them come to me and drink. For the one who trusts in me, it is just as the scripture said: rivers of living water flow from his insides." He was talking about the spirit those who trusted in him would receive: the spirit wasn't there yet, because Jesus hadn't yet been glorified.

Some of those in the crowd who heard these words said, "He is truly the Prophet"; others said, "This is the Anointed." Others said, "Doesn't the Anointed come from Galilee? Didn't the scripture say that the Anointed comes from the seed of David and from Bethlehem, the village where David was?" So a split developed in the crowd over him. And some of them wanted to seize him, but no one put their hands on him.

So the assistants came back to the high priests and Pharisees, who said to them, "How come you didn't bring him with you?"

The assistants answered, "No one ever talked like that in all the world!"

So the Pharisees answered them, "Don't tell us you've been fooled too! None of the rulers or the Pharisees believed in him, did they? But this crowd that doesn't know the law, they're all under his spell!"

Nicodemus says to them – the one who went to him earlier – since he was one of their number: "Surely our law doesn't judge a person without first hearing from him and finding out what he's doing?"

And they answered him, "You aren't from Galilee too, are you? Look it up, see for yourself: no prophet ever arises out of Galilee." And each of them traveled back to their own home.

8

BUT Jesus traveled out to Mount Olive. Come the dawn, he showed up in the temple and all the people were coming to see him, and he sat there teaching them. Then the canon-lawyers and Pharisees bring in a woman caught in the act of adultery and standing her up in front of everyone they say to him: "Teacher, this is a woman caught right in the act of her adultery. In the law Moses ordered us to stone women like her. So what do *you* say?" (They were saying this to test him, so they could have something to charge him with.)

Jesus bent down and started scratching with his finger in the soil. Then as they kept on asking him he raised his head and said to them, "Let whoever among you is guiltless be the first one to throw stones at her." And he bent back down and went on scratching in the soil.

On hearing that, they started going out one by one, starting with the eldest, till he and the woman standing in the middle were left alone. Looking back up, Jesus said to her, "Where are they, madam? Didn't anyone condemn you?"

She said, "No one, Lord."

Said Jesus, "I don't condemn you either. Go your way, and from now on stop doing wrong."

Then another time Jesus spoke to them saying: "I am the light of the world. The one who follows me will never walk in darkness, but instead will have the light of life."

So the Pharisees said to him, "You're testifying about yourself, so your testimony isn't valid!"

Answered Jesus, "Even if I am testifying about myself, my testimony is valid, because I know where I came from and where I'm going to, whereas you don't know where I came from *or* where I'm going to. You judge by the flesh; I don't judge anybody. And if I do judge, my judgment is valid, because I'm not alone, it's me and the Father who sent me. And it says in your law that the testimony of two people is valid. I'm one witness testifying about myself and then the Father who sent me testifies about me too."

So they said to him, "Where is your father?"

Answered Jesus, "You don't know either me or my Father. If you knew me, you'd know my Father too." He said these words standing near the collection-box while he was teaching in the temple. And no one seized him, because his time hadn't come.

Then he said to them another time: "I am going away, and you will look for me in vain and die in your errors. Where I go you cannot follow."

So the Jews said: "He isn't going to kill himself, is he? Is that why he says, 'Where I go you cannot follow'?"

And he said to them: "You are lower beings, I am a higher being. You come from this world, I don't come from this world. So I said that you'll die in your errors because if you don't believe that I am who I am, you _will_ die in your errors."

So they said to him, "Who are you?"

Said Jesus: "Just what I tell you in the first place. I have many things to say and judge about you, but the one who sent me is true, and what I heard from Him is what I say to the world." (They didn't understand he was talking about the Father.) So Jesus said to them: "When you raise the son of humanity on high, then you will find out that I am who I am, and that I do nothing on my own, but as the Father taught me, so I speak. And the one who sent me is with me. He hasn't left me alone, because I do just what He likes at all times."

When he said these things, many believed in him. So Jesus said to the Jews who had placed their faith in him, "If you stay with my words, you are truly my students, and you will know the truth, and the truth will free you."

They answered him, "We are Abraham's seed and were never the slave of anyone. How can you say, 'You'll be freed'?"

Jesus answered, "Truly, truly I tell you that everyone who does wrong is the slave of wrongdoing. The slave doesn't remain in the household forever, the son remains forever. So if the son frees you, then you will really be free.

"I know you're Abraham's seed, but you're looking to kill me, because you have no room for my words. I am speaking what I have seen at my Father's side, so whatever you hear from the Father, do it."

They answered him, "Our father is Abraham."

Says Jesus, "If you were children of Abraham, you'd do Abraham's work; but here you are trying to kill me, the person who has told you the truth that I heard from God. That's not what Abraham did! You're doing your father's work, all right."

So they said to him, "We weren't born out of wedlock, and we have one father: God."

Said Jesus, "If God were your father you would love me, because I come from God, I am here from God. Nor did I come on my own, He sent me. Why is it you can't make sense of my speech? Because you can't stand to hear my words. You come from your father the devil and you wish to carry out your father's fervent desires: he always was a killer from the beginning and never did stand for the truth, because there is nothing true about him. When he tells lies, he tells something of himself, since he's a liar and his father before him. But when I speak the truth you don't believe me. Which of you accuses me of a crime? If I speak the truth, how come you don't believe me? The one who comes from God listens to what God says: the reason you don't listen is that you don't come from God."

The Jews answered, " Aren't we correct in saying that you're a Samaritan, and crazy?"

Answered Jesus, "I'm not crazy. I honor my Father and you dishonor me. I'm not seeking my own glory; there is someone who seeks and who judges. Truly, truly, I tell you, if someone keeps my word, they will not see death ever."

So the Jews said to him, "Now we *know* you're crazy. Abraham died, and so did the prophets, and you say, 'If someone keeps my word, they will not taste death ever.' Are you greater than our father Abraham who died? Even the prophets died. Who are you making yourself out to be?"

Jesus answered, "If I glorify myself, my glory is nothing. It is my Father who glorifies me, about whom you say, 'He is our God.' But you haven't come to know Him; *I* know Him. If I ever say I don't know Him, I'll be as much of a liar as you. But no, I do know Him and I keep His words. Abraham your father was delighted that he should ever see my day, and he saw it and rejoiced."

So the Jews said to him, "You're not yet fifty years old and you've seen Abraham?"

Jesus said to them, "Truly, truly I tell you: before Abraham was born, I have already been." So they picked up stones to throw at him, but Jesus ducked out of sight and got out of the temple.

9

AND WALKING along he saw a fellow blind from birth, and his students asked him, "Rabbi, whose crime is it, his own or his parents', that caused him to be born blind?"

Jesus answered, "Neither his nor his parents': it was so the works of God could be manifested in him. We must do the work of the one who sent me while the day lasts: the night is coming when no one can work. As long as I am in the world, I am the light of the world."

Having said that much he spat on the ground and made mud with his spit and applied the mud to the man's eyes. And he said to him: "Go wash yourself in Siloam (which translates to 'Emissary') Pool." So he went off and washed himself and came away seeing.

So the neighbors and those who had previously observed that he was a beggar said, "Isn't this the guy who sits and begs?"

Some said, "Yes, it's him."

Others said, "No he just looks like him."

"It *is* me," he said.

So they said to him, "How did your eyes get opened up?"

He answered, "This fellow named Jesus made some mud and applied it to my eyes and told me, 'Go to Siloam Pond and wash.' So after going there and washing off, I could see."

And they said to him, "Where is that person?"

He says, "I don't know."

So they go to the Pharisees with the formerly blind man. Now it was the Sabbath on the day when Jesus made the mud and opened his eyes. So the Pharisees asked him again how come he could see now. And he said, "He put this mud on my eyes, and I washed myself, and now I can see."

So some of the Pharisees said, "That fellow can't be from God, because he doesn't keep the Sabbath."

Others said, "How could an evil man work such wonders?" So there was a split among them. So they said to the ex-blind man, "What do you say about him and the way he opened up your eyes?"

He said, "That he's a prophet."

So the Jews weren't convinced about him, how he was really blind and then became sighted, till they called on the parents of the newly seeing man and asked them, "This is your son, who you say was born blind? So how can he see all of a sudden?"

His parents answered, "We know that's our son and that he was born blind. How he comes to see now we don't know, and who opened up his eyes we also don't know. Ask him: he's an adult, he can tell you about himself." His parents said that because they were afraid of the Jews. You see, the Jews had already agreed among themselves that anybody acknowledging him as the Anointed would be barred from the synagogue. That's why his parents said, "He's an adult, you can ask him."

So they called the fellow in for a second time, the one who had been blind, and said to him, "Give glory to God! We know that this is a godless person."

Said the other, "Whether he's a godless person or not I don't know. One thing I do know: I was blind and now I can see."

So they said to him, "What did he do to you? How did he open up your eyes?"

He answered them, "I told you already and you didn't listen! Why do you want to hear it again? Do you want to become his students too?"

And they called him names and said, "You're one of his students yourself! We, on the other hand, are students of Moses. We know that Moses has been spoken to by God, but as for this guy, we don't know where he comes from."

The fellow answered them, "The amazing part about this is that you don't know where he comes from – but he opened up my eyes! We know God doesn't listen to the godless; instead, if somebody is God-fearing and does His will, that's who He listens to. In all history no one ever heard of anyone opening the eyes of a person blind from birth. If this person didn't come from God, he couldn't do anything."

They answered, "You were born in sin from head to foot and you're teaching us religion?" And they threw him out.

Hearing that they threw him out, Jesus found the man and said, "Do you believe in the son of humanity?"

Answered the other, "And who is it, sir, so I can believe in him?"

Said Jesus, "You have seen him: the person talking with you now is the one."

"I believe, sir," he said, and bowed before him.

And Jesus said, "I came into this world to bring it to judgment, that the blind might see and the seeing be blinded."

Some of the Pharisees who were with him heard that and said to him, "Then are we blind too?"

Said Jesus, "If you _were_ blind, you wouldn't be at fault, but since you say, 'We can see,' the fault remains with you.

10

"TRULY, TRULY I tell you, anyone who doesn't come into the sheep-pen by the gate but climbs over some other way, that person is a robber and a thief. The one who comes in by the gate is the shepherd of the sheep. The watchman opens up for him and the sheep respond to his voice, and he calls his own sheep by name and leads them out. When he's gotten all his sheep outside, he goes on his way at their head and the sheep follow him, because they know his voice. For a stranger they'll never follow along, they'll run away from him, because they don't know the voice of strangers." Jesus said this figure of speech to them, but they didn't know what those things were he was telling them.

So Jesus said again, "Truly, truly I tell you that I am the gate of the sheep-pen. All who came before me are robbers and thieves, but the sheep didn't listen to them. I am the door. Whoever enters through me will be saved and will go in and out and find grazing-land. The thief only comes to steal, slaughter, and destroy. I came so they would have life and more life.

"I am the good shepherd. The good shepherd puts his life down for his sheep. The hired hand is not the shepherd, and the sheep are not his own. He sees the wolf coming and leaves the sheep there and runs – and indeed the wolf attacks them and scatters them – because he's a hired hand and doesn't care about the sheep.

"I am the good shepherd, and I know my own, and my own know me, just as my Father knows me and I know my Father, and I put my life down for my sheep. I also have other sheep which are not from this fold; and I must bring them here, and they will respond to my voice, and then they will be one fold with one shepherd.

"That's why my Father loves me, because I lay down my life to get it back again. No one takes it from me, I lay it down myself. I have authority to lay it down, and authority to take it back again: I received just such orders from my Father."

Again a split developed among the Jews about those words. Many of them said, "He's possessed and he's stark raving mad. Why do you listen to him?"

Others said, "Those aren't the words of a possessed person. And a demon can't open the eyes of the blind, can he?"

Then it came to Hanukkah, the Feast of the Temple's Rededication, in Jerusalem during the winter, and Jesus was walking around in the temple in the porch of Solomon. So the Jews encircled him and started saying to him: "How long are you going to keep killing us? If you're the Anointed, say so outright."

Jesus answered them, "I told you, and you don't believe me. The deeds I do in the name of my Father testify for me. But you don't believe, because you aren't sheep of mine. My sheep respond to my voice; I know them and they follow me, and I give them everlasting life. And they will not perish ever, nor will anyone snatch them from my hands. What my Father has given me is greater than everything else, and no one can snatch anything from the hands of the Father. I and the Father are one."

Again the Jews picked up stones to throw at him. Jesus responded, "I showed you many fine deeds that came from the Father. Which one of those deeds will you stone me for?"

Answered the Jews, "We're not stoning you for fine deeds, we're stoning you for blasphemy, and for making a mortal like yourself into a god."

Answered Jesus, "Doesn't it say in your law, 'I have said you are gods?' If he called those people gods who were reached by the word of God—and the scripture can't be contraverted—how can you call it blasphemy if I, whom the Father sanctified and sent into the world, should say I am the son of God? If I don't do my Father's work, don't believe me. But if I do, and you still don't believe me, believe my deeds, so that you may know and understand that my Father is in me and I in my Father." So they tried to seize him again, but he slipped out of their hands.

And he went back across the Jordan to the place where John had first been bathing the people, and stayed there. And many came to see him and said, "John performed no miracles, but everything John said about him was true." And many came to believe in him there.

11

NOW THERE WAS a person sick, Lazarus of Bethany, from the same village as Mary and Martha her sister. Mary was the one who anointed the Lord with perfume and dried his feet off with her hair; it was her brother Lazarus who was sick. So the sisters sent word to him, saying, "Lord, look, your friend is sick."

Hearing that, Jesus said, "This is not a sickness to death, it is for the glory of God, that the son of God may be glorified through it." Now Jesus loved Martha and her sister and Lazarus dearly. So when he heard he was sick, he stayed in the place where he was two more days, then after that he says to his students, "Let's go back to Judea."

His students say to him, "Rabbi, the Jews were just trying to stone you, and you're going back there?"

Answered Jesus, "Aren't there twelve hours of daylight? If someone walks around by day, he doesn't bump into things, because he sees the light of this world; whereas if someone walks around by night, he bumps into things, because he has no light within him."

He said that much, and afterward he says to them, "My friend Lazarus is sleeping, but I'm going to go wake him up."

So his students said to him, "Lord, if he's sleeping, he's going to be all right." But Jesus was talking about his death, whereas they thought he was talking about going to bed and sleeping.

So then Jesus said to them outright, "Lazarus died, and I'm delighted with you for believing me, because I wasn't there; now let's go to him."

So Thomas, the one called the Twin, said to the other students, "Let us go too, and die with him."

Arriving, Jesus found he had spent four days in the tomb already. Now Bethany was near Jerusalem, about two miles away. So many of the Jews had come to see Martha and Mary and offer condolences to them about their brother. So when Martha heard that Jesus was coming she went out to meet him, while Mary stayed at home.

So Martha said to Jesus, "Lord, if you had been here, my brother wouldn't have died. But even now I know that anything you ask of God, he will give you."

Says Jesus, "Your brother will rise again."

Says Martha, "I know he will rise in the resurrection on the last day."

Said Jesus, "I am resurrection and life: whoever believes in me, even if he dies, will live, and everyone who lives and believes in me will never die ever. Do you believe that?"

She says to him, "Yes, Lord, I am convinced that you are the Anointed Son of God coming into the world."

And having said that she went and called Mary her sister aside, saying, "The teacher is here and calling for you." She, when she heard, got up quickly and came out to see him. Jesus hadn't gotten to the village yet, he was still at the spot where he had been met by Martha. So the Jews who were with her in the house and consoling her, seeing how Mary got up in haste and went out, followed her, thinking that she was going off to the tomb to mourn there.

So when Mary got to where Jesus was, seeing him she fell at his feet and said to him, "Lord, if you'd been here, my brother wouldn't have died."

Jesus, as he saw her crying, and all the Jews with her crying, went into an upheaval of the spirit and stirred himself up. And he said, "Where have you put him?"

They say to him, "Lord, come and see." Jesus wept.

So the Jews said, "See how much he meant to him." Some of them, though, said, "Couldn't the one who opened the eyes of the blind man also have kept the other from dying?"

So Jesus, still in an inner upheaval, comes to the tomb: it was a cave, and there was a stone blocking it. Says Jesus, "Take the stone away."

The sister of the deceased, Martha, says to him, "Lord, he'll be smelly by now: he's four days gone."

Says Jesus, "Didn't I tell you that if you believe you will see the glory of God?" So they took the stone away. Jesus then lifted up his eyes and said, "Father, I thank you for hearing me. I knew that you hear me at all times, but I said that for the benefit of the crowd around me, so that they might believe that you sent me." And after saying that, he shouted at the top of his voice: "Lazarus, come out here!" The dead man came out bound hand and feet with bandages and with his face covered by a cloth. Says Jesus, "Untie him and let him go."

So many of the Jews who had come to see Mary and then witnessed what he did believed in him. But some of them went to the Pharisees and told them what Jesus had done.

Then the high priests and Pharisees assembled in council, and they were saying, "What are we going to do about this fellow who works all these wonders? If we let him go on like this, they'll all believe in him, and the Romans will come in and take away both our land and our people."

One of them, Caiaphas, being the high priest for that year, said to them, "You don't know anything. Haven't you even considered that it's better for one person to die for the people than for the whole nation to die?"

He didn't say that on his own, but as high priest for that year he prophesied that Jesus was going to die for the nation – and not just for the nation, but to bring the scattered children of God together as one. So from that day on they were plotting to kill him.

So Jesus didn't walk around openly among the Jews, but went away to the country near the desert, to the town called Ephraim, and stayed there with his students.

Now it was close to the Jewish Passover, and many from that country were going up to Jerusalem before Passover to seek a blessing. So they were looking for Jesus and standing around in the temple saying to each other, "What do you say? He'll never show up for the festival, will he?" In fact, the high priests and Pharisees had given orders that anyone who knew where he was should alert them so they could seize him.

12

So SIX DAYS before Passover, Jesus came to Bethany, where Lazarus was, whom Jesus had raised from the dead. So they gave a dinner for him there, and Martha was serving, and Lazarus was one of the guests with him.

So Mary, taking a pound of genuine spikenard, very expensive, anointed the feet of Jesus and used her hair to dry his feet. The house was filled with the smell of the perfume. Says Judas Iscariot, one of his students, the one who was going to betray him, "Why wasn't that perfume sold for three hundred drachmas and given to the poor?" He said that not because he cared about the poor, but because he was a thief and as purseholder was dipping into the common funds.

So Jesus said, "Leave her alone, let this preserve me for my day of burial. Remember, you always have the poor around, but me you do not always have."

So a great crowd of the Jews found out he was there and came, not just to see Jesus, but also to see Lazarus, whom he had raised from the dead. But the high priests were plotting to kill Lazarus too, since on account of him many of the Jews were going off and believing in Jesus.

The next day, the great crowd that was there for the festival, on hearing that Jesus was coming to Jerusalem, took branches of palm-trees and came out to meet him and shouted:

"Hooray!
Bless him who comes in the name of the Lord,
The king of Israel!"

And Jesus found a donkey and sat down on it, just as it says:

Have no fear, daughter Zion:
Look! your king is coming,
Seated on the foal of a donkey.

(His students didn't think of it at first, but when Jesus was glorified, then they remembered that that is what was written about him and that's also what they did for him.)

So the crowd of people was bearing witness, those who had been with him when he called Lazarus out of the tomb and raised him from the dead. That's why the crowd was there to meet him: they had heard about his performing that miracle. So the Pharisees said to each other: "See how nothing you do does any good? Look, there went the world, all trooping off behind him."

Now there were some Greeks among those who were going up to worship on the feast-day. So they came up to Philip of Bethesda, Galilee, and asked him, "Sir, we want to see Jesus." Philip comes and tells Andrew, Andrew and Philip come and tell Jesus.

Jesus answered, "The time has come for the son of humanity to be glorified. Truly, truly I tell you, if the grain of wheat never falls to the ground and dies, it remains the only one. But if it dies it produces a great crop. The one who loves his life, loses it; the one who doesn't care about his life in this world will keep it safe for life everlasting. If someone serves me, let them follow me, and wherever I am, my servant will also be. If anyone serves me they will be honored by my Father.

"Now my soul is in consternation, and what shall I say? 'Father, save me from this hour'? But that is what I came to this hour for. Father, glorify your own name."

So a voice came from the sky: "I glorified it before and will glorify it again." The crowd standing around, when they heard that, said there had been thunder, while others said, "A holy messenger has spoken to him."

Answered Jesus, "That voice wasn't for me, it was for you. Now it is judgment time for this world, now the ruler of this world will be thrown out the door. And I, if I am raised high above the earth, will draw all people toward me." (He said that to signify by what death he would die.)

So the crowd answered, "We heard in the Law that the Anointed remains forever. So how can you say that the son of humanity must be raised on high? Who is this son of humanity?"

So Jesus said to them, "For a little while longer the light is among you. Walk around while you have light, so the darkness doesn't overtake you; the person walking in darkness doesn't know where he's going. While you have the light, believe in the light, so that you may become sons and daughters of the light." So spoke Jesus, and went away and hid from them.

After he had performed all those miracles in front of them, they still didn't believe in him, which fulfilled the word of Isaiah the prophet when he said,

Lord, who believed our report?
And to whom was the Lord's arm revealed?

The reason they couldn't believe was because of what Isaiah said elsewhere:

He has blinded their eyes
And petrified their heart
Lest they see with their eyes
And think with their heart,
And come back, and I heal them.

Isaiah said that because he saw his glory and spoke about him. However, though many of the ruling class came to believe in him, on account of the Pharisees they didn't admit it, so as not to be barred from the synagogue: they loved the glory of the world, it seems, even more than the glory of God.

Jesus cried out and said: "Whoever believes in me believes, not in me, but in the one who sent me. And whoever looks upon me looks upon the one who sent me. I the Light have come into the world so that anyone who believes in me will not remain in darkness. And if somebody hears what I say and doesn't keep it, I don't judge them, because I didn't come to judge the world, I came to save the world. The person who refuses me and won't accept what I say has his judge: the word I spoke will be his judge on the last day, because I didn't speak it on my own, the Father who sent me also gave me commands as to what to speak and what to say. And I know that his commandment means everlasting life. So as for the things I speak, it's just as my Father told me, that's how I speak."

13

BEFORE the feast of Passover, knowing that the hour had come for him to pass out of this world and back to the Father, Jesus, who had loved those who were his own in this world, loved them to perfection.

And as a dinner was going on – at a time when the devil had already put it in Judas Simon Iscariot's heart to betray him – knowing that his Father had given everything into his hands and that he had come from God and was going back to God, he got up from the table and put his clothes on and took a linen towel and tied it around his waist. Then he poured water into the basin and started washing his students' feet and drying them with the towel around his waist. So he comes to Simon Peter, who says to him, "Lord are *you* going to wash *my* feet?"

Answered Jesus, "For now you don't know what I'm doing, later you will know."

Says Peter, "Never in the world are you going to wash my feet."

Answered Jesus, "If I don't wash you, you will have no part of me."

Says Simon Peter, "Lord, wash not only my feet, but also my hands and my head!"

Says Jesus, "The cleansed person needs no more than to wash his feet: he's clean all over. And all of you are clean – well, not all." (He knew who would betray him; that's why he said, "Not all of you are clean.")

So after he washed their feet and took his clothes and sat down again he said to them, "Do you understand what I have done for you? You call me Teacher and Lord, and rightly so: that I am. So if I washed your feet, the Lord and the Teacher, you should also wash each other's feet. I gave you an example so that just what I did for you, you will also do yourselves. Truly, truly I tell you, there is no slave greater than his master, nor any emissary greater than the one who sent him. If you know these things, lucky for you if you do these things.

"It is not about all of you that I say 'I know those I have chosen'; it is so that the scripture may be fulfilled: 'He who eats my bread raised his heel against me.' I'm telling you now before it happens, so that you will believe when it happens that I am who I am. Truly, truly I tell you, whoever accepts the one I send accepts me, and whoever accepts me accepts the one who sent me."

Having said that, Jesus was stirred up in his spirit and bore witness, saying, "Truly, truly I tell you that one of you will betray me." His students looked at each other, at a loss as to whom he could be talking about.

One of his students, whom Jesus loved, was lying in Jesus's lap. So Simon Peter signals him to ask who it might be that he was talking about. So as the other lay there with his head on Jesus's chest he says to him, "Lord, who is it?"

Answers Jesus, "Whoever I dunk this piece of bread and offer it to, that's the one." So he dunks a piece of bread and offers it to Judas Simon Iscariot. And after he took the piece of bread, it was then that Satan entered into him. So Jesus says to him, "Do what you're doing and be quick about it." No one at the table understood what he was speaking to him about. Some thought because Judas held the purse that Jesus was saying to him, "Go buy what we need for the feast days," or that he should go give something to the poor. So the other took the piece of bread and went right out. It was night already.

So when he had left, Jesus says, "Now the son of humanity has been glorified, and God has been glorified in him. And if God was glorified in him, God will also glorify him in Himself, and He will glorify him without delay. Children, I am with you for a little longer: you will look for me, and just as I told the Jews that where I go you cannot come, I am telling you now. I give you a new commandment: to love each other, just as I loved you so that you would also love each other.

"That's how all will know you are my students: if you have love amongst yourselves."

Says Simon Peter, "Lord, where are you going?"

Answered Jesus, "Where I am going, you cannot follow me now, you will follow later."

Says Peter, "Lord, why can't I follow you right now? I'll give my life for you."

Answers Jesus, "You'll give your life for me, will you? Truly, truly I tell you that the rooster will not crow before you have said you don't know me three times."

14

"DON'T LET your hearts be troubled: believe in God and believe in me. In my Father's house there are many dwellings. If there weren't, would I tell you that I am going to prepare a place for you? And if I go and prepare a place for you, I will come again and bring you along with me, so that where I am you may also be. And where I am going, you know the way there."

Says Thomas, "Lord, we don't know where you're going. How can we know the way?"

Says Jesus, "I am the way, and truth, and life. No one comes to the Father if not through me. If you know me, you will know my Father too. And from now on you know Him and have seen Him."

Says Philip, "Lord, show us the Father and we will be satisfied."

Says Jesus, "All this time I've been with you and you don't know me, Philip? Whoever has seen me has seen the Father. How can you say, 'Show us the Father'? Don't you believe that I am in the Father and the Father is in me? The things I tell you, I don't say on my own: the Father does His work, remaining in me. Believe me that I am in the Father, and the Father is in me. If you don't believe me, believe my deeds themselves.

"Truly, truly I tell you, if someone believes in me, the deeds I do he will also do—indeed, he will do greater things than those, because I am going to the Father. And what you ask in my name I will do, so that the Father may be glorified in the son.

"If you love me, keep my commands. And I will ask the Father, and He will give you another Comforter to be with you forever. The breath of truth, which the world cannot receive because it doesn't see it or even know about it, is known to you because it stays with you and will continue to be in you. I will not leave you orphaned, I am coming to you. A little while longer, and the world will see me no more, but you will see me, because I am alive and you will be alive. On that day you will know that I am in my Father, and you in me, and I in you. The one who holds on to my commandments and keeps them, that's who loves me. Whoever loves me will be loved by my Father, and I will love him and reveal myself to him."

Says Jude—not Judas Iscariot—"Lord, how has it happened that you will reveal yourself to us and not to the world?"

Answered Jesus: "If anyone loves me, he will keep my words, and my Father will love him, and we will come to him and make our home with him. The person who doesn't love me doesn't keep my words. And the words you hear are not mine but those of the Father who sent me.

"I have told you these things while still remaining with you. But the Comforter, the sacred breath, whom the Father will send in my name, he will teach you everything and remind you of everything I told you.

"Peace I leave you, my peace I give to you; not as the world gives do I give to you. Don't let your hearts be troubled or intimidated. You heard how I told you, 'I am going away and coming back to you.' If you loved me you would be delighted that I'm going to the Father, because the Father is greater than me. And I have told you now before it happens, so that when it does happen you will believe. I will not talk much more with you, because the ruler of the world is coming, and in me there is nothing but that the world should know that I love the Father and that what the Father commanded me is just what I do. Arise, let us go on from here.

15

"I AM the true vine, and my Father is the farmer. Every branch of me that bears no fruit, He takes away, and every branch that does bear fruit He cleans so it will bear more fruit. Already you are clean because of the words I have said to you. Remain in me, as I in you. Just as the branch can't bear fruit by itself without staying on the vine, neither can you unless you remain in me. I am the vine, you are the branches. Whoever remains in me and I in him, bears fruit aplenty, because without me you can do nothing. If someone doesn't remain in me, he's already thrown out and withered like the branches which are collected and thrown into the fire and burned. If you remain in me and what I said remains in you, ask whatever you like and it will be done for you. My Father has made it his glory for you to bear fruit aplenty and become my students.

"Just as the Father loved me, I loved you; remain in my love. If you keep my commands you will remain in my love, as I have kept my father's commands and remain in His love. I have told you all this so that my joy may be in you and your joy may be complete. This is my command: to love each other just the way I loved you. No one has greater love than this: to lay down his life for his friends. You are my friends if you do what I command you. I do not call you slaves any more, because the slave doesn't know what his master does; you I have named my friends, because everything I heard from my Father I made known to you. You didn't choose me, I chose you; and I ordained that you should go and bear fruit and that your fruits should remain, so that whatever you ask the Father in my name He will give you. This is what I command you: to love each other.

"If the world hates you, know that it has hated me before it hated you. If you were of the world, the world would be friendly toward its own. But since you are not of the world, rather I have picked you out of the world, the world hates you for that. Remember the words I told you, that there is no slave greater than his master. If they hounded me, they will hound you too. If they kept my words, they will keep yours too. But they will do all these things to you because they don't know who sent me. If I hadn't come and talked to them, they would not be at fault, but now they have no excuse for their faults. Whoever hates me hates my Father too. If I had not done deeds in their midst that no one else ever did, they would not be at fault. But now they have seen and hated both me and my Father. But that is to fulfill the words written in their law: 'They hated me for nothing.'

"When the Comforter comes whom I will send you from the Father, the breath of truth that travels out from the Father, he will testify about me. And you will testify about me too, since you have been with me from the beginning.

16

"I HAVE TOLD you all this so you won't be caught off guard. They will ostracize you from their synagogues; indeed, the hour is coming when everyone who kills you will think he is doing God a service. And they will do that because they didn't know either the Father or me. But I have told you these things so that when their time comes you will remember that I told you of them. I didn't tell you these things from the beginning, because I was still with you.

"Now I go to the one who sent me, and now none of you are asking, 'Where are you going?' But because I have told you all this your heart has filled with grief. But I tell you the truth, it's better for you that I should go, because if I don't go, the Comforter will not come to you, whereas if I go, I will send him to you. And he when he comes will show the world better about wrongdoing and justice and condemnation. About wrongdoing, because they don't believe in me. About justice, because I go to the father and you see me no more; and about condemnation, because the ruler of this world has been condemned.

"I have much more to say to you, but you can't bear it just yet. But when the other comes, the breath of truth, he will guide you in the ways of all truth, because he will not speak on his own, but will speak what he hears and announce to you what's coming. He will glorify me, because he will take of what is mine and announce it to you. Everything the Father has is mine: that's why I said he will take of what is mine and announce it to you.

"A little while, and you see me no more, and again a little while, and you will see me."

So some of his students said to each other, "What is this that he's telling us – 'A little while, and you don't see me, and again a little while, and you will see me,' and 'I'm going to the Father'?" So they said, "What is this 'little while' he speaks of? We don't know what he's talking about."

Jesus realized that they wanted to ask him that, and said, "Are you arguing with each other about the fact that I said, 'A little while and you don't see me; and again, a little while, and you will see me'? Truly, truly I tell you that you will weep and wail, while the world rejoices. You will be grieved, but your grief will turn to joy. The woman is grieved when she gives birth because her hour has come, but when she bears the child, she no longer remembers her suffering for her joy that a person has been brought into the world. So you also are grieved now, but I will see you again, and your heart will rejoice, and no one will take your joy away from you.

"And on that day you will have no questions to ask me. Truly, truly I tell you, if you ask the Father something in my name, He will give it to you. So far you haven't asked Him anything in my name. Ask and receive, so that your joy may be complete.

"I have told you these things in figures of speech. The time is coming when I will no longer talk to you in figures of speech, I will give you the word straight out about the Father. On that day you will ask the Father, and I won't even say that I'll ask the Father on your behalf: because the Father Himself is your friend, since you have been my friends and have believed that I came forth from God. I came forth from God and have come into the world; now I am leaving the world again and traveling back to the Father."

His students say, "There! Now you're talking straight out, with no figures of speech. Now we know that you know everything, and do not need for anyone to ask you anything. By that sign we believe that you came forth from God."

Answered Jesus, "Now you believe? Watch: the time is coming – in fact it is here – for you to be scattered, each in a different direction, and leave me alone. But I am not alone, because the Father is with me. I have told you all this so that in me you may find peace. In the world you will find suffering; but courage! I have conquered the world."

17

JESUS SPOKE all this and lifted his eyes skyward, saying, "Father, my time has come. Glorify Your son so that Your son will glorify You, according as You have given him authority over every living thing, so that to everything You have given him, he may give life everlasting. That is what everlasting life is: for them to know You as the one true God and know the one You sent, Jesus the Anointed. I glorified You on the earth, completing the work You gave me to do. And now glorify me, Father, in Your own sight, with the glory I had in Your sight before there ever was a world.

"I have manifested Your name to the persons whom You gave me out of the world. They were Yours, and You gave them to me, and they have kept Your words. Now they have realized that everything You gave me comes from You; because the words You gave me, I have given them, and they accepted them and truly understood that I came forth from You, and believed that You sent me.

"I ask You for their sake, not for the world's sake but for the sake of those You have given me, because they are Yours, and all that is mine is Yours and what is Yours is mine, and I have been glorified in them, and I am no longer in the world, but they are in the world, while I am coming to You, holy Father: preserve them in Your name which You have given me, that they may be one, as You and I are. When I was with them I preserved them in Your name that You have given me, and guarded them, and none of them was lost except the son of perdition, so that the scripture could be fulfilled. But now I am coming to You, and I say these things in the world so they will have my joy completed in them. I have given them Your words, and the world has hated them because they aren't of the world, just as I am not of the world. I am not asking You to take them out of the world, but to keep them from the Evil One. They

226

are not of the world, just as I am not of the world. Consecrate them to the truth. Your words are truth. Just as You sent me into the world, I also sent them into the world. And I consecrate myself to them, so that they will also be consecrated to the truth.

"I ask not just for their sake, but also for those who believe in me through their words, so that all people will be one, just as You, Father, are in me and I in You; so that they will be in us; so that the world will believe You sent me. And the glory You have given me, I have given to them, so that they will be one as You and I are one, with me in them and You in me, so that they will be perfected into one, so that the world will realize that You sent me and that You loved them just as You loved me.

"Father, I want these – this gift You have given me – to be with me wherever I am, so that they may witness my glory, which You have given me because You loved me before the beginning of the world. Father of justice, still the world didn't know You, but I knew You, and these people knew that You sent me. And I made known Your name to them, and will go on making it known, so that the love You had for me will be in them, and I will be in them."

18

AFTER SAYING all this, Jesus went out with his students across the torrents of the Cedron to a place where there was a garden, which he and his students entered.

Judas his betrayer also knew the spot, since Jesus had frequently met there with his students. So Judas, with a band of soldiers and servants of the high priests and Pharisees, comes there with lanterns, torches, and weapons. So Jesus, knowing everything that was about to happen to him, came forward and says to them, "Who are you looking for?"

They answered, "Jesus of Nazareth."

He says to them, "Here I am." Judas his betrayer was standing with them. So when he said to them, "Here I am," they drew back and fell to the ground. So he asked them again, "Who are you looking for?"

They said, "Jesus of Nazareth."

Answered Jesus, "I told you, here I am, so if you're looking for me, let these people go" – that was to fulfill the words he'd said, "I have not lost any of those you gave me." So Simon Peter, who had a sword on him, drew it and hit the high priest's slave and cut off his right ear; the slave's name was Malchus. So Jesus said to Peter, "Put your sword back in its sheath: if this is the cup my father gave me, shall I not drink it?"

So the band of soldiers and the commander and the servants of the Jews took Jesus with them and tied him up and brought him first to Annas: he was the father-in-law of Caiaphas, who was high priest for that year. (Caiaphas was the one who advised the Jews, "Better for one person to die for the sake of the people.")

Now Simon Peter and another of Jesus's students were following him. The other student was known to the high priest and came into the high priest's courtyard with Jesus, while Peter stood outside the door. So the other student who knew the high priest came out and spoke to the doorkeeper and brought Peter inside. So the maid watching the door says to Peter, "You aren't one of that fellow's students too, are you?"

He says, "No, I'm not." Now the slaves and servants were standing around; they'd made a charcoal fire, since it was cold, and were warming themselves. So Peter was standing there with them and warming up.

So the high priest asked Jesus about his students and about his teaching. Answered Jesus, "I have publicly spoken to the world: I constantly taught in synagogues and in the temple, where all the Jews gather, and I said nothing in secret. What are you asking me? Ask the ones who heard me what I said to them. See these people? They know what I said."

When he said that, one of the servants standing near gave Jesus a slap, saying, "Is that how you answer the high priest?"

Answered Jesus, "If I said something bad, testify about the evil. If I spoke well, why are you beating me up?" So Annas sent him, still tied up, to Caiaphas the high priest.

Now Simon Peter was standing around and warming himself. So they said to him, "You aren't one of his students too, are you?"

He denied it and said, "No, I'm not."

Says one of the high priest's slaves, a relative of the one whose ear Peter cut off, "Didn't I see you in the garden with him?" Again Peter denied it, and just then a rooster crowed.

So they take Jesus away from Caiaphas to the governor's mansion – it was early morning by now – but they didn't go in themselves so they could eat the seder without being polluted.

So Pilate came out to see them, and he says, "What charge are you bringing against this person?"

They answered him, "If he wasn't doing something wrong, we wouldn't have handed him over to you."

So Pilate said to them, "Take him yourselves and try him by your own law."

Said the Jews, "We're not allowed to kill anybody" – to fulfill the words of Jesus in which he indicated by what death he was going to die.

So Pilate went back into the governor's mansion and summoned Jesus and said to him, "You're the king of the Jews?"

Answered Jesus, "Are you saying this on your own, or did others tell you about me?"

Answered Pilate, "Do I look like a Jew? Your people and high priests handed you over to me. What did you do?"

Answered Jesus, "My kingdom is not of this world. If my kingdom was of this world, my servants would fight to the death for me not to be handed over to the Jews; but in fact my kingdom isn't here."

So Pilate said to him, "So you are a king?"

Answered Jesus, "*You* say I am a king. What I was born for and what I came into the world for was to testify to the truth. Everyone who is of the truth responds to my voice."

Says Pilate, "What is truth?" And having said that, he went out to talk to the Jews again, and he says to them: "I don't see any charge against him. Now it's customary with you that I let one person go for you at Passover. So do you want me to let the 'king of the Jews' go?"

So they shouted again, "Not him – Barabbas!" (Barabbas was a robber.)

19

So THEN Pilate took Jesus and had him flogged. And the soldiers, weaving a crown of thorns, put it on his head and wrapped him in a robe of royal purple, and they were coming up to him and saying, "Good day, your majesty, king of the Jews" and then giving him a few slaps.

And Pilate came outside again, and he says to them, "See? I'm bringing him out here to let you know that I see no charge whatever against him." So Jesus came outside, wearing the thorny crown and the purple robe, and he says to them, "Here's the fellow."

So when the high priests and their servants saw him they raised a cry of "Crucify, crucify."

Says Pilate, "Take him yourselves and crucify him; I don't see any charge against him."

Answered the Jews, "We have our law and by that law he deserves to die, because he made himself out to be the son of God."

So when Pilate heard those words he really got scared and went back into the governor's mansion. And he says to Jesus, "Where are you from?" But Jesus gave him no answer.

So Pilate says to him, "You won't talk to me? Don't you know I have the power to let you go and also the power to crucify you?"

Answered Jesus, "You would have no power at all over me if it wasn't given you from above; so that the one who handed me over to you has the greater fault."

From that point Pilate was looking for a way to let him go, but the Jews shouted, "If you let this guy go, you're no friend of Caesar's. Anyone who makes himself out to be a king is speaking against Caesar."

So Pilate, on hearing those words, led Jesus outside and sat down on a podium at the place called Rockstrewn, or in Hebrew, "Gabbatha."

It was the Friday before Passover, about the noon hour, and he says to the Jews, "Here is your king."

They shouted, "Take him, take him and crucify him."

Says Pilate, "What, crucify your king?"

Answered the high priests, "We have no king but Caesar." Then he handed him over to them to be crucified.

So they took Jesus away, and carrying the cross on his back he came out to what they called Skull Place (which in Hebrew is called "Golgotha"), where they crucified him, and with him two others on this side and that, with Jesus in the middle. And Pilate lettered a sign and put it above the cross. It said, JESUS OF NAZARETH, KING OF THE JEWS. So many of the Jews read the sign, since it was a place near the city where they crucified Jesus, and it was written in Hebrew, Latin, and Greek. So the high priests of the Jews were saying to Pilate, "Don't write, 'The king of the Jews'; write, 'This man said, _I am the king of the Jews._'"

Answered Pilate, "What I have written, I have written."

So the soldiers there where they crucified Jesus took his clothes and made four shares, a share for each of the soldiers, plus the tunic. But the tunic was seamless, woven from top to bottom in one piece. So they said to each other, "Let's not tear it up; we'll roll dice for it to see who gets it," so that the scripture would be fulfilled that says,

They divided my clothes among them,
And for my vestments they cast lots.

So the soldiers did just that.

Among those standing by the cross of Jesus were his mother, his mother's sister, Mary wife of Cleopas, and Mary Magdalen.

So Jesus, seeing his mother and the student whom he loved standing near, says to his mother, "Madam, here is your son." Then he says to the student, "Here is your mother." And from that hour on the student took her for his own.

After that, Jesus, seeing that everything had already been accomplished, says, to fulfill the scripture, "I am thirsty." Now there was a jar lying there full of strong wine, so they put a sponge full of the wine on the end of a javelin and put it to his mouth. So when he had taken the wine, Jesus said, "It is finished," and bowed his head and gave up the ghost.

So the Jews, seeing as it was Friday, not wanting the bodies to remain on the cross for the Sabbath, especially since that was an important Sabbath-day, asked Pilate to break their legs and take them down. So the soldiers came and broke the legs of first the one and then the other crucified with him. When they got to Jesus, though, and saw he was already dead, they didn't break his legs, but one of the soldiers stuck a lance into his side, and blood and water came right out. And the one who saw that has testified about that, and his testimony is true, and he knows that he's telling the truth, so that you will also believe. That happened to fulfill the scripture, "Not a bone of his shall be broken." And again the scripture says elsewhere, "They will look upon the one they pierced."

After that Joseph of Arimathea, a student of Jesus in secret for fear of the Jews, asked Pilate if he could take the body of Jesus, and Pilate agreed. So he came and took his body, and Nicodemus also came, who had come to see him by night before, bringing a mixture of myrrh and aloes, about a hundred pounds of it. So they took Jesus's body and tied it with strips of cloth perfumed with the ointment, the customary way for the Jews to bury somebody. Now at the spot where they crucified him there was a garden, and in the garden a fresh tomb in which no one yet had ever lain. So, what with the approaching Jewish Sabbath and the tomb being near by, they put Jesus there.

20

ON THE FIRST day of the week, so early it was still dark, Mary Magdalen comes to the tomb and sees the stone taken away from the tomb. So she runs and finds Simon Peter and the other student whom Jesus was close to and says to them, "They've taken the Lord out of the tomb and we don't know where they've put him." So Peter and the other student came out and headed for the tomb. And they were both running, but the other student ran faster than Peter and got to the tomb first, and bent down and saw the wrappings lying there, but didn't go in. So Simon Peter gets there after him and goes into the tomb, and notices the wrappings lying there, and the cloth that had been over his head, which was not lying with the wrappings but rolled up separately in one place. So then the other student who got to the tomb first also went in, and saw and was convinced. (You see, they didn't know yet about the scripture passage that said he was to rise again from the dead.) So the students went back to their houses.

But Mary was standing outside by the tomb crying. So as she was crying, she bent down and looked into the tomb, and she sees two holy messengers dressed in white sitting there, one at the head and one at the foot of where the body of Jesus had lain. And they say to her, "Madam, why are you crying?"

She tells them, "They took my Lord away, and I don't know where they put him." So saying, she turned around, and she sees Jesus standing there, but she didn't know it was Jesus.

Jesus says to her, "Madam, why are you crying? Who are you looking for?"

She, thinking it was the gardener, says to him, "Sir, if you carried him someplace, tell me where you put him and I'll go get him."

Jesus says to her, "Mary?"

She, turning around, says to him in Hebrew, "Rabbuni!" (which means teacher).

Says Jesus, "Don't cling to me, I have not yet ascended to the Father. Go find my brothers and tell them I am ascending to my Father and your Father, and my God and your God."

Mary Magdalen goes and tells his students, "I have seen the Lord!" and what he said to her.

So when it was getting late on that first day after the Sabbath and the doors were shut where the students were for fear of the Jews, Jesus came and stood in front of them, and says to them, "Peace to you!" And after saying that he showed them his hands and his side. So his students were overjoyed to see the Lord. Jesus said to them again, "Peace to you! Just as the Father sent me, so I send you. And so saying, he breathed upon them, saying, "Receive the sacred breath. Whoever's wrongs you forgive, let them be forgiven; whoever you hold to their wrongs, let them be held."

Now Thomas, one of the twelve, the Twin, as he was known, wasn't with them when Jesus came. So the other students said to him, "We've seen the Lord!"

But he said to them, "Unless I see the nail-marks on his hands, and put my finger on the nailmarks, and put my hand in his side, I will never be convinced."

And a week later his students were indoors again, and Thomas with them. With the doors shut, Jesus came and stood in front of them and said, "Peace to you!" Then he says to Thomas, "Come here with your finger and look at my hands, and take your hand and put it in my side, and don't be a doubter but a believer."

Thomas answered him, "My Lord and my God!"

Says Jesus, "Because you have seen me, you are convinced? How lucky are the ones who never saw but still believed!"

There are many other wonders Jesus worked in the sight of his students which are not written in this book, but this much has been written so that you may believe that Jesus is the Anointed, the son of God, and by believing have life in his name.

234

21

AFTERWARDS Jesus revealed himself to his students on the Tiberian Sea. This is how he revealed himself: Simon Peter and Thomas the so-called Twin and Nathaniel from Cana, Galilee, and the sons of Zebedee and two more of his students were together. Simon Peter says to them, "I'm going fishing."

They say to him, "We're coming with you too." They went out and got in the boat, and during that night they caught nothing. When it was already morning Jesus stood on the shore; the students, however, didn't know that it was Jesus. So Jesus says to them, "Kids, do you have anything to eat?"

They answered, "No."

He said to them, "Cast your net on the right side of your boat, and you'll find something." So they did, and they couldn't even drag the net any more what with the great mass of fish.

So the student whom Jesus loved says to Peter, "It's the Lord!" Simon Peter, hearing that it was the Lord, put his tunic on and fastened his belt – he had been naked – and threw himself into the sea. The others came with the boat (since they weren't far from shore, only about two hundred feet off), dragging their netful of fish. As they got out onto land they see a charcoal fire there with a fish and a loaf of bread lying on it.

Says Jesus, "Bring some of the fish you just caught." So Simon Peter came up dragging the net full of big fish, a hundred fifty-three of them, and many as they were, the net didn't rip. Says Jesus, "Come have breakfast." None of the students dared to ask him, "Who are you?" knowing that it was the Lord. Jesus comes and takes the bread and gives it to them, and the fish likewise. That made three times already that Jesus revealed himself to his students after rising from the dead.

So when they'd breakfasted Jesus says to Simon Peter, "Simon Johnson, do you truly love me more than these others?"

He says, "Yes, Lord, you know I love you."

He says to him, "Shepherd my lambs." He says to him yet a second time, "Simon Johnson, do you truly love me?"

He says to him, "Yes, Lord, you know that I love you."

He says to him, "Pasture my sheep." For the third time he says to him, "Simon Johnson, do you love me?"

Peter was heartbroken that he could say to him a third time, "Do you love me?" And he says to him, "Lord, you know every-thing, you *know* that I love you."

Says Jesus, "Shepherd my sheep. Truly, truly I tell you, when you were a young man you used to fasten your own belt and walk around wherever you wished, but when you are an old man you will hold out your hands while someone else fastens your belt and takes you where you don't want to go." He said that indicating the death by which he was to glorify God, and after saying that he tells him, "Follow me."

Turning round, Peter sees the student whom Jesus loved following them, the same who lay with his head on his chest at the supper and said, "Lord, who is your betrayer?" Seeing him Peter says to Jesus, "Lord, what about him?"

Says Jesus, "If I wish him to stay till I come back, what is that to you? You follow me." So the word got out among the brothers that that student would never die. But Jesus didn't say to him that he wouldn't die, just "If I want him to stay till I come back, what is that to you?"

It is this same student who bears witness to these things and wrote these words, and we know that his testimony is true. There are many other things that Jesus did, such that if they were writ-ten down one by one, I don't think there would be room in the world for all the resulting volumes.

GLOSSARY

The following is a discussion of a few crucial words from the Gospels. With the reader's convenience in mind, the Greek words are alphabetized under the English words most traditionally used to translate them – not necessarily the words used in this version at all. Under "baptism," for instance, you will find reasons why the Greek word "baptisma" should be translated as "washing" or "bathing."

Abba (ἀββά, abba). This is an intimate Aramaic word for "father," for use inside the family rather than when talking with other people, and it sounds like one of a baby's first few words. In short, it's "Papa" rather than "Father." For centuries this word has been considered one of the most important and perhaps *the* most important word in the Gospels, the keystone of a religious message which is theological and mystical as well as ethical. Jesus, in short, is not just the nice person who helps people and tells us to be gentle. He is also – in fact, he is *rather* – the person who calls God "Papa."

Adultery (μοιχεῖα, moicheia). The word appears to be fairly specific: marriage-breaking, not just illicit sexual activity, which would be πορνεία (porneia, "whoring"). Though the general drift of Jesus's teaching is toward temperance and modesty in all things, his explicit commandments seem focused more on the sanctity of the marriage-bond than on the illicitness of sexual activity.

Amen (ἀμήν, amen). This Hebrew exclamation means literally "let it be" but is usually used with the force of "truly" or "believe me." Since "Amen" as an English word means "here ends my prayer," phrases like "Amen I say to you" have been rendered as something like "believe me" or "truly I tell you" so as not to leave the impression that Jesus ends his prayers before he begins them.

Angel (ἄγγελος, angelos); devil (διάβολος, diabolos). "Angelos" is the regular word for a "messenger" of any type. Most of the "messengers" in the New Testament are of the heavenly kind, but the same word is also used for human messengers, including John the Baptist, and the heavenly messengers are frequently though not always described as "messengers of the Lord" or "messengers of God." "Diabolos" means "slanderer" or "accuser," but in the Gospels is always used alone and never to describe humans (though human "accusers" are found in the Epistles).

Apostle (ἀπόστολος, apostolos). The word means "emissary" or "those sent out." Paul describes himself as an "apostle," and is generally conceded the title, but mostly it applies to the Twelve.

Baptism (βάπτισμα, baptisma); **baptize** (βαπτίζειν, baptizein). The most literal meaning is "dunking," but by extension it means "cleaning," "washing" or "bathing" and is so translated in this version. In the New Testament it means "baptism" too, but it is scarcely as abstract and consecrated a word as "baptism" is in English; another form of the word (βαπτισμός, baptismos) is used in Mark 7:4 to mean "washing the dishes."

Behold (ἰδού, idú). To modern readers, "behold" suggests "stand there goggle-eyed while the miraculous occurs," as in "behold, the Red Sea parted." But "idu" occurs much too often and too trivially for that. Instead, it is used as a storytelling device, to mark the point where a story's principal plot element is introduced ("I was walking down the street when idu,. . .") or the outcome is given ("so you know what he did? idu,. . ."). In this version, "idu" is rendered variously as "all of a sudden," "next thing you know," "just then," and "look" – whatever will serve the purpose.

Blessed (μακάριος, makarios). This word denotes the blessings of good fortune and even financial prosperity, not just the blessings of grace, which would be expressed more specifically by some form of χάρις, (charis), "grace." For that reason, the word is usually rendered here as "lucky" or "fortunate." In the Beatitudes, in particular, the word "blessed" is a trap: those who mourn, for example, are not "holier" in the present because they will be comforted, but destined to be "better off" in the future because they will be comforted.

Christ (Χριστός); **Messiah** (Μεσσίας). These are essentially the same word: "Christ" is Greek for "anointed," "Messiah" is Hebrew for "anointed," as John explains in 1:41. The Old Testament, of course, contains many references to Israel's hope that a savior will arise in its midst. However, the introspectively spiritual nature of Jesus's mission must have been a puzzlement and a disappointment to those who had expected a more militaristic Messiah – someone who would save the people not just "from their own wrongs," as in Matthew 1:21, but also from the Romans.

(Some commentators propose that Judas became disaffected for these reasons, and the explanation certainly looks plausible in the absence of any other satisfactory motive for the betrayal: if the money Judas gets is so little that he can throw it back in the high priests' faces, it's too little to be the sole reason.)

Church (ἐκκλησία, ecclesia). The word means "assembly" or "meeting," or even more literally, "calling everybody out to meeting." It will later mean "church," but it could scarcely mean that in the Gospels already. (Here essentially is the great struggle in reading the New Testament: not to view earlier events in light of later developments.) Certainly in Matthew 18:17, an injured party should if necessary "speak up at meeting," not "notify the authorities of the yet-to-be-established institutional church."

Disciple (μαθητής, mathetés); **master** (διδάσκαλος, didaskalos). "Mathetes" is the regular word for "student," the same that would be used of any other student, and "didaskalos" is likewise the regular word for any teacher. Furthermore, "students" and "teachers" is just what the initiates and adepts of various spiritual traditions call themselves to this day. Therefore, this translation calls the "students" and their "teacher" just that. The words ring a little strange, to be sure: in our day we don't normally think that wisdom qualifies as education.

Drachma (δραχμή); **denarius** (δηνάριον); **didrachma** (δίδραχμον); **stater** (στατήρ); **mina** (μνᾶ). This translation takes the lighthearted view that "it's only money" and doesn't try very hard to reproduce the exact details of ancient currencies, least of all as they figure in the parables.

It wouldn't work anyway. You can compare ancient sales of grain to modern sales of grain and conclude that "a drachma is so many dollars," but that's only true by the grain standard: you can't be assured that the other items in the ancient market-basket kept all the same relations to each other that they would keep in modern times; in fact you can be sure they didn't. Real estate was cheaper and imported spices more expensive, and if you used either of them as a standard instead of grain, there would be more or fewer putative dollars in your reconstructed drachma; so how much can your estimate ever really mean?

As a rough guide, you might think of either a drachma or a denarius as like a dollar, a didrachma as two dollars and a stater as four dollars; a mina would then be a hundred dollars, and a talent would be much larger, more like a thousand dollars.

Engaged (ἐμνηστευμένη, emnesteumènë). In his commentary on the first chapter of Matthew in the *Abingdon Bible Commentary*, J. Newton Davies explains that the engagements of Christ's time were more formal and unbreakable than those of our own day and carried with them both some of the rights and some of the responsibilities associated with marriage, possibly including cohabitation. Several words in Matthew and Luke seem to point in that direction: when Joseph considers if he should "break his engagement" to Mary in Matthew 1:19, the word is the same used elsewhere to mean divorce (as when Jesus condemns divorce). When Mary is found to be pregnant before she and Joseph have "gotten together" (Matthew 1:18), there seems to be the implication that they were about to set up housekeeping in anticipation of their coming marriage. Finally, in Luke 2:5 we see Joseph going to Bethlehem with his "fiancee," who is pregnant, with no suggestion of scandal on that account.

Faith (πίστις, pistis); **believe** (πιστεύειν, pisteuein). Does Jesus ask us to "believe" in him or just "trust" him? The words could be taken either way. In the public ministry as reported in Matthew, Mark and Luke, it doesn't seem plausible for Jesus to require a personal religious "faith" in his own person while trying to suppress premature reports that he's the Messiah. On the other hand, more than "trusting" is implied in John 1:7 when John the Baptist comes "to testify about the light, so that all might believe through him."

In fact, "pistis" seems to be a different word in John than in Matthew, Mark and Luke. It is only in John that the blessing is pronounced on those "who have not seen and have still believed." In the other three Gospels, Jesus wishes that the inhabitants of towns like Chorazin would trust him on the basis of what they *had* seen (Matthew 11:21).

Heaven (οὐρανός, uranos). As in French, German and Italian, the regular word for "sky" is also used to mean "heaven."

Hell (γέεννα, Gehenna). The word "Gehenna" derives from the Valley of Hinnom, south of Jerusalem. The place had been used in previous times as an incinerator, and at other times had been a center of Moloch worship, one of the darkest and most horrific forms of paganism, in which children were sacrificed by fire to the bull-god. The trashfire and the Moloch worshipers were gone by the time of Jesus, and the name of Gehenna, ceasing to be purely local, had taken on an identity fused with that of the Hebrew Sheol. Sheol was originally conceived of as simply a dark and dismal place like Hades, but not a place of fiery punishment. The idea of fiery punishment came later, perhaps in response to the observed tendency of robber-barons to die in bed. See Leslie E. Fuller's article "Religious Development of the Intertestamental Period" in the *Abingdon Bible Commentary* (New York, Doubleday, 1929).

Honor (τιμάειν). The word that underlies "timaein" is τιμή (timé), "honor" but also – in fact, primarily, the "price" or "worth" or "value" of anything. "Honor your father and mother," then, means "value them and be willing to pay the price of them." Jewish tradition has long interpreted this commandment specifically: not to be respectful toward parents during one's adolescent years, but to help aging parents.

Life (ζωή, zoë). Besides βίος "bios," the span of life (as in "biography"), and ψυχή, "psyche," the breath of life, there is also "zoë," being alive. All three words could be translated "life," but they could not be interchanged in Greek. In the Gospels, "zoë" is used only to mean the eternal life of those who are saved, and so in this version it is capitalized, "Life."

Love (ἀγάπη, agápë; φιλος, philos). Everyone has heard of the three Greek words for love: "eros," "philos," and "agapé" –wanting, liking, and loving. "Eros" is not much heard from in the Gospels, which speak often of adultery and whoremongering but seldom of lust in itself. "Philos" and "agapë" are both used quite a lot, particularly as verbs, *philō* and *agapō*. In this version, "philos" is sometimes rendered as "being a friend," whereas "agapë" is the love that could only be called love.

It is "philos" in John 11:36 ("see how much he meant to him"); and in John 16:27 ("and God Himself is your friend"). It is "agapë" in Mark 10:21, when Jesus feels love for the worldly young man; in Luke 7:47, when the fallen woman with the flask of ointment shows much love; in John 13:23, when the student Jesus loves, the teenaged John Evangelist, is resting his head on Jesus's chest; and in John 13:35, when Jesus says that love will be the mark of his followers. The difference, to be sure, does not always seem hard and fast.

In the last chapter of John the words are used strikingly together. Twice Jesus asks Peter if he feels agapë for him; twice Peter answers with philos; and finally Jesus says, "Well, so you feel philos, then?" Perhaps Peter is ashamed of exressing agapë for another man – though Jesus isn't and it appears to be a normal way of speaking – or perhaps in some subtler way he shies away from opening his heart full to the heart of Jesus. It's also possible that the difference means little or nothing and represents only an interchange of synonyms, as "sheep" and "lambs" and "feed" and "pasture" are interchanged in the same passage.

Magi (μάγοι, magoi). These would have been Persian priests versed in astrology and interpretation of dreams. Nothing in the Gospels says they were "three kings."

Men (ἄνθρωποι, anthropoi). "Anthropoi," a constant word in the New Testament, means either men or women, and this translation generally avoids expressions like "good will toward men" if they would leave women out of account in a way that the Greek words don't, especially since Jesus himself consistently includes women in his associations, his teachings, and the subjects of his parables.

At the same time, it is not always strictly true that "Anthropoi" are "people" and ἄνδρες ("andres") are "men." In fact, sometimes both words are used of men, but with a distinction in social status, "anthropoi" being "fellows" and "andres" being "gentlemen." In any event, the Gospels contain more people and fellows than men or gentlemen –"anthropoi" is much commoner than "andres."

Nations (ἔθνη, ethnë). Like the Hebrew "goyim," "ethnë" has the basic meaning of "nations," but also, by extension, "foreign countries." And since Israel is a religious state, the word is further extended to mean "pagan lands." Similarly, "ethnikoi," which means the "nationals" of a certain country, is extended to mean "foreigners" and "pagans." An example of the original meaning is "Go out and teach all nations" (Matthew 28:19). An example of the extended meaning is "Don't babble on like pagans" (Matthew 13:17).

O Ye of Little Faith (ὀλιγόπιστοι, oligopistoi). In Greek this is one word, "little-faithed-ones." In this translation it is rendered as "unbelievers."

Parable (παραβολή, parabole). The plainest translation would be "comparison," the most literal would be "putting things side by side." In short, the crucial thing about a parable is not the story element (there was a man who went sowing), but the comparison made and the way the comparison stands perhaps for something quite specific (the sower is the son of humanity, his seed is the word), though possibly also for something more general (each of us can be the Good Samaritan, everyone who needs our help is the man beset by thieves). In any case, a parable isn't just a story with a moral, it's a story with a key –which explains, for instance, why the high priests and Pharisees are so enraged to hear the story of the vineyard owner's son and the rebellious tenant-farmers: it doesn't just apply to them, it's about them.

Paraclete (παράκλητος, parákletos). The meaning of this word is hard to translate because it's hard to settle on in Greek.

"Comforter," "adviser" and "advocate" all have some accuracy. The closest thing to a literal rendering would be "someone who puts in a word for you."

Pharisee (Φαρισαῖος); **Sadducee** (Σαδδουκαῖος). Many people vaguely assume that the Pharisees were members of the priestly class and the biggest religious dinosaurs of their time. In fact, both descriptions fit the Sadducees instead. The Pharisees were a lay group, and considered more liberal and up to date than the Sadducees. They were flexible enough, for instance, to see a distinction between unthinking and deliberate swearing (Matthew 23:16) – though Jesus blasts the distinction as irrelevant – and they were "modern" enough to be open to the idea of bodily resurrection, which the Sadducees considered a newfangled romantic notion.

Publican (τελώνης, telónes). "Tax-collector." In Matthew, Mark and Luke tax-collectors are invariably named as the lowest form of male life, as whores are considered the lowest form of female life. Apart from the obvious drawback that they came demanding money, tax-collectors in Judea and Galilee were hated as traitors because they were collecting from their own kind in the service of Rome; as unclean because they were in constant contact with Gentiles; and as extortionary because they were working on commission.

Repent (μετανοεῖν, metanoein); **repentance** (μετάνοια, metanoia). The literal significance of the words is "changing your mind," but the usage of the words always implies "changing your mind and being sorry," not just "revising your opinion." The expression "a change of heart" suggests something of both the etymology and the meaning, and is sometimes used in this version.

Sanhedrin (συνέδριον, synedrion). The Romans of this period were still relatively tactful about allowing their subject peoples to govern themselves in small matters and worship in their own way. (The emperor hadn't declared himself to be God yet.) The Sanhedrin, the chief instrument of Jewish home rule, was both the "high court," as in this translation, and the "supreme council" of the Jews. It could try crimes, including religious crimes; but only the Romans could inflict the death penalty, and the Romans wouldn't do so for reasons involving an alien religion. That is why Jesus was arrested as a blasphemer and heretic but had to be executed as some kind of revolutionary.

Scandal (σκάνδαλον, scandalon); **scandalize** (σκανδαλίζειν skandalizein). Literally, a "scandal" is not a public embarrassment but a "stumbling-block," something – or someone – that trips you up, puts you off, leads you astray, or blocks your path. In this version the words are translated quite variously according to context: "let someone down," "lead someone astray," "offend someone," "be in someone's way."

Scribe (γραμματεύς, grammateus). Jesus spends quite a large part of his preaching time attacking the legalistic approach to religion and warning his followers not to get lost in the letter of the law. The best indication of what he is up against is the existence of a whole class of religious lawyers whose business it is to know whether Moses allows planting potatoes in months with an R in them. In this translation these people are called "canon-lawyers."

Servant (δοῦλος, doulos; διάκονος, diakonos; ὑπηρέτης, hyperétes). "Doulos," the word behind "servant" in most of the parables, means "slave" and not "servant" and is rendered as "slave" in this version. It may shock our liberal sensibilities to see how Jesus nowhere in the Gospels preaches against slavery *and* repeatedly makes slavery a prototype for humanity's total submission to God, but there it is.

Three considerations may make this seem less gross:

1) The startling omissions in the teaching of Jesus are two: one, just mentioned, is that slavery is an unsuitable social fabric. The other is that Rome is an unsuitable landlord. Espousing either theme would have cut short his mission: he would have been killed at once, not after a while. Also, speaking to either theme of outward social reform would have totally eclipsed his central theme of innermost reform: he would then have been Spartacus, or Joan or Arc, but not Jesus.

2) The description Jesus gives of humanity's submission to God uses the practice of slavery as a metaphor or starting-point but transcends realistic slavery both for good and for evil: if we're bad slaves of God, we'll be punished worse than any slave on earth; if we're faithful slaves of God, we'll be given such freedom and such rewards that our slavery will not seem in any way restrictive. If the conception of Jesus transcends his social framework, so should our judgment of his conception.

3) Calling yourself "God's servant" and not "God's slave" is open to some gross implications of its own: that you don't belong to God, He's just trying to run you, and if you don't like the way He runs you, you're always free to serve another god!

As for "diakonos" (the source of "deacon"), that word really does mean "servant," including waiters and waitresses. "Hyperetes" means something like "assistant"; notably, the high priests have such "assistants."

Sin (ἁμαρτία, hamartía; **sinners** (ἁμαρτωλοί, hamartoloi). As is in the cases of "baptism" and "heaven," the Greek word rendered as "sin" is less exclusively sacred and more of an everyday word than its traditional English translation; also, it may not have had quite so cursed and polluted a sound as "sin." Literally, "hamartia" is "missing the mark," as if we were aiming at something perceived as good, but picking the wrong targets and then also not shooting straight. For the reasons just given, and not to minimize the importance of human action for good or evil, this translation usually speaks of "errors" or "doing wrong" in place of "sin."

As for the "sinners," the term would apply not just to the authors of real crimes but to anyone not a good practicing Jew – which is why the expression "godless people" is sometimes used in this translation.

The question of who qualifies as a "sinner" has some bearing on the biography of Jesus. Certainly the actual criminals were admitted to his society, but we do not have to imagine Jesus surrounded by nothing but society's dregs, if some of the "sinners" were perhaps quite moral people who had turned away – or just fallen away – from the legalistic Judaism of that age. In fact, the Gospels show Jesus as "too free with his associations" in both directions, up as well as down. In Luke's narrative, for instance, the common people are just as aghast (Luke 19:7) that Jesus has dinner with the powerful chief tax-collector, Zaccheus, as the Pharisees are to see Jesus talking with women of *that* kind.

Son of Man (υἱὸς τοῦ ἀνθρώπου, huyos tu anthropu); **Son of God** (υἱὸς τοῦ θεοῦ, huyos tu theu). These crucial expressions probably do not mean exactly the same thing every time they appear. When the Devil says "If you're the Son of God . . ." the words clearly imply the unique status of Jesus as God's son. In other passages, such as the Beatitudes, Jesus invites us all to be God's sons and daughters. Furthermore, the expression "son of," as borrowed from Hebrew, can be used to mean something like "the soul of" or "the living embodiment of." A clear example of this last usage is in John 17:12, where Jesus says he has not lost any of the disciples God gave him "except for the son of perdition," meaning "except for Mister Perdition himself." Likewise, the Roman captain who exclaims in Luke 23:47, "Truly he was an innocent man," and in Matthew 27:54, "Truly he was the son of God," may have meant the same thing by either account: "Truly he was the soul of godliness."

As for "Son of Man" (rendered here as "Son of Humanity," that is one of the titles by which the coming Messiah is described in Old Testament writings, and has also been found as an expression current in those times meaning something more like "this mother's son." The explanation that it is a Messianic title is the most natural reason why Jesus persistently describes himself in those words. The more general expression, however, seems to occur in Mark 3:28, "the sons of humanity will be forgiven."

Soul ($\psi v \chi \acute{\eta}$, psyche). This word is decidedly shifty in meaning and cannot mean just the same thing every time; it also can't be translated consistently and still correctly. Basically, the belief in a person's immortal soul was beginning to displace an older belief in a *mortal* soul, a spirit in a person that lives with the person but dies with the person's death. In this older usage, "life" is a better translation than "soul": "those who wished the life of the child are dead" (Matthew 2:20). "Soul" is the right translation, on the other hand, in "Don't fear those who kill the body but cannot kill the soul" (Matthew 10:28). It's no wonder that the language should be ambiguous on the point of the soul's immortality when the religious question itself was in hot dispute, as between the Pharisees (immortal) and the Sadducees (mortal).

Spirit ($\pi v \epsilon \hat{v} \mu \alpha$, pneuma). This word, which contains an audible puff of air, is the regular word for "breath," and can even mean "wind," as in John 3:8. The notion of spirit as breath and breath as spirit links Christianity to such other major world religions as Hinduism and Buddhism, and is reflected in modern English by expressions like "breathing life into an enterprise." In this translation "breath" and "spirit" are both used freely as the context of each passage may suggest, but in Greek the two are always one.

Talent (*τάλαντον*). A silver talent is not a silver coin; in size and format it's more like a silver cannonball and weighs 50 or 60 pounds. It is sometimes translated here as "bar of silver" (though "bar" is a lie) so as not to sacrifice the point of a parable to a learned discussion of ancient Middle Eastern currency.

Tempt (*πειράζειν*, peirazein); **temptation** (*πειρασμός*, peirasmos). The most regularly mistranslated words in the New Testament. The Greek words do not have the seductive tone and certainly not the sexual tone of the English words "tempt" and "temptation," nor the same implication that what "tempts" a person must be something alluring. Instead, the words signify "testing," "examining" or "making trial of" a person's character; and while a flash of pretty leg could be a test of a man's character, so could a most unlovely disaster, such as the "temptation" of Job – how "tempting" is being covered with boils?

Virgin (*παρθένος*, parthenos). Though the virgin birth of Jesus is described in Matthew and Luke, the word "virgin" is not as crucial or as frequent a word in the Gospels as one might suppose. The passage from Isaiah (Isaiah 7:14) quoted as "a virgin shall conceive" in Matthew 1:23 could mean simply "a young woman will conceive." Also, the tradition of Mary's lifelong virginity is mentioned nowhere in the Gospels and doesn't seem to square well with passages like "he had no relations with her till she bore a son" (Matthew 1:25), "she bore her first-born son" (Luke 2:17), and "isn't he the son of Mary and brother of James, Joseth, Jude and Simon?" (Mark 6:3).

Roman Catholics consider that Joseph had no relations with Mary till she bore a son, nor thereafter; that she bore her first-, last- and only-born son, and that cousins could count as "brothers" in the countrified Aramaic sense of the term.

Catholic tradition has named Mary, wife of Cleopas, as the mother of the "brothers of Jesus." If that were true, it would still leave more than one passage in need of explanation.

On the other hand, the Mary-wife-of-Cleopas explanation squares well with Matthew 27:56 and Mark 15:40. In both cases, one of the faithful women watching as they bury Jesus is "Mary the mother of James and Joseph," according to Matthew, the Gospel that names James and Joseph as brothers of Jesus; and "Mary the mother of James and Joseth," according to Mark, the Gospel that names James and Joseth as brothers of Jesus. So is this "faithful woman" Mary, the mother of Jesus? If so, why the roundabout identification? Because Jesus has assumed such a special identity that his family isn't considered his family any more? A simpler explanation, at least of this case by itself, is that a different Mary is the mother of James and Joseth.

Mary, wife of Cleopas, is then mentioned by that name as standing at the cross in John 19:25, in words that may or may not describe her as the sister of Mary the mother of Jesus: "Among those standing by the cross of Jesus were his mother, his mother's sister, Mary wife of Cleopas, and Mary Magdalen." Probably those words do not describe the two women in question as sisters, for two reasons: 1) "Mary his mother's sister" would be the usual word order, not "his mother's sister Mary"; and 2) two sisters named Mary seems unlikely; most parents give each child a separate name.

The "brothers of Jesus" don't pass out of the record after the Ascension: they are mentioned as part of the faithful who gather between the Ascension and Pentecost. James in particular later becomes the head of the church at Jerusalem and is spoken of in the Acts of the Apostles, where he is still called "the brother of the Lord." The explanation that cousins count as "Aramaic brothers" seems supported by the faithful-women passages just mentioned in Matthew, Mark, and John. On the other hand, that explanation seems strained by the fact that only Jesus has such "Aramaic brothers," and that this supposedly lax usage is the only such lax usage in a genealogical vocabulary exact enough to include "brothers-in-law," "mothers-in-law," and generic "relatives."

In the end, neither a "virginal" nor a "non-virginal" reading of all passages comes out quite as simple and conflict-free as one might wish. However, the most important point is the one that *does* emerge most clearly from the Gospels as we have them: the Evangelists left no clear word on the subject of Mary's lifelong virginity *because they did not care*: as Jews, they believed in sexual modesty and temperance but did not have the kind of cult of virginity the Greeks and Romans maintained around Artemis and Diana. (Certainly we don't hear a cult of virginity in Elizabeth's cry of joy (Luke 1:25) that God gave her a child "on the day when he saw fit to lift my shame from before the world.") If Mary had been a lifelong virgin and the Evangelists had considered that important, they would have included a more explicit mention of the fact *and* excluded some of the ambiguous remarks they left in. "These things are written so that you may believe and have life in his name" (John 20:31) is an example of how explicit the Evangelists are when an important religious statement is to be made; and "he asked him this as a test, he himself knew what he would do" (John 6:6) is an example of how careful the Evangelists are not to leave a false impression. Certainly no such explicitness and no such care are expended on Mary's lifelong virginity. It doesn't even rate being mentioned.